US Foreign Policy and Defense Strategy

US Foreign Policy and Defense Strategy

The Evolution of an Incidental Superpower

Derek S. Reveron, Nikolas K. Gvosdev,
and Mackubin Thomas Owens

Georgetown University Press / Washington, DC

Library of Congress Cataloging-in-Publication Data

∞ This book is printed on acid-free paper meeting the requirements of the American National Standard for Permanence in Paper for Printed Library Materials.

16 15   9 8 7 6 5 4 3 2 First printing

Printed in the United States of America

Library of Congress Cataloging-in-Publication Data

Reveron, Derek S., author.
  US foreign policy and defense strategy : the evolution of an incidental superpower / Derek S. Reveron, Nikolas K. Gvosdev, and Mackubin Thomas Owens.
    pages cm
  Includes bibliographical references and index.
  Summary: This work analyzes the strategic underpinnings of US defense strategy and foreign policy since 1945. Primarily intended to be a supplemental textbook, it explains how the United States became a superpower, examines the formation of the national security establishment, and explores the inter-relationship between foreign policy, defense strategy, and commercial interests. It differs from most of the existing teaching texts because its emphasis is not on narrating the history of US foreign policy or explaining the policymaking process. Instead, the emphasis is on identifying drivers and continuities in US national security interests and policy, and it has a special emphasis on developing a greater understanding of the intertwined nature of foreign and defense policies. The book will conclude by examining how the legacy of the last sixty-five years impacts future developments, the prospect for change, and what US national security policy may look like in the future.
  ISBN 978-1-62616-158-0 (hardcover : alk. paper) — ISBN 978-1-62616-091-0 (pbk. : alk. paper) — ISBN 978-1-62616-159-7 (ebook)
  1. United States—Military policy. 2. National security—United States. 3. United States—Foreign relations—1945–1989. 4. United States—Foreign relations—1989– I. Gvosdev, Nikolas K., 1969– author. II. Owens, Mackubin Thomas, author. III. Title. IV. Title: United States foreign policy and defense strategy.
  UA23.R464 2015
  327.73--dc23

                                                                2014013043

Cover: Gore Studio Design
Cover Image: iStock/Gettey Images/earth maps courtesy of NASA: visibleearth.nasa.gov

Contents

Illustrations

Figure

Tables

Acknowledgments

A project like this is a product of many years of teaching, researching, and writing about foreign policy and defense issues. We each owe gratitude to past editors and colleagues at the Atlantic Council, the Foreign Policy Research Institute, *The National Interest*, *National Review*, *Orbis*, and *World Politics Review*. The short pieces we published there gave rise to deeper understanding of international security issues represented in this book.

While we proved invaluable to each other during the writing and editing process, we are also grateful to several colleagues who reviewed early versions of these chapters. They include Tom Nichols and Dean Zezeus of the Naval War College and Chris Fettweis of Tulane University.

The staff of Georgetown University Press impressed us with the attention they provided us and the care they exercised during the editing process. In particular we thank Don Jacobs for his guidance and patience as we worked through the complexity of understanding US national security.

Finally, we are grateful to our colleagues and students at the Naval War College. Successive leaders of the college value our ability to think and write objectively, without outside pressure. They continue to reaffirm the importance of academic freedom and its support in the college's role as the US Navy's home of thought. While we wrote this book on our own time and do not represent any official position, we hope this book contributes to the public debate of national security issues.

Introduction

Shall we protect our interest by defense on this side of the water or by active participation in the lands across the ocean?

—Nicholas Spykman, *America's Strategy in World Politics* (1942)

Even though the United States possesses the world's largest economy, its third largest population, and a very capable military, it has sometimes been described as an "accidental superpower," as if its rise to a position of global leadership could not have been anticipated. According to this narrative, while other nations had a conscious desire to gain power in the international system, Americans preferred to be left alone and only reluctantly became involved in world affairs.[1] This particular version of American exceptionalism appeals to many American political figures, who argue that the United States has no existential interest in organizing and maintaining the international system. Former secretary of state Colin Powell drew on this view, when in response to a question at the 2003 World Economic Forum as to whether the United States sought to dominate the world, he answered, "We have gone forth from our shores repeatedly over the last hundred years . . . and put wonderful young men and women at risk, many of whom have lost their lives, and we have asked for nothing except enough ground to bury them in, and otherwise we have returned home to seek our own . . . live in peace, to live our own lives in peace."[2] Americans, the "reluctant crusaders" in the formulation of Colin Dueck, are therefore said to approach international affairs as did the Roman consul Cincinnatus—willing to lead in the moment of crisis but prepared to return home once the threat has passed.[3] Indeed, the traditional attitude was that once a major conflict was concluded, "Americans could withdraw to more important domestic matters."[4]

The reality is somewhat more complex. Because the American nation has been formed largely from continuous waves of immigration, "there is no country in the world that does not touch us. We are a country of countries with a citizen in our ranks from every land. We are attached by a thousand cords to the world at large."[5] In the aftermath of the Second Great Awakening of the first half of the nineteenth century, a growing number of Protestant Americans heeded the call to become missionaries and go forth into the world to convert others not simply to a religious faith, but to the American way of life characterized by rugged individualism.[6] It seems the spirit of self-reliance and risk-taking moved from the North American frontier farther afield, to many parts of the world. Historically the United States may not have been an interventionist power, but by the end of the nineteenth century it possessed a network of global economic and security interests and was very much connected to world affairs.

By then, the United States had already assumed the role of the regional hegemon throughout the Western Hemisphere and developed a military infrastructure sufficient to intervene throughout the region to defend American interests. America's navy opened trade with Japan in 1855 and displaced the Spanish in Cuba, Puerto Rico, Guam, and the Philippines in 1898. President Theodore Roosevelt brokered peace between the Russians and the Japanese in 1905, and President Woodrow Wilson laid the groundwork for the contemporary international system in 1918.

Incidental, not Accidental

While the US government itself was not structured to play a decisive and leading role in world affairs, American business and society were very active on the global stage. This meant that American involvement in international relations was usually a more "informal" process occurring "through trade and political influence" rather than through direct state action of territorial annexation through invasion.[7] America could not be an isolationist state in the sense of ignoring the larger world scene since "a policy of aloof indifference to events outside of the western hemisphere was no longer possible to a State whose merchants and bankers were reaching out for profits all over the earth."[8]

By the start of the twentieth century, American political leaders recognized that the United States would have to play a growing role in the emerging international system. Both Theodore Roosevelt and Woodrow Wilson conceived of the United States as a great power that ought to take a leadership position in world affairs.[9] Roosevelt, in his 1910 Nobel Prize lecture, articulated his view that in search of lasting stability in global affairs, "such power to command peace throughout the world could best be assured by some combination between those great nations which sincerely desire peace and have no thought themselves of committing aggressions"—and he included the United States as one of those great powers who could help bring this about, a view expanded by Wilson in his own proposal for a League of Nations.[10]

The failure of the US Senate to ratify the Treaty of Versailles, which ended the First World War and created the League of Nations, has often been interpreted as the definitive resurgence of isolationism in US political thinking. Instead, as Bear F. Braumoeller has argued, the fight over the treaty should be understood as taking place largely "among different groups of internationalists"—between those who argued in favor of an assertive use of US military power placed at the disposal of an international organization to help regulate international affairs and those who either preferred a higher degree of US unilateralism or adhered to the earlier model of using American economic and financial power to manage security problems.[11]

Indeed, many of those who even embraced the moniker "isolationist" were not in favor of a complete withdrawal of the United States from the world scene. Charles Lindbergh, viewed as the archetypal isolationist, made it clear that isolationism did not mean "we will build a wall around our country and isolate ourselves from contact with the rest of the world." While he eschewed any involvement in Europe's wars, he made it clear that he would resist any attempt by other powers "to interfere with our hemisphere" and sketched out his vision that "with adequate leadership we can be the strongest and most influential nation in the world."[12]

The preference during the interwar period, therefore, was for using banks in place of battleships as the main tool for projecting American power overseas. While eschewing the use of the military instrument, the US government and the private sector marshaled a host of commercial and financial instruments to defend US interests. This meant that "America initiated and responded to such a broad range of international events that it could scarcely be called 'isolationist' in this period."[13] It was the decrease in the efficacy of such measures during the 1930s, culminating in the Second World War, that led to what might be considered a much more balanced approach after the war. US leaders realized that both "hard" military power and softer economic and cultural power would have to be deployed to protect key national security interests. The War Department (and the rest of the US government) and Wall Street would need to work together— hard power to deal with security threats and soft power to transform societies from foes into allies and trading partners. Thus, following World War II, the United States could militarily occupy Japan with leaders such as Gen. Douglas MacArthur but also revolutionize Japanese business through management gurus such as W. Edwards Deming, as part of a process of turning a former enemy into a friend and trading partner.

There was thus nothing "accidental" about the rise of the United States as a major force in international affairs. However, the emergence of the United States as a superpower with global reach (and global commitments) was not planned nor anticipated. Right up to the Second World War, and then in the short period of optimism following the Axis surrender in 1945, the preferred American position was "to protect its world interests without involving itself in entanglements abroad" to, in the words of President Franklin Delano Roosevelt in his address to Congress after the 1945 Yalta meeting, "take the responsibility for world collaboration."[14] When asked how long American troops might need to remain in Europe after the conclusion of hostilities, Roosevelt certainly did not anticipate their decades-long deployment overseas, telling army chief of staff Gen. George Marshall that he expected American soldiers to have to remain abroad for no more than two years.[15] Notably, there have been US forces in Germany since 1945, yet the mission there evolved from one of occupation to one of deterrence against the Soviet threat to one of logistical hub to deploy outside of Europe.

The Atlantic Charter as endorsed by Roosevelt during his meeting with British prime minister Winston Churchill on August 14, 1941, committed the United States to use its power to strive for a world that would create a "wider and permanent system of general security." This would guarantee free trade and freedom of navigation but did not presuppose that the United States would be required to be the principal underwriter of any postwar collective security arrangement.[16] Similarly the Declaration of the United Nations (January 1, 1942) bound each signatory "to employ its full resources, military or economic" in the struggle against the Axis powers, which meant that the United States would become one of the main pillars of the Allied group of nations. The prevailing attitude was summed up by a British economist, James Meade, who was part of the team assembled by John Maynard Keynes. After a 1943 visit to Washington, he remarked, "The Americans have already decided against isolationism, but don't for the life of them know what sort of interventionism to practice."[17]

Yet, at the time, it was not anticipated the degree to which the gulf would open up between US capabilities and those of its coalition partners. Moreover, Americans were optimistic that it would be possible to share power in the future UN structure with the Soviet Union. The agreements reached between the United States and the Soviet Union at the Tehran and Yalta conferences (1943 and 1945, respectively) assumed that the wartime alliance could endure in postwar conditions to preserve the peace, reflecting a position that many American diplomats would later regret as the decades-long Cold War unfolded.

The parameters of postwar American interventionism became clearer as the contradictions between the social systems of the West and of the Soviet regime, which could be sublimated in a common struggle against the Nazi threat, flared up once the peace was won and as the wartime partnership broke down. Joseph Stalin's famous formulation ("Whoever occupies a territory also imposes his own social system. Everyone imposes his own system as far as his army can reach. It cannot be otherwise."), combined with the weakness and debilitation of other US allies, meant that the United States would have to take on a more involved role in global security affairs than might otherwise have occurred.[18] Yet, as Robert Pollard has noted, there was "no pervasive, national security ideology" that characterized the US approach or provided concrete, actionable guidance to policymakers.[19] There was no American equivalent to the Soviet Union's Communist International, which promoted socialist revolution around the world.

Further, the government often struggled with recruiting the "best and brightest" to pursue careers in government. Instead, business leaders, missionaries, and civil society conveyed the American penchant for limited government and open markets.

This is why we have chosen the term the "incidental superpower." Much of what occurred that defined America's superpower status was incidental rather than accidental. There was no predetermined blueprint for achieving American global hegemony, and many of the building blocks of US power over the last half century have tended to be assembled in reaction to events rather than in anticipation of them.[20] Indeed, the initial catalyst for catapulting the United States to becoming a global superpower was the "dramatic unraveling of the geopolitical foundations and the socioeconomic structure" of the planned post–World War II international system rather than any deliberate choice of US policymakers.[21] The nature of the Soviet threat required the United States to develop a global logistical system to reinforce its allies in Europe and Northeast Asia. This system later becomes the hallmark of superpower status, as the United States is the only country that can deploy and sustain hundreds of thousands of military personnel thousands of miles from the homeland. Had the United States been forced to confront an existential threat on its borders, today's military would resemble those of US allies—defined by a territorial defensive posture rather than the expeditionary shape it finds itself in today.

In 1945, the United States was prepared to be the leading *primus inter pares* of a group of powers. Faced with the Soviet challenge for supremacy, it shifted its approach. The postwar realities changed US optimism about the willingness of Moscow to work with Washington to ensure international peace and security through the United Nations (UN); this in turn forced a reversal of postwar demobilization. To contain Soviet expansionism, the United States moved to create a strong defensive infrastructure and then a series of binding alliances around the world and to promote regional and global economic integration. This in turn created a global economic and security infrastructure that laid the foundation for the United States to become a superpower. In Europe this meant dozens of countries bound through the North Atlantic Treaty Organization (NATO) and pledged to defend one another. In Asia alliances took the shape of a "hub-and-spoke," where the United States was independently bound with Japan, the Philippines, Thailand, Australia, New Zealand, and South Korea.

At the same time, there was unprecedented growth in the national security establishment to support this global posture. In 1940, the United States fielded a grand total of approximately 460,000 men in active duty across all of its military services and relied on conscription for wartime. At the height of the Cold War, that number had nearly quintupled, augmented by a large reserve component and civilian workforce, making the Department of Defense the largest part of the federal government and the world's largest employer. In addition, the massive expansion of the capabilities of the US government—including the creation of new intelligence agencies and the growth of the diplomatic corps—helped to bolster the size, importance, and reach of the national security establishment.[22] Today some 854,000 people in the federal government hold a "top secret" security clearance.[23] Empowered by the enabling legislation passed by Congress and fueled by the preponderance of discretionary federal spending, the national security organizations of the US government enable the United States to be a superpower. To be sure, there are calls to reduce the national security establishment, but we are not any closer to answering the question about levels of internationalism that Nicholas Spykman posed in 1942, used as the epigraph of this chapter.

While there has been continuity in US foreign policy since 1945, democratic politics and national crises tend to drive US international behavior. Given the robust field of actors in the national security agenda, there is little that one person, even the president, can do to guide such a large, diverse, and complex government in the international system. Rather, enduring national interests, a stable national security establishment, and international partners generate a steady set of demands that drive US internationalism. Even today the United States enables France to intervene in Africa, Saudi Arabia to improve its deterrence posture in the Middle East, and Japan to protect its interests from a rising China.

Chapter Outline

To make sense of the US path to hegemony, this book begins by understanding the transformation of the United States from a regional great power into a global superpower in the years following the Second World War. Far from having any master plan to ascend to superpower status, the US government formulated an entirely new national security apparatus largely in reaction to external events. The Pentagon, for example, was built in just fifteen months during World War II to give the War Department the space it needed to direct operations in Europe, Africa, and Asia. Unlike Britain's abandoned war bunkers, the Pentagon did not disappear in 1945; instead, it became a symbol of American power.

After World War II, a series of ad hoc responses to Soviet expansionism created a global infrastructure for the projection of power and altered America's strategic outlook from its prewar position as the reluctant offshore balancer of last resort to viewing newfound allies in Europe, the Middle East, and Asia as the first lines of homeland defense. When the Soviet threat evaporated after the collapse of the USSR in 1991, America did not "come home," nor did it dismantle this global security architecture. In fact the government embraced a new conception of the United States as the world's indispensable nation, as the "hub" uniting the various regional "spokes" into a coherent whole. Demands from partners such as Germany, the United Kingdom, South Korea, Japan, Saudi Arabia, and Qatar kept US military forces engaged in stability operations, deterrence missions, and security cooperation around the world. The US finds itself both leading international coalitions and enabling coalitions of countries that rely on the intelligence and logistical capabilities American power brings.

From the days of the early Republic until the end of World War II, the United States essentially dealt with security issues on an ad hoc basis. The efforts of the War, Navy, and State Departments, if they were coordinated at all, were coordinated by joint boards and similar organizational constructs. But the lack of direction among the various components of the US government during World War II and the emergence of a hostile Soviet Union after the war led policymakers to create a formal national security establishment. To make sense of this process, the second chapter traces the evolution of the establishment from the National Security Act of 1947 to the Goldwater-Nichols Defense Department Reorganization Act of 1986 and to current efforts to reorganize not only the Department of Defense, but all national security components of the US government. The chapter explores contemporary challenges of the national security establishment and considers how thirteen years of war, a fiscal crisis, and a rising China will reshape the bureaucracy for the future.

As the defense establishment became permanent and the military was professionalized, civil-military tensions emerged. The third chapter examines how the balance between civilian and military authority has been kept, both during the days of the Cold War and continuing in current conditions where the lines between peacetime and wartime are often blurred and unclear. From the time of the American Revolution, the ideal civil-military relationship in America has been defined by an essential *bargain*, the goal of which is to allocate prerogatives and responsibilities between the civilian leadership on the one hand and the military on the other. The parties to the bargain are the American people, the government, and the military establishment. From time to time, certain circumstances—political, strategic, social, and technological—have changed to such a degree that the terms of the existing civil-military bargain became obsolete. The resulting disequilibrium and tension has led the parties to renegotiate the bargain in order to restore equilibrium.[24] The bargain has been tested by the creeping "militarization" of US foreign policy—especially with the emergence of the geographic combatant commands, whose commanders are sometimes described as latter-day American viceroys, and the rise of new technologies that allow for much greater civilian (and thus political) control over not only the strategic but even operational details of military missions.[25] This was demonstrated during the rescue of the crew of the *Maersk Alabama*, the ship hijacked in the Indian Ocean in 2009, and the 2011 Abbottabad raid that killed Osama bin Laden. Incidents like these illustrate that the traditional model of civil-military relations is in flux, which raises the question as to whether the current civil-military relations bargain is being renegotiated. To explore this, chapter 3 examines five questions that lie at the heart of the civil-military bargain at any time: Who controls the military? What is the proper role of the military? What is the appropriate level of military influence in a liberal regime? What pattern of civil-military relations best ensures military success? And who serves?

The civil-military bargain, in turn, shapes and is shaped by the debate over the nature and role of US global leadership and about how American power—military, economic, political, social, and cultural—ought to be deployed—the theme of chapter 4. Even though the incendiary rhetoric at election time might suggest otherwise, a fairly enduring bipartisan consensus about America's role in the world has endured for the past several decades.[26] This is due, in part, to the fact that while administrations may change, fundamental US interests have not, including the need for securing access to reliable sources of energy, protecting the US homeland from catastrophic attack, sustaining a global system marked by open sea lanes to facilitate commerce, and preserving regional balances of power to prevent powers hostile to the United States from being able to dominate important areas of the world. Combined with this is an enduring idealistic vision of spreading the benefits of democracy to other parts of the globe, with a corresponding assumption that democracies will be friendly to the United States and supportive of its global agenda. These perspectives guarantee that the United States is not likely to return to the isolationist approach that defined its foreign policy prior to World War II. In spite of calls for retrenchment, culturally Americans are connected to the world, and there is bipartisan support for a global foreign policy. At the same time, however, America's ability to sustain its current foreign policy is eroding, as the US share of the global economy decreases and as current engagements sap away at its economic and military strength. The main challenge for the future, therefore, will be to find enduring partners capable of and willing to join with the United States in promoting a common global security agenda. Given how little European countries spend on defense, this may force a relook at US commitments in Europe, in spite of recent Russian provocations.

Since 1945, the United States has deployed military forces to a different area of the world about every four years. Some deployments were for high-intensity conflicts, such as the Korean War in 1950–53 and the Gulf War in 1990–91. Some deployments were short, such as those to Panama in 1989 and Libya in 2011. Other deployments were for long-term efforts to defeat insurgencies and build functioning states, such as in Vietnam from 1959 to 1975 and Afghanistan from 2001 to 2014. These conflicts or the American cause to war cannot be explained alone by reference to Thucydides's assertion that "three of the strongest motives" for why a state acts are "fear, honor and interest."[27] Rather, US military action can be driven by a particular strategic narrative such as containment, the global war on terrorism, or the responsibility to protect, where the immediate mission, operation, or intervention may not fulfill any of Thucydides's criteria but are believed to support the overall strategy. Underlying these narratives are efforts to situate US military action beyond immediate tactical or strategic objectives, such as expanding the number of allies, offering humanitarian assistance, and facilitating UN and NATO military operations around the world. This approach reinforces the belief that the United States has no permanent enemies, so that Russian paratroopers can serve alongside American infantry in Bosnia in the 1990s or Chinese warships can participate in US-led exercises in the Pacific in the 2010s. This moves beyond classical understandings of the cause to war and explains why deterrence or geographic location does not restrain presidents from deploying military forces for missions that rarely neutralize existential threats to the United States. This is why we need to examine the important role political culture plays in driving US military interventions.

This sets up an examination of how the United States fights—the subject of the fifth chapter. Russell Weigley's classic 1960 work *The American Way of War: A History of United States Military Strategy and Policy* charted key characteristics of how the United States organized and fought, from the founding through World War II. While many of the conclusions were relevant in the Cold War, key changes in the national security establishment occurred in the aftermath of Vietnam. Among these changes are a decades-long effort to move away from conscription to professionalize the force, incorporating key capabilities in the reserve component (the Abrams Doctrine, developed by army chief of staff Gen. Creighton Abrams [1972–74]; the predilection to integrate new technology to support core warfighting capabilities; and the adoption of coalition warfare through partnerships around the world. Tempered with the realities of frustrated stability operations in the Balkans of the 1990s and stubborn counterinsurgency operations in the 2000s, this chapter identifies the new American way of war. Characterized as joint (all services), coalition (international partners), and interagency (nonwarfighting arms of the federal government), the US military is postured to operate in all domains from cyberspace to outer space and perform many missions from major combat to humanitarian assistance. None of this would be possible without the global logistics system that gradually developed over the last seventy years. When called into combat, operations do not cease when the adversarial government falls. Rather, the American way of war seeks to remove preconditions of insecurity and support economic development, build institutions, and professionalize former foes. At times this approach has been successful in countries such as Japan, Germany, and South Korea; more recently, however, Haiti, Afghanistan, and Iraq illustrate the limits of this broad concept of the American way of war.

Chapter 6, the "American Way of Peace," flows directly from the "American Way of War." It places an emphasis on the reconstruction and transformation of the formerly "enemy" society with the stated goal of transforming former foes into new friends. Since the Second World War, part of the US strategy for securing the peace has been to construct collective security organizations and to promote closer economic integration through free trade, based on the assumption that US interests are best served through a global order that promotes the spread of open societies lightly defended, tied to the United States through shared economic and security interests. This approach, which has been most successful in Western Europe and East Asia, has had more mixed results in other parts of the world. Yet there seems to be little competition to the US dollar, Washington-based institutions, and American partnership. In spite of strategic missteps and occasional government paralysis, Washington is still viewed as essential to the global system.

The American way of peace has also influenced the US focus on creating international rules-based institutions (such as the UN, the International Monetary Fund, the World Bank, and the World Trade Organization) reflecting its faith in the value of international cooperation—but with a caveat: trying to find ways for the United States to either maintain a preponderance of influence (by controlling the largest bloc of voting shares in international financial organizations) or building in some form of veto power for Washington.[28] This tension—between the stated desire for a rules-based order and preserving the right of the United States to bend or break those rules—continues to be a major fault line within US foreign policy to this day. With fiscal challenges weighing on the United States and fiscal prosperity facilitating China's rise, the next twenty years will test American ambivalence for the institutions it created and largely funds. However, given that China (and other emerging economies) benefit from the Americanized international order, institutions will remain unreformed, and these powers will cultivate bilateral relations in a similar way. In short, Beijing, New Delhi, or Brasilia will not replace the importance of Washington anytime soon. Not only do these countries face significant internal challenges, they also tend to accept the status quo since their development is largely dependent on maintaining the existing international system (and Western levels of consumption).

The seventh chapter addresses the critical question of how the United States finances its ways of war and peace. Over the past sixty years, the United States has enjoyed enormous financial and fiscal advantages not shared by its rivals or predecessors. At various points during the Cold War—and afterward—the United States has been able to tap into a broader resource flow emanating from allies and partners (and sometimes even potential rivals) to pay for its national security enterprise. The United States possessed an advantage over other challengers: its ability to create a truly global economic system that attracted other countries by offering a stable currency and the prospect of free trade—what Walter Russell Mead has labeled "sticky power."[29] Even with record deficits incurred during the George W. Bush and Barack Obama administrations—which calls into question whether the United States can maintain its level of activity in the international system—Mead and others have noted that US sticky power, having been integral to the prosperity of other states, has created an "interest in maintaining the strength of the US-led system."[30] This explains why the largest foreign holder of US debt is potential rival China.

The creation of the Bretton Woods financial architecture enshrined the US dollar as the de facto global currency of trade, making it difficult for emerging powers to "unstick" themselves from the dollar. This power is reaffirmed by the decision of major energy producers to price their products in dollars. Further, this advantage provides a major stimulus for the expansion of US business overseas that helped to fuel American corporate dominance. While they are based in the United States, companies such as Boeing, General Electric, and Apple are truly global. This reality also creates a worldwide demand for the dollar as a trading instrument and storehouse of value. However, global interest in the fate of the dollar has allowed the US government to run deficits, secure in the knowledge that there is a built-in demand for dollars as well as an incentive not to let the dollar lose significant value.

The concluding chapter offers a speculative look forward over the next two decades and offers the outline for a foreign and defense strategy for the United States. In contrast to the Cold War (when countering a "peer competitor" such as the Soviet Union was the organizing principle for US foreign policy) and to the immediate post–Cold War period (when the emphasis was placed on preserving America's unique status as the "sole superpower" by discouraging other countries from acquiring greater security capabilities), future foreign policy will center around reinforcing capable partners who can take on more of a role in stabilizing their regions and who can help to deter the possible rise of challengers intent upon changing the existing global order in partnership with others as well as with the United States. Over the last twenty years, the United States expanded the number of partnerships at record levels—focusing on quantity. The next twenty years will emphasize the cultivation of a smaller number of partners who can make definitive contributions to economic prosperity and international security and who share the US vision for a world defined by secure lines of communication, free trade, and collective security against regional hegemons and transnational threats.

Conclusion

In his 1951 State of the Union Address, President Harry S. Truman made the case to the American people why the United States needed to be the incidental superpower. It could not survive as a free and independent nation, he noted, if the "free nations" of Asia and Europe and the resource base of Africa fell under

Soviet control. Then "the Soviet Union could impose its demands on the world, without resort to conflict, simply through the preponderance of its economic and military power. The Soviet Union does not have to attack the United States to secure domination of the world. It can achieve its ends by isolating us and swallowing up all our allies."[31]

Today the United States no longer faces one, single, overarching threat. Instead, the world of the early twenty-first century is characterized by "interconnectedness, multiple power centers, shared vulnerabilities and dramatic change."[32] The Pentagon noted that the "global security environment presents an increasingly complex set of challenges and opportunities."[33] Under such conditions, it is unclear if the institutions and focus of the world's "incidental superpower" can change and evolve, leaving behind Cold War legacies. At the same time, the foreign policy community of the United States, as well as the general public more broadly, must continue to believe that continued and sustained US engagement to shape and direct the international system is in the national interest. We hope to provide a definitive answer in the succeeding chapters.

Notes

1. See, for instance, Matthew C. Price, *The Wilsonian Persuasion in American Foreign Policy* (Amherst, NY: Cambria Press, 2007), 142.

2. The transcript of his remarks can be found at http://web.archive.org/web/20050223091222/http://www.weforum.org/site/homepublic.nsf/Content/Remarks+from+Colin+Powell,+US+Secretary+of+State.

3. Colin Dueck, *Reluctant Crusaders: Power, Culture and Change in American Grand Strategy* (Princeton, NJ: Princeton University Press, 2006), 2.

4. Lawrence A. Kaplan, "The United States and the Origins of NATO, 1946–1949," *Review of Politics* 31, no. 2 (April 1969): 211.

5. "Excerpts from Powell's Opening Statement to Foreign Relations Committee," *New York Times*, January 18, 2001, at www.nytimes.com/2001/01/18/us/excerpts-from-powell-s-opening-statement-to-foreign-relations-committee.html?src=pm.

6. See, for instance, Andrew Preston, "Bridging the Gap between the Sacred and the Secular in the History of American Foreign Relations," *Diplomatic History* 30, no. 5 (November 2006): 783–812.

7. "The American Evangelical Missionary Impulse," interview with Professor Mark Noll of Wheaton College, *Religioscope*, June 29, 2002, at www.religioscope.com/articles/2002/005_noll.htm.

8. Frederick L. Schuman, *International Politics: An Introduction to the Western State System*, 2nd ed. (New York: McGraw-Hill, 1937), 472.

9. John Milton Cooper Jr., *The Warrior and the Priest: Woodrow Wilson and Theodore Roosevelt* (Cambridge, MA: Harvard University Press, 1983), xii–xiii.

10. A copy of the text of the address is archived at www.nobelprize.org/nobel_prizes/peace/laureates/1906/roosevelt-lecture.html.

11. Bear F. Braumoeller, "The Myth of American Isolationism," *Diplomatic History* 6, no. 4 (October 2010): 350–51.

12. Charles Lindbergh, "Election Promises Should Be Kept: We Lack Leadership That Places America First," speech delivered at Madison Square Garden, New York, at an America First Committee rally, May 23, 1941. The full text appears in *Vital Speeches of the Day* 7, no. 16 (June 1941), 482.

13. Braumoeller, "Myth of American Isolationism," 367.

14. Schuman, *International Politics*, 481; Franklin D. Roosevelt, "Address to Congress on Yalta (March 1, 1945)," archived by the Miller Center at http://millercenter.org/president/speeches/detail/3338.

15. Quoted in Michael Beschloss, *The Conquerors: Roosevelt, Truman and the Destruction of Hilter's Germany, 1941–1945* (New York: Simon & Schuster, 2002), 23.

16. A copy of the charter is archived by the Avalon Project of the Law School at Yale University at http://avalon.law.yale.edu/wwii/atlantic.asp.

17. Warren F. Kimball, *The Juggler: Franklin Roosevelt as Wartime Statesman* (Princeton, NJ: Princeton University Press, 1991), 104.

18. Milovan Djilas, *Conversations with Stalin*, trans. Michael B. Petrovich (New York: Harcourt, Brace and World, 1962), 114.

19. Robert A. Pollard, *Economic Security and the Origins of the Cold War, 1945–1950* (New York: Columbia University Press, 1985), 23.

20. Steven Metz, "Strategic Horizons: Planning for America's Next War," *World Politics Review*, April 24, 2013, at www.worldpoliticsreview.com/articles/12896/strategic-horizons-planning-for-america-s-next-war.

21. Melvyn P. Leffler, "The American Conception of National Security and the Beginnings of the Cold War, 1945–48," *American Historical Review* 89, no. 2 (April 1984): 365.

22. To some extent in discussing the "national security establishment," we follow the usage of Melvyn Leffler, who himself used the generic term "defense official" in a broad sense to refer to military officers and civilian officials in the Department of Defense as well as in the intelligence agencies and on the staff of the National Security Council (Leffler, "American Conception," 348n6). We would expand that to also include much of the Department of State as well as those sections of other departments that touch on foreign and defense policy.

23. Dana Priest and William M. Arkin, "A Hidden World, Growing beyond Control," *Washington Post*, July 19, 2010, at http://projects.washington post.com/top-secret-america/articles/a-hidden-world-growing-beyond-control/.

24. One of the present volume's authors, Mac Owens, is indebted to Andrew Bacevich for this formulation of the problem when he commented on an early version of his proposal for a book tentatively titled *Sword of Republican Empire: A History of U.S. Civil-Military Relations*.

25. As Derek Reveron and Michelle Gavin note about the geographic combatant commanders, "no other office in the U.S. government is as sweeping or as well funded as the regional combatant commands are." This means that "a regional commander provides clear, unambiguous policy to an entire region." See their "America's

Viceroys," in *America's Viceroys: The Military and U.S. Foreign Policy*, ed. Derek S. Reveron (New York: Palgrave Macmillan, 2004), 3.

26. We accept, however, that a general bipartisan consensus on foreign policy does not necessarily translate into the opposition party giving the president a blank check in foreign affairs and that even when there is agreement on the outline of policy, "bitter partisan conflict and Congressional attempts to block presidential foreign policy initiatives remain the norm" in current American politics. Steven Hurst, "Parties, Partisanship and US Foreign Policy: The Growing Divide," in *New Directions in US Foreign Policy*, ed. Inderjeet Parmar, Linda B. Miller, and Mark Ledwidge (Abingdon, Oxon: Routledge, 2009), 80.

27. Cited in his Book 1, *The Landmark Thucydides: A Comprehensive Guide to the Peloponnesian War*, ed. Robert B. Strasser (New York: Free Press, 1996), 43.

28. John Lewis Gaddis, *Surprise, Security, and the American Experience* (Cambridge, MA: Harvard University Press, 2004), 53.

29. Walter Russell Mead, "America's Sticky Power," *Foreign Policy*, March 1, 2004, at www.foreignpolicy.com/articles/2004/03/01/americas_sticky_power ?page=full.

30. Ibid.

31. "Annual Message to the Congress on the State of the Union," January 8, 1951, archived by the Truman Library at www.trumanlibrary.org/publicpapers/ index.php?pid=202.

32. Franklin D. Kramer, *NATO Global Partnerships: Strategic Opportunities and Imperatives in a Globalized World* (Washington, DC: Atlantic Council, 2013), 2, at www.acus.org/files/publication_pdfs/403/NATOPartnerships2013.pdf.

33. Department of Defense, *Sustaining U.S. Leadership: Priorities for 21st Century Defense* (Washington, DC: Department of Defense, 2012), 1.

1

From Regional Power to Global Superpower

What we need in this coming period is faith in ourselves, courage to do the difficult and distasteful things, consideration and forbearance for our allies, without whose confidence and help our purposes will not be accomplished.

—Harry S. Truman, address to the National War College, 1952

In August 1943, speaking before the Canadian parliament, President Franklin Delano Roosevelt reiterated a statement that he had delivered five years earlier: "The vast amount of our resources, the vigor of our commerce, and the strength of our men have made us vital factors in world peace whether we choose it or not."[1] With this recognition, Roosevelt envisioned the United States playing a much greater role in postwar international affairs as one of the dominant powers of the global system. Yet as he and other senior American leaders began to strategize about the shape of international relations once the Second World War concluded, they had no master plan for ascending to superpower status. Further, there was no expectation that American leadership—seen primarily at this time to mean American coordination of joint efforts undertaken by a coalition of major powers—required massive American military, economic, and political engagement with other parts of the world, the maintenance of a huge military establishment, or continued, sustained deployments of US forces outside the territory of the United States. Instead, the United States conceived of a postwar world where the allies could maintain peace through regional hegemony.

The Four Policemen

Without intention or master plan, the United States did not want to inherit the British Empire or establish its own empire. Yet the destroyed industrial base of Europe and Asia and the killing of 60 to 85 million people in World War II (both combat fatalities plus associated war deaths) put the United States on a path to global hegemony. In 1945, the United States became the de facto global economy, responsible for more than half of the world's gross domestic product. Further, while there were some four hundred thousand US casualties in World War II, that number was low relative to an entire generation of Europeans, Soviets, Chinese, and Japanese that the war claimed; this demographic advantage set up the US industrial base to expand rapidly when the war ended, which was later sustained through the baby boom.

While some privately advised the president that the United States should take the world for itself following the war, Roosevelt eschewed sole global dominance.[2] He conceived of the United States as one of the world's "Four Policemen" (along with the Soviet Union, Great Britain, and Nationalist China)—with each bearing primary responsibility for creating security in different parts of the world.[3] Collectively the Four Policemen would maintain sufficient armed forces to discourage future aggressors and would "jointly blockade the disturber of the peace and confront him militarily if he would not abandon his aggressive stand."[4] He believed that this vision of international peace and security could cross ideological lines, accommodating capitalist, communist, and nationalist perspectives, and unlike Woodrow Wilson's blueprint for a League of Nations, which was predicated on liberal-democratic values, this system would be more durable.

Within each region, each "policeman" would be expected to do what the United States had achieved at the 1940 Havana Meeting of Ministers of Foreign Affairs of the American Republics. At this conference, the nations of the Western Hemisphere had agreed to form an emergency committee to take over the administration of any European colony whose home country had fallen under occupation. In addition, the countries of the region agreed "that any attempt on the part of a non-American state against the integrity or inviolability of the territory, the sovereignty or the political independence of an American state shall be considered as an act of aggression against the states which sign this declaration" and committed them to "consult among themselves in order to agree upon the measure it may be advisable to take."[5] The Havana Conference signaled that a majority of Latin American states agreed with the US view of hemispheric defense and set up a pattern in the future whereby US policy would be voluntarily endorsed by a larger coalition of states.[6]

At the Tehran Conference (November 28 to December 1, 1943), Roosevelt built on this idea of the Four Policemen in his proposals to Joseph Stalin and Winston Churchill for dealing with postwar issues. He also briefed Stalin on US policy in Latin America, holding it out as a model for how the Soviet Union could police the Eurasian space.[7] In envisioning the US international role, Roosevelt expected the United States, although serving as the de facto "chairman of the board" of the great powers, to work collaboratively and in concert with the other major powers in settling disputes and preventing the outbreak of further wars as well as taking over and administering via trusteeship both the overseas territories and colonies of the Axis powers. However, while Roosevelt anticipated that the United States would play a much more active role around the world, not simply in the Western Hemisphere, he was still thinking largely in terms of the nation functioning as an offshore balancer, working with the other policemen to tip the balance against aggressors that might rise. Indeed, rather than foreseeing the forward deployment of a large number of US forces to forestall aggression, Roosevelt believed that the other policemen, in the event of any security challenge arising outside the Western Hemisphere, would provide the bulk of the ground forces needed to deal with any situation, with the United States providing naval and air support when needed.[8]

Uniting the Nations

Roosevelt "democratized" his concept of the Four Policemen by vesting their authority within a proposed new international organization, the United Nations (UN), to which other states could add their voice, although the addition of a Security Council defined by the presence of five veto-wielding permanent members (through the addition of France because of its global presence through colonies in Africa and Asia) meant that the policemen would still bear much of the responsibility for the maintenance of international peace and security in the postwar world.[9] While the UN would form the backbone of international politics—and the major powers would control the Security Council—the Bretton Woods institutions would form the backbone of international economics. However, just as with the Security Council, the new economic institutions were deliberately crafted to give the "Big Four the greatest voting power as well as permanent seats on the boards of directors."[10] In the proposed International Bank for Reconstruction and Development, the top shareholders were envisioned to be the United States, the United Kingdom, and the Soviet Union.

At the same time the international order was being shaped by diplomacy and economic policy, the US military establishment crafted plans for the postwar world that operationalized the Rooseveltian vision. The first consideration was to provide for "defense in depth" of the Western Hemisphere by creating "a defensive ring of outlying bases" that would "enable the United States to possess complete control of the Atlantic and Pacific oceans and to keep hostile powers far from American territory."[11] The second was to ensure that American power, particularly air and naval forces, could be quickly and easily deployed to other parts of the world from the continental United States.[12] The latter was based on the assessment that North America would not become a battlefield. Instead the United States would fight its enemies abroad, and it would do so by developing an expeditionary-oriented military (a theme that we explore further in chapter 6).

Roosevelt was also confident that he had found a solution to dealing with the Soviet Union. With hindsight, we can criticize the apparent naiveté of the

Roosevelt administration expecting that the USSR would be a reliable partner with the United States in maintaining global security, but it is important to recall that the prevailing view in 1944 and early 1945 (when the USSR and the United States were allies) was that the Soviet Union was indeed "in a mood to accept decent compromises" and that it "needs no more territory, but badly needs several decades of peace."[13] Similarly, US officials who had engaged with their Soviet counterparts at the conferences at Bretton Woods and Dumbarton Oaks, where the architecture of the postwar world was being assembled, had left these sessions confident that the Soviet Union would play an active and constructive role in the new institutions.[14]

In assessing the reason for his confidence that the Soviet Union under Stalin could be a responsible partner for peace, Roosevelt noted, "I bank on his realism. He must be tired of sitting on bayonets."[15] At the Yalta Conference in February 1945, after initial discussions with the Soviets faltered on a variety of issues (notably the composition of a postwar Polish government), Roosevelt sent a personal letter to Stalin on February 6th stressing the importance of finding a "meeting of minds" on these matters. He noted that if the major powers could find satisfactory compromises, it would enable the continuation of the wartime partnership in order to "get an understanding on even more vital things in the future."[16] The transcripts of subsequent sessions indicate that compromise agreements could be reached, providing for governments in Eastern Europe that would be pro-Soviet in terms of their foreign and defense policies but otherwise permitted to retain their domestic institutions.[17] Roosevelt and British prime minister Winston Churchill were prepared to recognize a "pre-eminent role" for the Soviet Union in Eastern Europe but insisted that noncommunists be part of coalition governments and that reasonably free elections be held in the region.[18]

Roosevelt and Stalin also again expanded on the idea of joint Soviet-American trusteeships for former colonies in Asia. Both seemed confident that they could work together to provide security for these territories and prepare them for full independence, with only a short occupation period required.[19] Roosevelt's expectation was that there would be a free flow of ideas and goods between the different spheres policed by each of the major powers, by which he hoped to prevent the emergence of rival and hostile blocs.[20]

By and large, Americans themselves believed that the outcome of the Yalta Conference had been positive. This included a series of compromises on Eastern Europe, Soviet entry into the Pacific war, and the creation of a new international organization. It seemed to validate Roosevelt's instinct that the major powers could cooperate to maintain international peace. Opinion polls taken in March 1945 noted that some 51 percent of Americans rated the Yalta meetings a success, and satisfaction with the tenor of cooperation between the major powers rose from 46 percent (prior to the Yalta Conference) to 71 percent.[21] In the month prior to his death, Roosevelt had, in his mind, laid the foundations for what he believed was an "appropriate international role" (and one that was sustainable in terms of US domestic politics) for the United States—regional hegemony in the Western Hemisphere and a consultative role on ensuring security in other parts of the world—without committing it to being dragged into their day-to-day issues and quarrels. Americans reluctantly accepted that they would have to play a greater role in global affairs, but Roosevelt himself realized that there was little appetite for global interventionism. Instead, the preferred American position was one "of regional leadership combined with great power consultation at the international level."[22]

The Soviet Challenge

The Rooseveltian vision for the role the US would play in international affairs, however, was based on several assumptions that ended up being invalid. The first was that his concept of regional policemen assumed that other powers were capable of exercising this function, thus freeing the United States from having to assume direct responsibility. This assumption overlooked the devastation to European economies and European distaste for remilitarizing. Indeed, the structure of the proposed UN Security Council envisioned four other major powers, each capable of playing a leading role. In commenting on the first draft of the UN Charter after the 1944 Dumbarton Oaks conference, Robert Arthur James Gascoyne-Cecil, the Viscount Cranborne, the Conservative leader in the House of Lords, noted that the UN system would place "the responsibility for international security four-square on the shoulders of the nations best able to bear it."[23] While Roosevelt certainly hoped that the Soviet Union would be a constructive player, he also assumed that other powers would be able to balance and contain Soviet expansionism.

However, a US military estimate provided by the Joint Staff to the secretary of state in the summer of 1944 was already calling into question the whole notion of the regional policemen: "After the defeat of Japan, the United States and the Soviet Union will be the only military powers of the first magnitude. This is due in each case to a combination of geographical position and extent, and vast munitioning potential."[24] As much as Roosevelt wanted it to be, the world was not going to be a multipolar one where the United States would function as a "chairman of the board" delegating significant responsibility for regional security to other partners. Instead, it was trending in the direction of becoming a bipolar one where Europe was sandwiched between the Soviet Union and the United States, and Asia would become a focus of competition rather than cooperation.

Even as it became clearer that the Roosevelt policeman model would not function, the other core assumption—that the United States and the Soviet Union could continue to work together in common cause to shape the postwar world—was also being challenged. Roosevelt had assumed that, as the Soviet Union extended its sphere of influence, "Stalin would be discreet and operate with some appearance of democratic method."[25] A number of senior US military figures also hoped that, if presented with clear signals that the United States would not seek to take advantage of Soviet weakness in the immediate postwar period to extend American power, this "might be reciprocated by the Soviets, providing time for Western Europe to recover and for the British to reassert some influence on the Continent"—thus holding out the possibility that the Four Policemen model might prove workable in the future.[26]

However, Stalin and his associates decided that Soviet security required complete control in the countries that were occupied by the advancing Red Army to provide the country strategic depth and some spoils for a very costly war. The Soviet position was that it was entitled to "special security arrangements" in Turkey, Eastern and Central Europe, and East Asia that entailed a much greater degree of Soviet supervision than Roosevelt had envisioned. Moscow's imperial streak appeared when Soviet foreign minister Vyacheslav Molotov argued that the Soviets "had to introduce order" in these areas to consolidate the Soviet position.[27] Starting only weeks after the Yalta Conference, the first steps were already taken to replace the "broad-based" coalitions in Eastern Europe with communist-dominated governments, which in American eyes represented a violation of the Yalta accords.[28] American public opinion reflected the dramatic drop in popular confidence that the United States and the Soviet Union could work together; by the fall of 1945, only 44 percent of respondents agreed with the proposition that the United States could cooperate with the Soviet Union. By February 1946, that number had dropped to 35 percent.[29] The following month, at Westminster College in Missouri, Winston Churchill delivered his famous "Iron Curtain" speech that is often used as a symbolic starting point of the Cold War.

Yet, even faced with the growing evidence that the wartime alliance with the Soviet Union would give way to a postwar rivalry for influence—an impression certainly solidified by Truman's experiences in meeting with Stalin at the Potsdam Conference during the summer of 1945—the Truman administration was not initially inclined to respond more aggressively to the Soviet posture or to keep US forces deployed overseas to check Soviet power, in part because there was no immediate perceived threat to US security.[30] Roosevelt's preference for a short postwar occupation period (of one to two years) was endorsed by his successors.[31] Moreover, in the months after the German and Japanese surrenders, there was enormous pressure on the part of Congress and the general public to accelerate the demobilization of US forces and return servicemen from Europe and East Asia. Secretary of War Robert Patterson expressed his concerns in a memo of November 1, 1945, that the rapid pace of demobilization would leave the United States with diminished leverage in the international arena, but his

Table 1.1: The Soviet Bloc, 1955

Country	Population	Land Area (square miles)
Soviet Union	216,200,000	8,602,700
Albania	1,625,000	11,100
Bulgaria	7,798,000	42,796
People's Republic of China	669,000,000	3,911,209
Czechoslovakia	13,648,874	49,354
German Democratic Republic	16,500,000	41,380
Hungary	9,977,870	35,905
North Korea	10,750,000	49,114
Mongolia	954,000	614,350
Poland	29,731,000	120,442
Romania	18,403,000	91,654
North Vietnam	15,903,000	62,808
Total, Soviet bloc:	1,010,490,744	13,632,812
Total, world:	2,780,296,616	57,308,738
Percentage of Soviet bloc:	36 percent	24 percent

views were not shared by others in the Truman cabinet.[32] By the end of 1945, the US Army had already released nearly half of its personnel from service, and when delays were contemplated in the repatriation of remaining forces from overseas stations, there were heated protests not only from the servicemen but also from many US politicians.[33]

In Search of New Ideas

Truman's initial preference was to return to the prewar approach of relying on American "economic rather than military power to achieve its foreign policy aims" and concentrating on the Western Hemisphere.[34] Even before FDR's death, the United States and Latin American nations, meeting at Mexico City in March 1945, had reaffirmed their commitment to mutual defense in the Act of Chapultepec, noting that "any attempt on the part of a non-American State against the integrity or inviolability of the territory, the sovereignty or the political independence of an American State shall be considered as an act of aggression against all the American States" and pledging to "consult amongst themselves in order to agree upon the measures it may be advisable to take."[35] One other recommendation that grew out of this conference was the proposal to enshrine this understanding in a formal treaty providing for collective self-defense, which occurred at Rio de Janeiro in September 1947 when the Inter-American Treaty of Reciprocal Assistance was signed.[36] Significantly this agreement committed the United States, as a matter of treaty obligation, to view an "armed attack" against any other American state as an attack on the United States and to offer assistance "in meeting the attack" (Article 3).

But when it came to the rest of the world, the first preference was not for the United States to become directly involved but to prop up other nations, starting with the British and the French, so that they would be able to better contain and balance Soviet power.[37] In keeping with Roosevelt's vision of the United States as the provider of air and naval "backup" for other powers, the nation, instead of "folding up" its naval command in the Mediterranean Sea once the European war was over and turning responsibility for security over to the British (which had been the plan communicated to Rear Adm. Jules James in 1945), now began to build up its presence in the region, including destroyers, battleships, and aircraft carriers—and to patrol from Gibraltar through to the Persian Gulf.[38]

But the traditional methods for ensuring American security—hemispheric consolidation combined with some military and financial assistance to partner countries in the Old World—was, by the end of the 1946, proving inadequate in coping with the Soviet challenge.[39] China was convulsed by civil war, while Britain was running out of resources to sustain the efforts to prop up pro-Western governments in Greece and Turkey. Dean Acheson, who was then serving as undersecretary of state, recalled his shock when, in February 1947, he received a confidential communication from the British government informing Washington that "British aid to Greece and Turkey would end in six weeks."[40]

The prospect of a British withdrawal from the eastern Mediterranean was an important catalyst in forcing the Truman administration to consider the question as to "how far did the American sphere of responsibility have to extend in order to ensure American security?"[41] Acheson, Secretary of State George Marshall, and others were willing to articulate a fundamental redefinition of what constituted the vital interests of the United States. If left unchecked, Soviet gains in Turkey and Greece—themselves two countries remote from the American heartland and not in and of themselves major trading partners of the United States nor important sources of raw materials for its economy—"might open three continents to Soviet penetration. Like apples in a barrel infected by one rotten one, the corruption of Greece would infect Iran and all to the east. It would also carry infection to Africa through Asia Minor and Egypt, and to Europe through Italy and France, already threatened by the strongest domestic Communist parties in Western Europe."[42] US officials began to realize that "the Soviet presence in Eastern Europe, the vacuums of power in Western Europe and northeast Asia, and the emergence of revolutionary nationalism" as decolonization began in what would be known as the "Third World" (including the insurgencies then under way in French Indochina and the Dutch East Indies) could pose a threat to American well-being and power at home and abroad, meaning that the United States needed to be able to "mobilize and project its own power to protect its core values."[43]

Redefining the National Interest

During this time an evolution was under way in how senior officials conceived of the vital interests of the United States. The first was a geographic shift, in which pivotal countries in Europe and Asia, as opposed to Latin America, were seen as the necessary "outposts" to guarantee US security.[44] The second was the importance of the "economic health" of the Old World. Initially the US approach had been, particularly with regard to the former Axis powers, to ensure that they did not possess an economic base from which to reconstruct their military power—a vision that had taken root in the plan developed by Henry Morgenthau during the Second World War and ratified by the Quebec Summit between Roosevelt and Winston Churchill in September 1944, which called for "converting Germany into a country primarily agricultural and pastoral in its character."[45] Over time, however, the American attitude shifted from a strategy of denial to one of guided economic reconstruction. Truman himself had come to the realization that the United States itself "cannot enjoy prosperity in a world of economic stagnation."[46] US security was threatened if the resource potential and economic base of Western Europe, Africa, the Middle East, and South and East Asia were to fall under Soviet domination. At the same time, "long-term American prosperity required open markets, unhindered access to raw materials, and the rehabilitation of much—if not all—of Eurasia along liberal capitalist lines."[47] A first step had occurred in January 1947, after the British and the Americans had agreed to merge their two occupation areas in Germany to form "Bizonia" as a way to accelerate economic and political redevelopment in northwestern Germany.

Truman's own evolving view of what the US role ought to be in the world was on full display when he gave his now-famous address before a joint session of Congress on March 12, 1947. Identifying the crisis in Greece and Turkey as directly affecting US national security, he noted that there were no other "policemen" able to help and that "should we fail to aid Greece and Turkey in this fateful hour, the effect will be far reaching to the West as well as to the East." Anticipating resistance from those who would argue that the fate of Greece and Turkey themselves were not of vital importance to the United States, Truman offered a redefinition of US national security beyond hemispheric defense to argue that America must be "willing to help free peoples to maintain their free institutions and their national integrity against aggressive movements that seek to impose upon them totalitarian regimes. This is no more than a frank recognition that totalitarian regimes imposed on free peoples, by direct or indirect aggression, undermine the foundations of international peace and hence the security of the United States." However, at this point, Truman retained his preference that US assistance "should be primarily through economic and financial aid."[48]

After Truman obtained congressional approval for this initial request, the next step (beyond the provision of immediate, short-term emergency assistance to Greece and Turkey) was to promote a more systematic and institutionalized "form of assistance that would treat the economic chaos left in the wake of war."[49] This reflected a shift from the immediate postwar disaster relief, "limited aid for maintaining minimal civilian consumption to broader aid for increasing production as a way to limit imports, increase exports and eliminate the need for further external assistance."[50] This required a more "global" view in which the United States committed itself to the "sustained rejuvenation" of the economies of Western Europe and Northeast Asia and ensuring the free flow of vital resources from the Near East and Africa as well as enhancing their linkages to the United States.[51] During his famous commencement address at Harvard University on June 5, 1947, Secretary of State George Marshall declared that US policy would be to promote "the revival of a working economy in the world so as to permit the emergence of political and social conditions in which free institutions can exist." The United States had a compelling interest in assisting "the return of normal economic health in the world, without which there can be no political stability and no assured peace."[52] This was not based on solely altruistic considerations; rather, a restored global economy was critical for American firms to expand their markets, secure access to raw materials, and to pursue new investment opportunities.[53]

In the spring of 1948, Congress passed the Economic Cooperation Act of 1948 (the ECA, Public Law 472, Eightieth Congress, Second Session), in which US legislators formally recognized that economic stagnation in Europe and other parts of the world "endangers the establishment of a lasting peace" and the "general welfare and national interest of the United States." Countries located "wholly or partly in Europe" were eligible for assistance, provided that they agreed to participate in a joint pan-European recovery program. This entailed joining the Organization for European Economic Cooperation (established on April 16, 1948) and then concluding a bilateral agreement with the United States setting out the terms under which US aid would be used. In turn, the U.S. encouraged European states to work together and to integrate their economies. By promoting a united Europe the United States hoped to achieve greater economies of scale and to encourage countries, particularly smaller ones, to view their prosperity as indivisible from their neighbors'. Subsequent modifications of the act allowed for Asian countries to receive aid (without the proviso that they join a common European economic effort). The main objective "was to establish conditions in which sound economic relations among the European countries, and of European countries with the rest of the world, would exist. These sound economic relations include maximization of trade."[54] In so doing, policymakers hoped to address "the vulnerability of American strategic and economic interests" that were threatened by "postwar economic dislocation and social and political unrest."[55] From 1948 to 1953, aid provided under the rubric of the "Marshall Plan" (as aid to Europe provided as a result of the ECA was popularly termed) as well as other kinds of economic development assistance totaled over $44 billion.[56] This also marked the beginning of linking American strategic aims with economic tools—in particular, the assessment that promoting growth in other countries by extending access to the US market would benefit both American national security as well as its overall prosperity.[57] Leaders seemed to recognize that the goal of sharing the burden for international security required national economies that could generate the wealth and capabilities needed to police their spheres of influence.

The ECA also mandated the "greatest possible utilization of private trade channels" so that while the US government was providing the grants to assist countries in recovery, it would be private businesses that would benefit from the increased ability of other countries to import US-produced equipment and raw materials.[58] The act also required that 50 percent of "the gross tonnage of commodities procured within the United States out of funds made available" were to be shipped on US-flagged vessels—thus building up and extending the ability of American shipping firms to reach markets.[59] The ECA also tied together US strategic imperatives with an appeal to the self-interest of American companies; Undersecretary for Economic Affairs William L. Clayton noted plainly, in early 1947, that American businesses "need markets—big markets—in which to buy and sell."[60] Not only did domestic businesses benefit, but, under the aegis of the Economic Cooperation Authority, the agency set up to disburse ECA funds, American companies were engaged in the effort to build projects, particularly those connected with infrastructure, all throughout Europe.[61]

The final stage in the transformation of the United States into a global superpower came with the realization that "economic recovery was impossible without military security."[62] Moving beyond the Rooseveltian demand for capabilities to permit the rapid egress of US forces from the American continent (which would otherwise remain garrisoned within US territory), US policymakers (some quite grudgingly) accepted the need for more open-ended security arrangements with other states. (They were aided by a growing sense from the business community that the United States needed to safeguard its investments in Europe's recovery.[63]) This, of course, flew straight in the face of the advice that America's first president, George Washington, had provided in his 1796 Farewell Address, with its warning to avoid "entangling alliances."

The Rio Pact was a first step, a legally binding treaty between the United States and other countries of Latin America that went beyond earlier recommendations for collective security or resolutions that were binding only for the duration of the Second World War.[64] But the main challenge was in taking the Rio Pact's provision for collective defense, especially an American commitment to come to the aid of another treaty partner if attacked—and extending that principle beyond the Western Hemisphere. This was done, in part, by reframing the American defensive perimeter from the Atlantic and Pacific Oceans to the dividing lines between the Soviet sphere and the rest of the world on the continents of the Eastern Hemisphere (in other words, to make places such as Western Europe "honorary members" of the Western Hemisphere).[65]

In 1948, the first steps were taken to start discussions on a possible Atlantic security pact that would bind the United States in an alliance with the countries of Western Europe. These initial conversations took place against the backdrop of the coup d'état in Czechoslovakia in February, which had replaced a democratically elected government with a communist regime. At a conference convened in Brussels in March, Belgium, Britain, France, Holland, and Luxembourg concluded the Treaty of Economic, Social and Cultural Collaboration and Collective Self-Defense, which provided for a consultative council to promote joint decision making and contained a clause committing the signatories to mutual defense. Initially some US officials hoped that the Brussels Treaty signaled that Western European states could collectively counterbalance the Soviet Union without the need for US involvement.[66] However, the signatories made it clear that they required the active support of the United States to sustain their efforts.[67] A signal of the evolving American attitude came when Sen. Arthur Vandenberg sponsored a Senate resolution (number 239, passed in June 1948), which in part called for the "Association of the United States, by constitutional process, with such regional and other collective arrangements as are based on continuous and effective self-help and mutual aid, and as affect its national security."[68] Vandenberg's public efforts were mirrored by discussions within the National Security Council (NSC), where memoranda were prepared to justify US support for the Brussels process, finding ways to induce other European states to join the existing signatories and to proceed with negotiating a "defense agreement for the whole North Atlantic area."[69]

The passage of the Vandenberg Resolution, coupled with the start of the Soviet blockade of the land routes that guaranteed access to the western sectors of Berlin in July 1948, "forced the United States to grapple with the problems" of defending Western Europe against possible Soviet aggression and highlighted the need for more permanent security arrangements than the ad hoc provision of military assistance to a country on a bilateral basis (as had occurred for Greece and Turkey in 1947) or simply providing targeted economic support to a group of countries (as the Marshall Plan was meant to do).[70] Representatives of the Brussels Treaty signatory states, along with US and Canadian officials, convened during the summer for the "Washington Exploratory Talks" for a proposed Atlantic security pact. Reaching the conclusion that the security of North America was impacted by the Soviet threat to Western Europe, the talks reached the conclusion that the only solution was for the United States to associate with the Europeans in a North Atlantic security arrangement. In developing a draft for a "North Atlantic Treaty," US negotiators then borrowed language from both the Rio and Brussels Treaties, particularly the proviso that an attack against one treaty member would be considered an attack against all.[71] In order to deal with lingering isolationist concerns that the United States was being "entangled" in a military alliance that would drag the country into new wars, the proposed North Atlantic alliance was redefined as a "partnership for peace"—language that would be resurrected decades later to characterize further expansions of US-led alliances around the world.[72]

The North Atlantic Treaty was signed in Washington on April 4, 1949. In order to lessen the chances that the Senate might not choose to ratify the agreement, the final version did not automatically commit the United States (or any other member) to have to go to war; the famous Article 5 guarantee simply requires each member to "assist the Party or Parties so attacked" but noted that any action, including the use of armed force, would be taken as each member "deems necessary."[73] Moreover, the agreement was couched as a treaty of "political guaranty" with the aim of making "Europeans feel secure so that they could get on with the task of economic recovery."[74] It is important to note that at the time of ratification, there was no expectation that the treaty required a unified command structure or for US forces to be stationed in Europe.[75] By a vote of 82–19, the Senate approved the treaty (on July 21, 1949), "a margin sufficient to suggest that the United States had abandoned its isolationist tradition," but at the same time the United States took no steps to deploy its combat troops, and in many ways the North Atlantic Treaty Organization "remained largely symbolic."[76]

From Shattered Dream to Americanized International Order

The successful Soviet test of its own atom bomb and the fall of mainland China to the communists in 1949 shook America's geopolitical confidence. But it was the impact of the first months of the Korean War—when South Korean troops and a small contingent of US forces were nearly driven off the peninsula by the North Korean army—that led US policymakers to a wholesale reassessment of the US approach, including the desirability of forward-deploying American military units in support of security commitments.[77] This was the catalyst for a number of events. First, it freed the National Security Council report NSC-68 from the interagency process and formally acknowledged the United States was the bulwark to Soviet expansionism.[78] Further, by signing NSC-68 in September 1950, with its recommendations calling for the United States to "lead in building a successfully functioning political and economic system in the free world" in order to contain Soviet power and ultimately to "foster a fundamental change in the nature of the Soviet system," Truman made this official US policy.

The second was the transformation of the North Atlantic Treaty "from a loose mutual defense pact into a permanent military alliance, with U.S. troop commitments and a formal command structure under U.S. leadership."[79] This built on Gen. Omar Bradley's observation that the United States could not count on friends and partners in other parts of the world "if our strategy dictates that we shall first abandon them to the enemy with a promise of later liberation."[80] At the first meeting of the North Atlantic Treaty Organization (NATO) Council after the start of the Korean War, the United States pledged to enact "substantial increases in the strength of the United States forces to be stationed in Western Europe in the interest of the defense of that area."[81] In turn, the Europeans pushed hard for the creation of "an integrated force in Europe commanded by an American" and lobbied for Dwight D. Eisenhower to become the first Supreme Allied Commander.[82] NATO thus acquired its "unprecedented integrated multinational command structure" in order to provide for "the efficient pooling of military power," which required "coordination of military deployments, operational doctrine, and plans, and . . . reliable mechanisms for the immediate exercise of centralized command."[83]

Finally—fulfilling the fears of a number of US policymakers that the Rio and Washington Treaties might "lead to pressure on the United States to agree to similar agreements in other parts of the globe"—there was the expansion of America's security commitments beyond the Western Hemisphere and Western Europe, what Robert Jervis has termed the "globalization of U.S. commitments."[84] The fighting in Korea gave new impetus to a "Pacific pact" proposal that had been advanced by the Australians and that served as the basis for the trilateral Australia–New Zealand–United States alliance concluded in 1951. This ANZUS Pact, along with bilateral security agreements the United States reached with Japan and the Philippines, set the stage for a US-constructed regional security architecture for the Pacific Rim.[85] Elements of the Pacific Pact proposal then found their way into the creation of the Southeast Asia Treaty Organization (SEATO), set up by the 1954 Manila Treaty, and to complete the links between the geographic regions, the United States encouraged a number of Middle Eastern countries to follow the model of the Brussels Treaty. The Baghdad Pact (1955) bound Britain and several Middle Eastern states in a mutual-security treaty, which created the Central Treaty Organization (CENTO); the United States had essentially underwritten its creation and formally joined the military committee of this alliance in 1958.

Managing Global Security, 1950–89

Within the decade following the end of World War II, therefore, the United States moved from a strategy that limited itself to controlling the Western Hemisphere in favor of embracing an approach predicated on global management of security.[86] In so doing, the plea of former president Herbert Hoover for the United States to pull back and focus on becoming the "Gibraltar of Western civilization" in a radio address on December 20, 1950, fell largely on deaf ears.[87] Instead many American policymakers embraced the notion of creating "security communities" with other like-minded states, which in turn might facilitate the spread of a liberal order defined by free markets and democratic forms of governance.[88]

Part of this process of global management required the United States, as Paul Nitze noted in a 1952 State Department Policy Planning Staff memorandum, to take up "the effective organization, direction and leadership" of the "actual and potential capabilities of the US and of allied and friendly states." A second memorandum observed that such coordination was required in order to achieve a "limited mobilization designed to develop and maintain a favorable power position without resort to an armament effort that would disrupt the economies of the free nations and thus undermine the vitality and integrity of free society."[89] What was particularly noteworthy was the speed in which American policymakers embraced "the belief that the world was tightly interconnected" and that threats in different parts of the globe, in areas before World War II that would have been seen as remote, were now believed to "threaten vital American interests."[90]

In turn the United States rapidly developed a security network that extended its reach far beyond its continental borders. In 1938, the United States "had no military alliances and no U.S. troops were stationed on territory it did not control."[91] Two decades later, the United States had some 450 bases spread around the world in thirty-six different countries. Moreover, many of these facilities were no longer viewed as temporary in nature but as permanent outposts.[92] In contrast to FDR's expectation of the United States as a balancer of last resort, by 1963 one half of the active-duty military forces and most of the combat-ready units of the US military were based overseas in sixty-five host countries, while the United States also committed to train the military personnel of seventy-two nations.[93]

The United States also developed a truly global presence, in contrast to the Soviet Union, whose bloc was largely concentrated around its immediate borders, most notably in Eastern Europe. Reflecting its maritime character, America's influence penetrated nearly all parts of the world.[94] Moreover, America's rise to global superpower status was facilitated by the active cooperation and indeed invitation of other countries, which cultivated the US presence as a way to obtain concrete security and economic benefits. Unlike its European partners (and to their chagrin), the United States promoted decolonization.

The "unprecedented network" of American global commitments was seen as critical to cementing US relations with partners all over the world—including having US forces stationed as a visible and tangible sign of the American security pledge.[95] The United States offered many countries alliance on easy terms (in contrast to the demands often placed by the Soviet Union on its satellites), providing, in addition to military security, generous amounts of economic and military assistance as well as open access to the US market for their exports.[96] As a result, over time "many of the countries that welcomed American influence were also able to do considerably better, at least in long term material terms, than . . . the United States itself."[97]

Behind the protection of the US security umbrella, American businesses benefited from the creation of zones of stability in other parts of the world, starting with Western Europe. By 1970, some thirty-five hundred American companies had foreign direct investments in approximately fifteen thousand enterprises around the world. In turn, many large corporations adopted "global" management structures, which better integrated domestic operations with international operations. The end result was that the "top management of the companies became more involved in worldwide operations than before," and this also led to the development of a strong internationalist constituency within the American business community.[98]

The Discontents of a Superpower

America embraced superpower status because it saw no plausible alternative to protecting its own interests as long as the Soviet Union remained a peer competitor. Given Soviet expansionism and its active program to promote communism around the world, oceans provided no protection against ideological expansionism. Consequently Secretary of Defense James Forrestal had argued that the keys to maintaining American dominance in the global system revolved around the abilities to "outproduce the world" and to "control the sea and . . . strike inland."[99] Forward presence, alliances, and economic integration were all key elements of the strategy.

The US-led system began to falter in the 1960s. During the second Nixon-Kennedy presidential debate (on October 7, 1960), Sen. John F. Kennedy expressed his concerns that the United States had "not maintained our position and our prestige" and that the "relative strength of the United States both militarily, politically, psychologically, and scientifically and industrially . . . has deteriorated." Kennedy might have been speaking hyperbolically, but as the decade went on US economic problems made it far more difficult to sustain US commitments (and also caused some American companies to sell off their foreign subsidiaries. This was exacerbated by the recovery of Europe and East Asia, which lessened their dependence on the United States for help, the collapse of some of the regional alliances created by the United States (such as CENTO and SEATO), the emergence of Soviet capabilities that permitted Moscow to project its power beyond its immediate Eurasian range to points further around the world, and the end of the Bretton Woods arrangements, which had enshrined American financial dominance of the Western world.[100]

Yet even after these setbacks, the United States remained "the acknowledged leader of the Western world."[101] The United States—and the international system it created—showed tremendous resiliency. Despite the economic shocks of the 1970s, the major powers of the Western world had too much invested in the stability of the institutions created by the United States and Washington's ability to sustain them to allow complete collapse—and could see a far less appealing future in a world more dominated by the Soviet Union. It is true that America's share of "world production and wealth had shrunk," but the United States could draw upon an "increasingly integrated economic bloc"—including the nations of Western Europe and East Asia—in order to help assist (and fund) the management of common military and economic affairs.[102] Ronald Reagan's presidency helped to fully reestablish America's global leadership as well as provide a renewed narrative for efforts to promote further consolidation and integration among the nations of the "Free World."

Thus, Mikhail Gorbachev would lament that the Soviet Union was "surrounded not by invincible armies but by superior economies."[103] However, the US role in maintaining the military security of the noncommunist world was not neglected. Michael Howard's observation, while made specifically of Europeans, could also be applied to others in the Free World; he commented on the "degree to which we Europeans have abandoned the primary responsibility for our defense to the United States" and "have come to take the deterrence provided by others for granted."[104]

Beyond the Cold War

As the Cold War began to wind down in the late 1980s—and as the original goal of NSC-68 (modifying Soviet behavior) appeared to be achievable, the question was raised as to what might follow. After the USSR collapsed in 1991, some expected that the United States would "come home." Patrick Buchanan argued that "NATO, CENTO, SEATO, the ANZUS and Rio pacts, and security treaties with Korea, Japan, [and] Taiwan" were meant to "be temporary alliances to endure only as long as the crisis endured." With the Soviet threat over, the United States now "had the opportunity to pull up our 'trip wires' around the world and shed unwanted commitments—to recapture our freedom of action and restore a traditional foreign policy."[105] Buchanan and others argued that the United States could return to a pre–World War II posture in international affairs, using primarily commercial instruments to retain US influence in the world.

But others argued it would be irresponsible for the United States to dismantle its global security architecture. The Soviet Union might have disappeared, but concerns were raised that the "withering away" of the Cold War might "release previously contained forces and generate fresh contradictions" that would take advantage of any post–Cold War vacuum caused by US disengagement.[106] Wars in the Balkans and parts of Africa seemed to reinforce this concern.

Any American withdrawal could also put vital interests at risk. Even with the USSR gone, America's forward presence and direct engagement were needed to "(1) to prevent, deter, and reduce the threat of nuclear, biological, and chemical weapons attacks on the United States; (2) to prevent the emergence of a hostile hegemony in Europe or Asia; (3) to prevent the emergence of a hostile major power on United States borders or in control of the seas; (4) to prevent the catastrophic collapse of major global systems (trade, financial markets, supplies of energy, and environmental); and (5) to ensure the survival of United States allies."[107]

A rejoinder to Buchanan's thesis was provided by Henry Nau, who argued: "Strengthening alliances . . . makes expanding markets possible. A larger NATO in Europe and widening U.S. alliances in Asia are not alternatives to trade and economic cooperation: they are prerequisites."[108] Without security and stability, economic development and global trade were not possible. Furthermore, the argument was advanced that the United States needed to retain its position in order to guarantee an "international system, which provides for open seas, open trade and open societies lightly defended."[109]

Moreover, even when the Cold War came to an end, preventing any future power—whether a resurgent Russia, a rising China, or some other combination of states—from dominating the Eurasian land mass remained a core US national security objective. Former national security adviser Zbigniew Brzezinski summed up this view in his 1997 *Foreign Affairs* essay: "A power that dominated Eurasia would exercise decisive influence over two of the world's three most economically productive regions, Western Europe and East Asia. A glance at the map also suggests that a country dominant in Eurasia would almost automatically control the Middle East and Africa. . . . What happens with the distribution of power on the Eurasian landmass will be of decisive importance to America's global primacy and historical legacy."[110] Preventing the rise of a new peer competitor to replace the Soviet Union was seen as a desirable strategic aim of the United States—and remains the strategic rationale for continuing US engagement across the Eurasian landmass and the Pacific Rim, particularly vis-à-vis a rising China.[111] In so doing, the United States hopes to shape the architecture of the region and to encourage China to become, in

Robert Zoellick's words, a "responsible stakeholder" of the status quo.[112] By so doing, it would guarantee, as Thomas Donilon said, "the United States' security and prosperity in the 21st century."[113] In an attempt to avoid precipitating a new Cold War with China, Secretary of State Condoleezza Rice concluded that China should rise within the larger context of a series of US-inspired security and economic relationships—both older ones that were forged during the Cold War with the Soviet Union as well as new ones that have emerged in the early twenty-first century—with other countries of the region that would guarantee that China would be "more likely to play a positive role."[114]

The risk, of course, is that Beijing will perceive US intentions quite differently. In assessing the US strategy, some Chinese commentators conclude that it is "setting a limit on China's rise and growth."[115] Some see US efforts to bring together Japan, South Korea, the nations of Southeast Asia, and India as designed to create a "crescent-shaped ring of encirclement" intended "to diminish China's influence in this region and to safeguard and expand U.S. strategic interest in Asia"—to contain China (*ezhi Zhongguo*).[116]

Creating a New Order

For many American policymakers, the US rise to superpower status had not only been about containing the Soviet Union, but also creating a better global order.[117] The existence of the USSR meant that the United States tended to adopt a defensive crouch in safeguarding the noncommunist world, but its disappearance opened up new possibilities for realizing Wilsonian and Rooseveltian aspirations for molding the global system. Rather than "coming home," US power ought to be maintained (and even expanded) in order to better shape the international environment.[118] During the Cold War, the United States had focused its attention on helping other states resist outside pressure. After 1991, there was a pronounced shift in favor of actively spreading liberal political and economic institutions (usually covered under the rubric of "democracy promotion) to other states. Samuel Huntington wrote, "The pervasiveness of democratic norms rested in large part on the commitment to those norms of the most powerful country in the world."[119] This was not to be done purely for altruistic reasons, although US policymakers often embraced such rhetoric in their public statements. Rather, it was based on the assessment that "tying American security to global democracy" was the "cheapest way to keep the peace."[120] The democratic peace thesis—that democracies tend to not fight each other, to settle their disputes in a pacific manner, to cooperate in creating rules-based international organizations, and to trade with each other—was formally incorporated into US strategic documents. The 1996 National Security Strategy declared: "Democracies create free markets that offer economic opportunity, make for more reliable trading partners, and are far less likely to wage war on one another."[121]

The post–Cold War paradox saw the expansion, rather than the retraction, of America's presence around the world. Indeed, during Bill Clinton's tenure as president, US military forces were deployed in more countries (not fewer) than at any point during his immediate predecessors' time in the Oval Office, even though the Cold War had been in full force.[122] This trend has continued, with the United States today having military personnel present in more than 140 countries.[123] If "economic engagement . . . [would] eventually lead to greater political liberalization," and if renewed security guarantees were essential to safeguarding the growth of zones of peace and prosperity around the world, then it would make sense to commit the United States to a "strategy of enlargement . . . of the world's free community of market democracies."[124] This would mean expanding the scope and responsibilities of existing alliances and groupings (such as NATO) and expanding their geographic reach, from their cores in Western Europe and East Asia into the larger Eurasian and Asia-Pacific regions.

In the 1990s, the focus of American efforts was on creating conditions for extending zones of security and prosperity on the theory that "political as well as economic globalization would make the world safer—and more profitable— for the United States."[125] After the terrorist attacks of September 11, 2001, the emphasis shifted toward counterterrorism. While military force was an essential part of the response, the United States also committed itself to making "substantial economic and political investment designed to reconstruct regimes" in order to strengthen states around the world and to prevent "scattered, localized cells from transforming into a potent network with a global reach," rather than withdrawing to a more isolationist position.[126] The 9/11 attacks acted as a "shock" not dissimilar to the Korean War fifty years earlier, focusing American policymakers' attention on why the United States needed to deploy its power to shape the global order and to build up the capacity of its allies for its own security.[127] Under the rubric of "security assistance," the United States focused on "enabling partners and reinforcing allies" in order "to see its partners fulfill regional and global security roles."[128] In the last several years, there has been yet another shift in US focus—away from terrorism toward preventing a rising China from reaching a geopolitical position whereby it might threaten US interests. Yet even the pivot to Asia is couched in terms of making a positive impact on regional and global orders rather than simply balancing China. The pivot to Asia is based on the assessment that it would be possible "to ease China's revisionist aims and convince China that it can achieve its goals within the existing and evolving international system" by "a concerted effort to develop and strengthen regional institutions—in other words, building out the architecture of Asia."[129] At the same time, the United States wants to shift its attention to the Pacific Rim with a degree of confidence that other parts of the world, starting with Europe, will require less direct US involvement.

Indeed, the common thread through the Clinton administration's "democratic enlargement" strategy, the George W. Bush–era "global war on terror," and the Pacific pivot announced by the Barack Obama team is the importance placed on creating far-reaching partnerships with a growing number of "middle powers" that can act as security providers (rather than consumers) and that can contribute to rising global prosperity.

Thus in recent years the United States has moved to offer even closer security and economic relationships to its partners—guaranteed protection against attack, combined with complete access to the American market. A number of US allies already enjoy free-trade agreements with the United States and the proposed Trans-Pacific Partnership and Transatlantic Trade and Investment Partnership (linking the United States to Europe) would cover most of the rest of America's close allies. This means that "trade policy is the pursuit of diplomacy by other means. Accordingly, a central aim of trade negotiations across both the Pacific and the Atlantic is to cement alliances between countries that share interests in security, democracy promotion, and many other areas."[130]

In turn these associations give the United States an unparalleled advantage over any potential adversary. They provide the United States a pool of potential volunteers to augment America's own internal military and economic resources as well as the ability to utilize hundreds of facilities—naval bases, communications centers, and airfields among them—located around the world, which allows the United States to project power anywhere in the world.

For instance, the US–South Korean relationship exemplifies the type of strategic and economic partnership Washington hopes to create with its allies around the world. Originally bound together by the Mutual Defense Treaty of 1953, this security relationship has expanded beyond the immediate defense of the Korean Peninsula. Since 1999, for example, South Korea has taken part in the stabilization operation in East Timor, sent forces to Iraq and Afghanistan (including taking over the management of a provincial reconstruction team), and dispatched warships to take part in the antipiracy operation off the coast of Somalia. South Korea has also accepted the notion of "strategic flexibility"—that is to say, that US forces stationed on the Korean Peninsula can be deployed to other contingencies, thus making South Korea an important staging area for the global projection of US military power. The change reflects South Korea shifting from a consumer of US security guarantees to an active participant in US-led global operations.

At the same time Korea developed an independent and complementary military, the economic relationship evolved too. Today Korea is America's seventh largest trading partner, and products by Samsung and Hyundai are a part of Americans' daily lives. Likewise the United States is Korea's third largest trading partner, with bilateral trade exceeding $100 billion. In recognition of this economic relationship, the two countries ratified a free-trade agreement that went into force in 2012. Once fully implemented, the agreement will remove nearly all tariff barriers and clears the way for the completely free movement of goods and capital between the two countries.

As South Korea has benefited from US assistance in the past, today it is a net donor of assistance to other countries, doing its part to help other countries develop—which supports an overall US strategy of attacking some of the root causes for instability in the world. Further, when asked, South Korea also deployed with American forces to Iraq in the 2000s. As a key industrial power, South Korea forms part of the network of states cooperating with the United States on defense projects, augmenting the research and defense capabilities of US-led alliances. All of this helps to cement South Korea's status as one of the most important strategic and economic partners of the United States—and serves as a model for the type of partnerships Washington hopes to forge with other countries.

Conclusion

Reflecting on the events that defined the post–World War II world, Robert Kagan wrote: "No divine providence or progressive teleology, no unfolding Hegelian dialectic required that liberalism triumph after World War II. Those who live in this remarkable world tend to assume that both the global explosion of democracy and the liberal economic order of free trade and free markets that have spread prosperity these past sixty years were simply a nature stage in humankind's upward progress. We like to believe that the triumph of democracy is the triumph of an idea and the victory of market capitalism is the victory of a better system, and both are irreversible." Yet Kagan argues that the United States is essential to this system, sardonically noting: "The better idea doesn't have to win just because it is a better idea. It requires great powers to champion it."[131]

The economic crisis of 2008–9 weakened the US position, but even with its diminished capacities, the United States remains at the center of the international security system. As the 2014 Quadrennial Defense Review noted: "People around the world gravitate toward the freedom, equality, rule of law, and democratic governance that American citizens are able to enjoy. From setting global norms to defeating terrorist threats and providing humanitarian assistance, the United States collaborates with allies and partners to accomplish a wide range of strategic, operational, and tactical goals."[132] Even with recent declines in US power, the United States remains at the top of the hierarchy of power and "also the foremost impresario of the world's major politico-strategic relationships."[133] The United States has served as a "hub," creating institutions that "upheld international security and free trade and thus cemented America's preponderance by giving other key players potent reasons for choosing cooperation over ganging up."[134] Because other countries continue to gain tangible benefits from association with the United States, they have incentives for the continuation of American leadership and the preservation of the system it has created.

Notes

1. "Address by the President before the Canadian Parliament at Ottawa," August 25, 1943. Excerpts are archived at http://avalon.law.yale.edu/20th_century/decade07.asp.

2. For instance, Francis Cardinal Spellman, archbishop of New York and someone utilized by Roosevelt for diplomatic missions during the conflict, was a proponent of a de facto American hegemony following the war. See John Cooney, *The American Pope: The Life and Times of Francis Cardinal Spellman* (New York: Times Books, 1984), 135.

3. Frederick W. Marks IIII, *Wind over Sand: The Diplomacy of Franklin Roosevelt* (Athens: University of Georgia Press, 1988), 284. The Soviet Union would have primarily responsibility for the Eurasian landmass from Germany to China; the British would take care of Western Europe, the Middle East, and Africa; China the Asia-Pacific region, and the United States the Western Hemisphere.

4. Georg Schild, "Planning for the Postwar Economy and the United Nations," in *World War II in Asia and the Pacific and the War's Aftermath, in General Terms,* ed. Loyd E. Lee (Westport, CT: Greenwood, 1998), 424.

5. *Report of the Secretary of State on the Second Meeting of the Ministers of Foreign Affairs of the American Republics, Habana, July 21–30, 1940,* Department of State publication 1575, Conference Series 48, 71–72.

6. Van Alstyne, Richard W. *American Diplomacy in Action: Security, Expansion, Neutrality* (Stanford, CA: Stanford University Press, 1947), 235.

7. Warren F. Kimball, *The Juggler: Franklin Roosevelt as Wartime Statesman* (Princeton, NJ: Princeton University Press, 1991), 110.

8. Townsend Hoopes and Douglas G. Brinkley, *FDR and the Creation of the U.N.* (New Haven, CT: Yale University Press, 1997), 99–102.

9. See, for instance, the discussion in C. L. Lim, "The Great Power Balance, the United Nations and What the Framers Intended: In Partial Response to Hans Köchler," *Chinese Journal of International Law* 6, no. 2 (2007), esp. 307–10, and Stanley Michalak, *A Primer in Power Politics* (Wilmington, DE: Scholarly Resources, 2001), 202.

10. Raymond F. Mikesell, "The Bretton Woods Debates: A Memoir," *Essays in International Finance* (International Finance Section, Department of Economics, Princeton University), no. 192 (March 1994): 5.

11. Melvyn Leffler, "The American Conception of National Security and the Beginnings of the Cold War, 1945–48," *The American Historical Review* 89, no. 2 (April 1984): 350, citing the set of memoranda prepared by the Joint Chiefs of Staff, dated November 2, 1943, and transmitted by Adm. William J. Leahy, the president's chief of staff, to the president, on November 15, 1943.

12. See, for instance, the Joint Chiefs of Staff memorandum "Over-All Examination of United States Requirements for Military Bases and Rights," September 27, 1945, RG 218, ser. CCS 360 (12-9-42), JCS 570/34. See also the discussion in Leffler, "American Conception," 351–54.

13. W. L. White, *Report on the Russians* (New York: Harcourt, Brace, 1945), 308, 309.

14. See, for instance, Mikesell, "Bretton Woods Debates," 42.

15. Quoted in Susan Butler, ed., *My Dear Mr. Stalin: The Complete Correspondence between Franklin D. Roosevelt and Joseph V. Stalin* (New Haven, CT: Yale University Press, 2005), 9.

16. The letter from Franklin Roosevelt to Joseph Stalin forms part of the "Attachment to Notes, Fourth Formal Meeting of Crimean Conference, 4 P.M., February 7, 1945," and is part of the cache of documents released by the National Security Archive related to the Yalta Conference on October 4, 1998, which is archived at www.gwu.edu/~nsarchiv/coldwar/documents/episode-2/06-01.htm.

17. Roosevelt and his staff may have had in mind the provisions of the 1944 armistice between Finland and the Soviet Union, in which Finland gave up some territory to the USSR and accepted limits on its armed forces but where the Soviet Union agreed not to interfere in Finland's domestic affairs and "left her democratic institutions intact"—a state of affairs reconfirmed by the 1948 Finno-Soviet Treaty. See Victor S. Mamatey, *Soviet Russian Imperialism* (New York: Van Nostrand Reinhold, 1964), 85.

18. Vladislav Zubok and Constantine Pleshakov, *Inside the Kremlin's Cold War: From Stalin to Khrushchev* (Cambridge, MA: Harvard University Press, 1996), 32.

19. See, for instance, the "Memorandum of Conversation—Crimean Conference: Meeting of the President [Roosevelt] with Marshal Stalin" (February 8, 1945), part of the cache of documents released by the National Security Archive related to the Yalta Conference on October 4, 1998, and archived at www.gwu.edu/~nsarchiv/coldwar/documents/episode-2/07-05.htm.

20. Kimball, *Juggler*, 102.

21. Michael Dobbs, *Six Months in 1945: From World War to Cold War* (New York: Knopf, 2012), 107.

22. Kimball, *Juggler*, 109.

23. House of Lords Debates, October 11, 1944, vol. 133, 487.

24. Cited in Maurice Matloff, *Strategic Planning for Coalition Warfare, 1943–1944* (Washington, DC: Government Printing Office, 1959), 523–24, quoting from a memo of the Joint Chiefs of Staff, no. 973 (July 28, 1944), "Fundamental Military Factors in Relation to Discussions Concerning Territorial Trusteeships and Settlements." This memo, drawn up by the Joint Strategic Survey Committee (JSSC) was, with minor amendments, forwarded by the Joint Chiefs of Staff on August 3, 1944, to the secretary of state. See JCS 973/4, 9 Jan 45 title: International Trusteeships.

25. Jerald A. Combs, *The History of American Foreign Policy* (New York: Knopf, 1986), 10.

26. Lefler, "American Conception," 357.

27. Zubok and Pleshakov, *Inside the Kremlin's Cold War*, 98.

28. American president Ronald Reagan wrote in his autobiography *An American Life* (New York: Simon & Schuster, 1990, 305) that as president he sincerely

wrote to the Soviet leaders and insisted that they honor their commitment to freedom in Eastern Europe as expressed in the Yalta agreement. He noted that "at Yalta, I reminded them, Stalin had promised Poland and all the countries of Eastern Europe the right of self-determination, but the Soviets had never granted it to any of them."

29. Cited in John Lewis Gaddis, *The United States and the Origins of the Cold War, 1941–1947* (New York: Columbia University Press, 1972), 289.

30. Truman's initial impressions of Stalin were favorable, but over the time of the conference his assessments became more negative. See Ralph B. Levering and Verena Botzenhart-Viehe, "The American Perspective," in *Debating the Origins of the Cold War: American and Russian Perspectives*, ed. Ralph B. Levering, Vladimir O. Pechatnov, Verena Botzenhart-Viehe, and C. Earl Edmondson (Lanham, MD: Rowman & Littlefield, 2001), 34. Truman also began to question whether or not the Soviet government would honor the agreements it had signed, expressing his doubts, for instance, in a letter to former secretary of war Henry Stimson several months before the latter's death in 1950. Cf. *Mr. President: The First Publication from the Personal Diaries, Private Letters, Papers, and Revealing Interviews of Harry S. Truman, Thirty-Second President of the United States of America*, ed. William Hillman (New York: Farrar, Straus and Young, 1952), 55; Robert A. Pollard, *Economic Security and the Origins of the Cold War, 1945–1950* (New York: Columbia University Press, 1985), 20, 22.

31. Michael Beschloss, *The Conquerors: Roosevelt, Truman and the Destruction of Hitler's Germany, 1941–1945* (New York: Simon & Schuster, 2002), 23.

32. Melvyn P. Leffler, *A Preponderance of Power: National Security, the Truman Administration and the Cold War* (Stanford, CA: Stanford University Press, 1992), 43.

33. Richard W. Stewart, ed., *American Military History, Volume II: The United States Army in a Global Era, 1917–2003* (Washington, DC: Center of Military History, 2005), 201, at www.history.army.mil/books/AMH-V2/AMH%20V2/chapter7.htm.

34. Pollard, *Economic Security*, 22.

35. Quoted in *Pillars of Peace: Documents Pertaining to American Interest in Establishing a Lasting World Peace, January 1941–February 1946* (Carlisle Barracks, PA: Book Department, Army Information School, 1946), 73, 74.

36. Josef L. Kunz, "The Idea of 'Collective Security' in Pan-American Developments," *Western Political Quarterly* 6, no. 4 (December 1953): 678.

37. Paul Kennedy, *The Rise and Fall of the Great Powers: Economic Change and Military Conflict from 1500 to 2000* (New York: Vintage Books, 1987, 1989), 366–68.

38. Jonathan Knight, "American Statecraft and the 1946 Black Sea Straits Controversy," *Political Science Quarterly* 90, no. 3 (Autumn 1975): 454.

39. Herbert Feis, *From Trust to Terror: The Onset of the Cold War, 1945–1950* (New York: Norton, 1970), 126.

40. Dean Acheson, *Present at the Creation: My Years at the State Department* (New York: Norton, 1969), 196.

41. John Lewis Gaddis, *Surprise, Security and the American Experience* (Cambridge, MA: Harvard University Press, 2004), 39.

42. Acheson, *Present at the Creation*, 198.

43. Melvyn P. Leffler, "National Security," *Journal of American History* 77, no. 1 (June 1990): 147.

44. See, for instance, an October 1946 memorandum prepared by Loy Henderson, then the director of the Office of Near Eastern Affairs, for Secretary of State James F. Byrnes, and Byrnes's own comments to Secretary of War Patterson and Secretary of the Navy James Forrestal. Cf. Arnold A. Offner, *"Another Such Victory": President Truman and the Cold War, 1945–1953* (Stanford, CA: Stanford University Press, 2002), 196.

45. Nicholas Thompson, *The Hawk and the Dove: Paul Nitze, George Kennan, and the History of the Cold War* (New York: Henry Holt, 2009), 17.

46. Gaddis, *Origins of the Cold War*, 342.

47. Leffler, "American Conception," 358.

48. A copy of the address is archived at http://avalon.law.yale.edu/20th_century/trudoc.asp.

49. Lawrence A. Kaplan, "The United States and the Origins of NATO, 1946–1949," *Review of Politics* 31, no. 2 (April 1969): 216.

50. Young-Iob Chung, *South Korea in the Fast Lane: Economic Development and Capital Formation* (Oxford: Oxford University Press, 2007), 307–8.

51. Leffler, "American Conception," 375.

52. Marshall's address is archived at www.oecd.org/general/themarshallplan speechatharvarduniversity5june1947.htm.

53. Leffler, "National Security," 147.

54. Walter S. Surrey, "The Economic Cooperation Act of 1948," *California Law Review* 36, no. 4 (December 1948): 512.

55. Leffler, "American Conception," 349.

56. See table 1075, *Statistical Abstract of the United States: 1954* (Washington, DC: Bureau of the Census, 1955), 899. The Marshall Plan accounted for $12.5 billion. Cf. Alan S. Milward, *The Reconstruction of Western Europe, 1945–51* (Berkeley: University of California Press, 1984), 94.

57. Jan S. Prybyla, *The American Way of Peace: An Interpretation* (Columbia: University of Missouri Press, 2005), 26.

58. Surrey, "Economic Cooperation Act," 512.

59. Ibid., 524.

60. Scott Jackson, "Prologue to the Marshall Plan: The Origins of the American Commitment for a European Recovery Program," *Journal of American History* 65 (March 1979): 1055.

61. Diane B. Kunz, "The Marshall Plan Reconsidered: A Complex of Motives," *Foreign Affairs* 76, no. 3 (May/June 1997), 168.

62. Kaplan, "United States and the Origins," 217.

63. Kunz, "Marshall Plan Reconsidered," 169.

64. Ibid., 678.

65. Kaplan, "United States and the Origins," 222.

66. John D. Hickerson, then the head of the Office of European Affairs at the State Department, expressed his hope that the Brussels agreement would lead to the creation of a "real European organization strong enough" to resist Soviet pressure. John Milloy, *The North Atlantic Treaty Organization 1948–1952: Community or Alliance* (Montreal and Kingston: McGill–Queens University Press, 2006), 18.

67. Kaplan, "United States and the Origins," 217.

68. S. Res. 239, 90th Cong., 2d sess., June 11, 1948. A copy is archived at http://avalon.law.yale.edu/20th_century/decad040.asp.

69. Geir Lundestad, "Empire by Invitation? The United States and Western Europe, 1945–1952," *Journal of Peace Research* 23, no. 3 (1986): 270.

70. Kaplan, "United States and the Origins," 219, 218.

71. Wilson D. Miscamble, *George F. Kennan and the Making of American Foreign Policy, 1947–1950* (Princeton, NJ: Princeton University Press, 1992), 132, 137.

72. Kaplan, "United States and the Origins," 222.

73. For more on the changes made with an eye to accommodating the Senate, see Nicholas Henderson, *The Birth of NATO* (Boulder, CO: Westview, 1983), 91–92, and Don Cook, *Forging the Alliance, NATO 1945–1950* (London: Secker & Warburg, 1989), 214.

74. Robert Jervis, "The Impact of the Korean War on the Cold War," *Journal of Conflict Resolution* 24, no. 4 (December 1980): 569, 570.

75. Michael G. Roskin, "NATO: The Strange Alliance Getting Stranger," *Parameters*, Summer 1998: 30.

76. Kaplan, "United States and the Origins," 222; Jervis, "Impact of the Korean War," 571.

77. Roskin, "NATO," 31; Jervis, "Impact of the Korean War," 580–81.

78. NSC-68 observed: "Soviet efforts are now directed toward the domination of the Eurasian land mass. The United States, as the principal center of power in the non–Soviet world and the bulwark of opposition to Soviet expansion, is the principal enemy whose integrity and vitality must be subverted or destroyed by one means or another if the Kremlin is to achieve its fundamental design." A copy can be found in the *Naval War College Review* 27 (May/June, 1975): 51–108. Jervis, "Impact of the Korean War," 585.

79. David Reynolds, "The Origins of the Cold War: The European Dimension, 1944–1951," *Historical Journal* 28 (June 1985): 510.

80. Robert E. Osgood, *NATO: The Entangling Alliance* (Chicago: University of Chicago Press, 1962), 30.

81. Per the commitment of President Truman in September 1950. Cf. Phil Williams, *The Senate and U.S. Troops in Europe* (New York: St. Martin's, 1985), 24.

82. Lundestad, "Empire by Invitation?," 272.

83. Richard K. Betts, "U.S. National Security Strategy: Lenses and Landmarks," paper presented for the launch conference of the Princeton University project "Toward a New National Security Strategy," November 2004 (originally presented May 2004), 14, at http://www.princeton.edu/~ppns/papers/betts.pdf.

84. Jervis, "Impact of the Korean War," 574, 585.

85. See Sandra Penrose, "Percy Spender and the Origins of ANZUS: An Australian Initiative," paper presented to the Australian Political Studies Association Conference, University of Adelaide, September 29–October 1, 2004, at www.adelaide.edu.au/apsa/docs_papers/Aust%20Pol/Penrose.pdf.

86. Gaddis, *Surprise*, 48.

87. Cited in *Congress and the Nation, 1945–1964* (Washington: Congressional Quarterly, 1965), 264.

88. Betts, "U.S. National Security Strategy," 4, 15.

89. Memorandum by the Director of the Policy Planning Staff (Nitze) to the Deputy Under Secretary of State (Matthews), July 14, 1952, G/PM files, lot 68 D 358, "NSC 135"; Statement of Policy Drafted by the Director of the Policy Planning Staff (Nitze), July 30, 1952, PPS files, lot 64 D 563, "NSC 68 & 114."

90. Jervis, "Impact of the Korean War," 584.

91. Lundestad, "Empire by Invitation?," 265.

92. Anne R. Pierce, *Woodrow Wilson and Harry Truman: Mission and Power in American Foreign Policy* (New Brunswick, NJ: Transaction, 2007), 240.

93. George Stambuk, "Foreign Policy and the Stationing of American Forces Abroad," *Journal of Politics* 5, no. 3 (August 1963): 472–73.

94. Lundestad, "Empire by Invitation?," 263.

95. Stambuk, "Foreign Policy," 473.

96. David B. H. Denoon, *Real Reciprocity: Balancing U.S. Economic and Security Policies in the Pacific Basin* (New York: Council on Foreign Relations Press, 1993), 1.

97. Lundestad, "Empire by Invitation?," 263–64.

98. Mansel G. Blackford and K. Austin Kerr, "The Company in the Postwar World," in *History of the United States Economy since World War II*, ed. Harold G. Vatter and John F. Walker (Armonk, NY: M. E. Sharpe, 1996), 138–39.

99. James Forrestal, *The Forrestal Diaries*, ed. Walter Millis (New York: Viking, 1951), 350–51.

100. Michael Cox, "From the Truman Doctrine to the Second Superpower Détente: The Rise and Fall of the Cold War," *Journal of Peace Research* 27, no. 1 (February 1990): 31–35; Lundestad, "Empire by Invitation?," 273; Betts, "U.S. National Security Strategy," 16; Blackford and Kerr, "The Company," 352.

101. Lundestad, "Empire by Invitation?," 274.

102. Kennedy, *Rise and Fall*, 435.

103. Quoted by Dusko Doder and Louise Branson, *Gorbachev: Heretic in the Kremlin* (New York: Viking, 1990), 207.

104. Michael Howard, "Reassurance and Deterrence: Western Defense in the 1980s," *Foreign Affairs* 61, no. 2 (Winter 1982–83): 319.

105. Patrick J. Buchanan, *A Republic, Not an Empire: Reclaiming America's Destiny* (Washington, DC: Regnery, 1999), 310, 327.

106. Cox, "From the Truman Doctrine," 35–36.

107. *America's National Interests: A Report from the Commission on America's National Interests*, Graham Allison, Dimitri Simes, and James Thomson, executive

directors (Cambridge, MA: Center for Science and International Affairs, John F. Kennedy School of Government, Harvard University, 1996), 2–3.

108. Henry R. Nau, *At Home Abroad: Identity and Power in American Foreign Policy* (Ithaca, NY: Cornell University Press, 2002), 57–58.

109. Charles Krauthammer's comment in the foreign policy section of the symposium "After September 11: A Conversation," *National Interest* (Thanksgiving 2001), 68.

110. Zbigniew Brzezinski, "A Geostrategy for Eurasia," *Foreign Affairs* 76, no. 5 (September/October 1997), at www.foreignaffairs.com/articles/53392/zbigniew-brzezinski/a-geostrategy-for-eurasia.

111. Under direction of then undersecretary of defense Paul Wolfowitz, the Draft Defense Planning Guidance (of 1992) outlined strategy to prevent the rise of "potential competitors," to discourage advanced countries "from challenging our leadership," and to extend security commitments to countries that had been Soviet allies only a short time before. When the draft was leaked, controversy, especially among allies, produced a toned-down version with more politic packaging. Betts, "U.S. National Security Strategy," 24.

112. Zoellick used this phrase in his speech, "Whither China: From Membership to Responsibility?," remarks of the deputy secretary of state to the National Committee on U.S.-China Relations, New York City, September 21, 2005, archived at http://2001-2009.state.gov/s/d/former/zoellick/rem/53682.htm.

113. Thomas Donilon, speech to the Asia Society, New York on March 11, 2013, http://asiasociety.org/new-york/complete-transcript-thomas-donilon-asia-society-new-york.

114. "Remarks by Condoleeezza Rice at Sophia University, Tokyo," March 19, 2005, http://2001-2009.state.gov/secretary/rm/2005/43655.htm.

115. Nikolas K. Gvosdev, "Horsetrading with Beijing," *World Politics Review*, November 20, 2009, at www.worldpoliticsreview.com/articles/4671/the-realist-prism-horse-trading-with-beijing.

116. The quotes are taken from Qin Jize and Li Xiaokun, "China Circles by Chain of US Anti-Missile Systems," *China Daily*, February 24, 2010, and from an editorial in *Renmin Ribao* of August 19, 2005.

117. Kenneth N. Waltz, "The Emerging Structure of International Politics," *International Security* 18, no. 2 (Autumn 1993): 47–48.

118. Betts, "U.S. National Security Strategy," 23.

119. Samuel P. Huntington, *Third Wave: Democratization in the Late Twentieth Century* (Norman: University of Oklahoma Press, 1993), 47.

120. Paul Miller, "The Pitfalls of Practicing Strategery," *Foreign Policy*, March 13, 2013, at http://shadow.foreignpolicy.com/posts/2013/03/14/the_pitfalls_of_practicing_strategery?wp_login_redirect=0.

121. William J. Clinton, *The National Security Strategy of Engagement and Enlargement* (Washington, DC: White House, 1996), 2.

122. Douglas Brinkley, "Democratic Enlargement: The Clinton Doctrine," *Foreign Policy* 106 (Spring 1997): 112.

123. Department of Defense, "Active Duty Military Personnel Strengths by Regional Area and by Country (309A)," September 30, 2010, at http://siadapp .dmdc.osd.mil/personnel/MILITARY/history/hst1009.pdf.

124. Nau, *At Home Abroad*, 38; Brinkley, "Democratic Enlargement," 116.

125. Betts, "U.S. National Security Strategy," 25.

126. Ray Takeyh and Nikolas K. Gvosdev, "Do Terrorist Networks Need a Home?," *Washington Quarterly* 25, no. 3 (Summer 2002): 107, 106.

127. Betts, "U.S. National Security Strategy," 25.

128. Derek Reveron, "Security Force Assistance: It's Not Just for Weak States," *New Atlanticist*, February 23, 2013, at www.acus.org/new_atlanticist/ security-force-assistance-its-not-just-weak-states.

129. Nau, *At Home Abroad*, 40; remarks by Tom Donilon, national security adviser to the president, "The United States and the Asia-Pacific in 2013," the Asia Society, New York, March 11, 2013, at www.whitehouse.gov/the-press-office/2013/03/11/remarks-tom-donilon-national-security-advisory-president-united-states-a.

130. Uri Dadush, "Cold Water for Hot Trade Deals," *National Interest*, May 13, 2013, at http://nationalinterest.org/commentary/cold-water-hot-trade-deals-8460.

131. Robert Kagan, *The World America Made* (New York: Knopf, 2012), 20–21.

132. Department of Defense, *Quadrennial Defense Review* (Washington, DC: Department of Defense, 2014), 9.

133. Josef Joffe, "Hubs, Spokes, and Public Goods," *National Interest*, October 30, 2002. http://nationalinterest.org/article/hubs-spokes-and-public-goods-2159?page=1

134. Ibid.

2

The American Way of Organizing for Defense

A standing military force, with an overgrown Executive will not long be safe companions to liberty. The means of defence ag[ain]st foreign danger, have been always the instruments of tyranny at home.

—James Madison, speech at the Constitutional Convention, June 29, 1787

It is to be expected that a superpower, of necessity, would possess a large national security establishment. In the American case, however, its creation and expansion went against the grain of US political culture. In fact, America's founders might be shocked at the size of both the standing military and the bureaucracy that serves it, as they were preoccupied with the threat that a large national security establishment might pose to individual liberties. James Madison expounded on this theme:

> Of all the enemies to public liberty war is, perhaps, the most to be dreaded, because it comprises and develops the germ of every other. War is the parent of armies; from these proceed debts and taxes; and armies, and debts, and taxes are the known instruments for bringing the many under the domination of the few. In war, too, the discretionary power of the Executive is extended; its influence in dealing out offices, honors, and emoluments is multiplied; and all the means of seducing the minds, are added to those of subduing the force, of the people. The same malignant aspect in republicanism may be traced in the inequality of fortunes, and the opportunities of fraud, growing out of a state of war, and in the degeneracy of manners and of morals engendered by both. No nation could preserve its freedom in the midst of continual warfare.[1]

Madison's thoughts guided much of the country's early history. Even as the country developed and expanded its commercial interests, it was not particularly interested in maintaining a large permanent armed force, and the focus was, as Capt. Alfred Mahan noted, on "providing for rapid development in a time of war."[2] When wars concluded, American tradition dictated that the military establishment demobilize and return to a peacetime state of a small, skeletal force.

However, in keeping with Mahan's precept that a nation, particularly one with global economic interests, needed to be able to develop permanent naval forces capable of protecting the approaches to the United States while securing its interests overseas, Mahan and others called for a policy of "maintaining an armed navy, of a size commensurate with the growth of its shipping and the importance of the interests connected with it."[3] Mahan was on solid constitutional ground, drawing from both the founders' expressed caution against standing armies and the specific provision in Article I, Section 8, that gave Congress the power to raise armies in time of war but maintain a navy.

The navy became more important in US foreign affairs as land-expansion efforts from the Atlantic to the Pacific subsided by the end of the nineteenth century. Consequently, the US Navy went from 38 vessels on active duty in 1886 to a total of 245 by 1916, which made it the third largest force in the world after the navies of Imperial Germany and Britain.[4] But the two-ocean responsibility meant that US naval power could not be easily concentrated.[5] At the same time, the Marine Corps possessed a robust ability for mounting police-action expeditions and fighting small wars in the Western Hemisphere. But even these developments did not herald the emergence of formidable power-projection capabilities on the part of the US military, which still did not have a large standing force, nor was the government organized to marshal American power to play an effective role in world affairs. Even as the United States emerged to take its place as one of the great powers, it still lacked any unified defense establishment, a general staff, or any sort of national security council. A massive ramping-up of US military power to take part in World War I and the creation of a "Council of National Defense" to coordinate the war effort across the departments of the US government were reversed after 1918, and a similar desire to demobilize after World War II initially guided postwar policy. Some policymakers hoped that the US monopoly of the atomic bomb would be sufficient to act as a deterrent to any future aggressors, obviating the need to maintain a large and permanent military establishment.[6]

Breaking the Boom-and-Bust Cycle of Defense

The breakdown of Franklin Delano Roosevelt's postwar arrangements began to reluctantly convince the American government that the traditional American way of defense organization was no longer sustainable. Roosevelt's own "preference for backstairs negotiations, his immobility and the lack of institutional arrangements" in how he conducted national security policy also contributed to this assessment.[7] The "boom-and-bust" cycle of American defense was deemed insufficient for a world that became characterized by US-Soviet rivalry. In 1946, the Joint Chiefs of Staff, accepting the premise that the Soviet Union was bent on global domination, "advocated the development of an immediately usable military force—one that did not require mobilization time," marking a clear break with past precedents.[8] Civilian advisers agreed: Clark Clifford, Harry S. Truman's White House counsel, and George Elsey, a military assistant to Clifford, advised the president that "the United States should maintain military forces powerful enough to restrain the Soviet Union and to confine Soviet influence to its present area."[9] The enunciation of the Truman Doctrine in 1947 (and the extension of commitments to Greece and Turkey), the Berlin Crisis of 1948, the Soviet detonation of its own atomic bomb in 1949, and the start of the Korean War in 1950 all shattered any illusion that the United States could meet its commitments without ramping up its military capabilities.[10] Moreover, National Security Council Report 68 (NSC-68) committed the United States to "increase as rapidly as possible our general air, ground and sea strength and that of our allies to a point where we are militarily not so heavily dependent on atomic weapons."[11]

In examining how a new US defense posture to meet the Soviet challenge was created, however, it is important to remember that military considerations alone have rarely shaped US military policies and programs. Defense matters have always been constrained by the political system, especially the Constitution, availability of finite resources and manpower, and societal values. Lingering suspicions about a powerful military establishment threatening US liberty—concerns echoed yet again in President Dwight D. Eisenhower's valedictory address at the end of his presidency warning about the dangers of the military-industrial complex—had an impact on creating institutional and structural constraints to keep the armed forces in check.[12] Perhaps most important has been the nation's firm commitment to civilian control of military policy, which requires careful attention to civil-military relations. (Explored in depth in chapter 3, this commitment makes military policy a paramount function of the federal government, where the executive branch and Congress vie to shape it.)

Factors That Shape the National Security Establishment

The massive organization of the US defense establishment that took place after World War II did not occur in a vacuum but within the context of an American approach to military affairs that dates back to the beginning of the Republic. In particular, five factors have governed how the country has created organizations for directing US military forces: the Constitution, especially its division of power between the executive and legislative branches; changes in the military resulting from technology and the industrial base; the relationship between the services and the executive departments that administer them; the various interpretations of the meaning of civilian control of the military; and operational failures.

The Constitution's provisions regarding direction and administration of the military are very broad. To paraphrase the adage of constitutional scholar William Corwin, the Constitution is "an invitation to struggle" between the executive and the executive branches for control of the military instrument. The president is the commander in chief of the army and navy, but Congress has the authority to declare war, raise and support armies, provide and maintain a navy, make rules for governing and regulating the land and naval forces, and "make all laws, which shall be necessary and proper for carrying into Execution the foregoing Powers." For the most part, Congress has delegated the authority to organize executive departments to the executive branch, while maintaining overall oversight. Nonetheless, since the end of World War II, Congress has been very active shaping the military departments, beginning with the National Security Act of 1947 and culminating in the Goldwater-Nichols Defense Department Reorganization Act of 1986.

The changing character of the American military, especially the growth of professionalism after the Civil War, also influenced the direction and administration of the US military, including relations between the uniformed military and the War and Navy Departments. Advances in technology led to the creation of technical bureaus in both the War and Navy Departments in the nineteenth century and to the proliferation of assistant secretaries of defense since World War II. (The development of the airplane rendered old defense organizations obsolete, leading eventually to the creation of an independent air force. New military organizations were also created, over time, to support operations in space and the cyber realm.)

Finally, the various interpretations of "civilian control" have affected defense organization and management. Far too often the term has been reserved for members of the executive branch—the president and cabinet members—forgetting the role of Congress. This is a significant oversight, because most of the debates concerning defense organization and policy have illustrated an important point about civil-military relations: For the most part, civil-military conflicts have not per se pitted "civilians" against the military. Instead battles have raged between different coalitions made up of both civilians and members of the uniformed military. For instance, President Truman's decision to fire Gen. Douglas MacArthur—often cited as the preeminent example in modern US history of the civilian power opposing the wishes of the military—was supported by many high-ranking officers, including George Marshall and Dwight Eisenhower—and opposed by many prominent civilians, such as a majority of the Republican members of Congress. As we shall see, most of the debates over defense unification following World War II pitted the army, the air force, and their civilian supporters in Congress and the press against the navy and Marine Corps—and their civilian supporters in Congress, in the media, and in the emerging think-tank and expert communities.

Defense Organization before World War II

From 1775 to 1945, the United States dealt with security issues on an ad hoc basis, reacting to immediate threats or challenges rather than preparing for sustained conflict with a set group of adversaries. Following the constitutional division of any US military in Article I, Section 8, into an army and a navy, Congress authorized in 1789 the creation of a War Department to coordinate all land-based forces and, after lobbying on the part of James McHenry, a separate "Department of the Navy" in 1798 with responsibility for all maritime military capabilities. The activities of the War and Navy Departments remained mostly uncoordinated because during the nineteenth century there was, for the most part, little need for coordination or cooperation: The army focused on supporting western expansion and other internal, domestic operations; the navy, in contrast, concentrated on "showing the flag" abroad (such as the expedition to "open" Japan led by Commodore Matthew Perry in the 1850s)—but did not otherwise serve as a credible arm for projecting American land-based power abroad.

However, many operations during the Mexican War, the Civil War, and the Spanish-American War required army-navy cooperation. What is now called a "joint" operation was largely conducted under the principle of "mutual cooperation," the idea that the army and navy commanders would come to an ad hoc, friendly agreement about how best to coordinate their forces in combat. Some of these operations were successful—for example, those during the Civil War against Forts Henry and Donaldson (coordinated by Gen. Ulysses S. Grant and Adm. Andrew Hull Foote), the Vickburg Campaign (coordinated by Grant and Adm. David Dixon Porter), and the second attack on Fort Fisher, the bastion defending Wilmington, North Carolina. But many were not—for example, the army-navy campaign to capture Santiago, Cuba, during the Spanish-American War in 1898.

At the department level, the effectiveness of army-navy coordination depended a great deal on the attitudes of the individuals involved. For instance, when President Woodrow Wilson's secretary of the navy, Josephus Daniels, raised the issue of better army-navy cooperation with the secretary of war, Lindley Garrison, the latter replied: "Joe, I don't care a damn about the Navy and [you don't] care about the Army. You run your machine and I will run mine. I am glad if anyone can convince me I am wrong, but I am damn sure nobody lives who can do it. I am an individualist and am not cut out for cooperative effort. I will let you go your way, and I will go my way."[13]

Not all secretaries of war and the navy were as indifferent to cooperation as Garrison, but for the most part each department did, in practice, go its own way, in part because there was no pressing need for coordination, and when there were failures of or breakdowns in coordination, the consequences were not particularly dire. Indeed, so distinct were the two departments that they were overseen in Congress by separate committees in each house, the Navy Department by the naval affairs committees and the War Department by the military affairs committees.

Dissatisfaction over the lack of army-navy cooperation at Santiago and during other operations in Cuba and Puerto Rico in 1898, as well as jurisdictional disputes over administration of newly acquired overseas possessions after that conflict, led to the creation of a Joint Army and Navy Board in 1903. Its purpose was to institutionalize cooperation between the services.

Unfortunately the high-ranking officers who composed the board (four army and four navy) retained their primary service duties, which rendered them incapable of devoting sufficient attention to joint matters. Lacking a subordinate group to do detailed staff work, the board focused on minutiae rather than joint issues of major importance. As a result of these factors—as well as the hostility of President Wilson—the board was little used during World War I.

A more effective version of the Joint Board was established in 1919. Its membership was designated by position rather than by name, ensuring continuity of operations. More important, the Joint Board was provided with a subordinate staff organization, the Joint Planning Committee, made up of officers from the General Staff's War Plans Division and the Office of Naval Operations' Plans Division, whose primary duty was to the Planning Committee.

After 1923, the Joint Board was composed of the army chief of staff, the deputy chief of staff, and the chief of the General Staff's War Plans Division from the War Department and, from the Department of the Navy, the chief of naval operations (CNO), the assistant CNO, and the director of the Naval Operations' Plans Division. In July of 1941, the army's deputy chief of staff for air and the chief of the navy's Bureau of Aeronautics also became members.

But the interwar Joint Board was marginalized until World War II (when it would evolve into the Joint Chiefs of Staff) by two movements that shifted the discussion from simply better cooperation to the idea of the unification of military affairs within a single department. The first of these movements focused on achieving comprehensive administrative reform.

As part of a 1922 plan to improve the "efficiency and economy in the conduct of Government business," a joint congressional committee proposed merging the Department of War and the Department of the Navy into a department of defense under a single cabinet secretary, assisted by undersecretaries for the army, the navy, and national resources. During hearings before the joint committee, both the secretary of the navy and the secretary of war opposed unification of their departments, arguing that such a move would reduce military effectiveness. As a result, the joint committee's final report to Congress did not even mention unification.

The emergence of the airplane as a major instrument of war complicated land-sea coordination.[14] During hearings before a subcommittee of the House Military Affairs Committee in 1919, the heads of the War and Navy Departments, nonaviator army officers, and all navy officers opposed the creation of a separate cabinet department for military aviation, while all active and former army aviators supported the proposal. This division would continue for the next two and a half decades before an independent air force was created in 1947.

Brig. Gen. William "Billy" Mitchell and other advocates of air power continued to press for the creation of a separate aviation department and an independent air force. Indeed, Mitchell's vociferous advocacy of air power led to his conviction by court martial for "conduct prejudicial to military discipline" and his retirement from the army. But it also led President Calvin Coolidge to appoint a panel ("the Morrow Board") to look at how best to apply air power to the national defense. These discussions led to the Air Corps Act of 1926, which among other things changed the name of the Army Air Service to the Army Air Corps, authorized higher rank for its officers, and created an assistant secretary within the Department of War "to aid the Secretary of War in fostering military aeronautics."[15]

The Great Depression led to calls for greater governmental efficiency, including another proposal to unify the War and Navy Departments. During the Seventy-Second Congress, three bills were introduced to create a Department of National Defense. In testimony before the House Committee on Expenditures in the Executive Departments, both the secretary of war and the secretary of the navy opposed these bills, along with Gen. Douglas MacArthur, the army chief of staff.

World War II

The Joint Board was not designed to provide strategic guidance of military operations in the field. However, it did accomplish something of great importance during the interwar period: the preparation of the Joint Basic War Plans. Initially these were the so-called color plans, which were designed to deal with individual countries that might pose a strategic threat (e.g., War Plan Orange was focused on a possible war against Japan in the Pacific theater). Later "rainbow plans"—so called because they drew from existing color plans to develop contingencies for the US military fighting multiple adversaries simultaneously—dealt with enemies operating in combination (e.g., Germany and Italy in Europe). The Joint Board's last plan, Rainbow 5, provided the strategic plan that the United States followed during World War II. The board also issued a command guide titled *Joint Action of the Army and Navy* that outlined the military tasks of the respective services as well as the methods of cooperation during combat operations.[16]

Until 1939, both the secretaries of war and of the navy had to approve the board's decisions before they were implemented. But with war seemingly imminent, President Roosevelt directed in July of that year that the Joint Board report to him directly concerning issues of strategy and operations. In May 1941, the Joint Board established a Joint Strategical Committee under the Joint Planning Committee to relieve the latter's workload as the details of operational plans were being developed in expectation that the United States would soon be at war.

Joint Chiefs of Staff

In December 1941, with the tacit approval of the president, Gen. George Marshall, chief of staff of the army, Adm. Howard Stark, chief of naval operations, Adm. Ernest King, commander of the US Fleet (CINCUSFLEET), and Gen. Hap Arnold, chief of the army air forces, formed the Joint Chiefs of Staff as the counterpart to the British chiefs of staff. The US-UK Combined Chiefs of Staff (CCS) first addressed strategy for the Southwest Pacific and subsequently for all operations undertaken by the United States and Britain against the Axis powers of Germany, Italy, and Japan. As a consequence, the Joint Board ceased to operate, and the Joint Chiefs of Staff (JCS) became the primary national defense organization.[17]

During the war, the JCS fulfilled two sets of responsibilities.[18] First, the body represented the United States on the CCS and, subject to the authority of the president and British prime minister Winston Churchill, negotiated the development of a grand strategy for the war and the allocation of resources among the various combined commands. Second, the JCS served as the supreme command and planning body for US forces within American areas of responsibility, subject only to the authority of the president.

On the one hand, the Joint Chiefs gave a great deal of leeway to the theater commanders, reserving to themselves only the choice of who would command the theater, the strategic objectives within the theater, and the timing of campaigns. Theater commanders were responsible for developing detailed operational plans, in cooperation with planners within the War and Navy Departments and subordinate planning staffs of the JCS. On the other hand, the JCS was also involved in areas considered to be outside the purview of the military: industrial mobilization, distribution of manpower, management of critical resources, and the economics of financing the war.

During the war the JCS operated on the basis of consensus, not majority vote. As Admiral King remarked at the end of the war, "We usually found a solution. Sometimes it was a compromise."[19] The services cooperated but without abandoning what Samuel Huntington called their "strategic concepts," which he defined as "the fundamental element of [a] service, . . . its role or purpose in implementing national policy." A service's strategic concept answers the "ultimate question: What function do you perform which obligates society to assume responsibility for your maintenance?"[20]

The army's strategic concept centered on defeating an enemy's army. The navy's strategic concept centered on defeating an enemy's fleet and projecting power across the ocean. The strategic concept of the army air forces centered on destroying the enemy's war-making capacity and will. Thus the navy concentrated on executing its strategic concept in the Central Pacific, although there were substantial army forces in that theater. The army focused on defeating German and Italian land forces in the North African, Mediterranean, and European theaters of operations, albeit supported by the navy. The army air forces focused its main effort on daylight, precision strategic bombing.

Unifying Defense

In November of 1943, General Marshall forwarded a formal memorandum to the JCS calling for a "single Department of War in the postwar period," which, he contended, would achieve economies of scale, improved operational outcomes, and enhanced civilian control over military affairs. Marshall's proposal contemplated a single defense department headed by a cabinet-level secretary of national defense, supported by undersecretaries for ground, naval, and air elements. It also called for a single "Chief of Staff of the Armed Forces" who, along with a military chief of staff to the president and the service chiefs, would constitute the "Armed Forces General Staff."

The chiefs agreed to forward the proposal to a subordinate committee of the JCS, the Joint Strategic Survey Committee, for further study. It went no farther, but in early 1944 Marshall convinced Rep. James W. Wadsworth to introduce a House resolution creating a "Select Committee on Post War Military Policy." This committee, chaired by Rep. Clifton A. Woodrum, began hearings on April 24, 1944. The first proposal considered by the Woodrum Committee was that of army air forces lieutenant general Joseph McNarney, who made a proposal similar to Marshall's but with some noteworthy additions.

Like Marshall's proposal, the McNarney Plan created a single defense department headed by a secretary for the armed forces and three undersecretaries for the army, navy, and air as well as a director of common supplies. On the one hand, the service chiefs were subordinate to their respective undersecretaries. But on the other, as members of the JCS, they had direct access to the president, to whom they were expected to provide advice regarding budgets and military strategy.

At about the same time, the JCS undertook an examination of postwar organization on its own, establishing a committee chaired by retired admiral James O. Richardson. The JCS plan insulated the military from civilian authority other than the president, placing a great deal of power in the "Commander of the Armed Forces," answerable to the president alone, with the "Chiefs of Staff" operating in an advisory capacity alone and with a civilian secretary of the armed forces who would act only as an administrator.[21]

The report was so radical that even the committee chairman, Admiral Richardson, dissented, submitting his own minority report. He preferred endowing the existing JCS with statutory permanence. Within the JCS, General Marshall and General Arnold favored the report, while Admiral Leahy and Admiral King opposed it, preferring Admiral Richardson's minority report. This was the last opportunity the Joint Chiefs had to design their own organization. From then on, the defense reorganization arena would be the civilians in Congress.

Architecture, Civilian Control, and Strategic Orientation

Within Congress, the McNarney Plan generated debate over the issues that would dominate the debate over defense organization ever after: the degree of acceptable centralization, the architecture of a national security establishment, civilian control, and the impact of the defense organization on strategic orientation.

The United States has contemplated three alternative architectures for defense organization over the years: the *vertical* system, the *divided* system, and the *balanced* system. Under the vertical system—the system that Elihu Root established in the War Department in 1903, which continued until 1947— the president issued orders to the army through the secretary of war; however, the army chief of staff retained direct authority over the entire department as well as direct access to the president as commander in chief. In this system, civilian control of the department was minimal, since the civilian secretary and his assistants depended on the chief of staff and the general staff for information and advice. The McNarney Plan reflected the army's preference for a vertical architecture.

The second alternative, the divided system, provided for greater civilian control. In this system, the military chief has operational control of the fighting forces and is answerable to both the president and secretary. However, the latter is mainly responsible for managing the administrative and support elements of the department. The Navy Department has tended to favor this architecture.

The third alternative is the balanced system, in which the secretary has authority over the administrative and support elements of the department, and the military chief commands the forces. This was the approach that President Abraham Lincoln and Secretary of War Edwin M. Stanton employed during the Civil War, but otherwise it has been little used.[22]

Strategic Monism versus Strategic Pluralism

For the most part, the debate that began in 1944 pitted the vertical system against the divided system. Those who advocated the former tended to be proponents of "strategic monism," which refers to primary reliance on a single strategic concept, weapon, service, or region and "presupposes an ability to predict and control the actions of possible enemies."[23] Those favoring the latter were usually supporters of "strategic pluralism," which "calls for a wide variety of military forces and weapons to meet a diversity of potential threats."

The clearest example of strategic monism was the "New Look" defense policy of the Eisenhower administration, which subordinated the aviation capabilities of the army and navy to the air force in regard to long-range strategic bombing. The US emphasis on NATO's central front in the 1970s also reflected a strategic monist perspective. The John F. Kennedy administration's adoption of "Flexible Response" in the 1960s and the defense policy of the Ronald Reagan administration in the 1980s were examples of strategic pluralism.

As a rule of thumb, the naval services have usually preferred strategic pluralism and have feared a more centralized defense organization because of concerns that such an organization could impose strategic monism on the country's defense policy, as happened during the Eisenhower administration and the New Look. The air force traditionally has been the strongest advocate of strategic monism and the creation of a vertical, centralized defense organization to impose it. The army has generally been in both camps at different times.

The National Security Act of 1947

The navy's preference for strategic pluralism led it to oppose the McNarney Plan, giving rise to the charge of obstructionism. To counter this charge, Secretary of the Navy James Forrestal asked Ferdinand Eberstadt, the former chairman of the Munitions Board, to look at the various proposals and offer his own views on the proper form of postwar defense organization. In a letter to Eberstadt on June 19, 1945, Forrestal asked him to prepare a report based on the following questions: (1) Would unification of the Navy and War Departments under a single head improve national security? (2) If not, what changes would improve national security? (3) What form of postwar organization should be established?

By September 25, Eberstadt and his staff had produced a 250-page report. It concluded that unification would not improve national security. The real problem, the report asserted, was the lack of coordination between the State Department and the military departments and between the military and agencies responsible for mobilization. As for the future, Eberstadt recommended the maintenance of the War and Navy Departments, with the addition of a separate Air Department to control aviation assets then within the army. He recommended that the JCS be given statutory permanence, responsibility for strategic guidance and control of the military forces, and a full-time, subordinate Joint Staff.

To coordinate and integrate national security efforts, the report recommended creation of a National Security Council (NSC) and a National Security Resources Board (NSRB). The former would formulate and coordinate overall national security policy and make recommendations regarding the defense budget. The latter would formulate plans for industrial mobilization. The report also recommended the creation of a Central Intelligence Agency (CIA) subordinate to the NSC.

The Marshall, McNarney, Richardson, and Eberstadt plans merely constituted the prelude to the main event, which commenced in October of 1945 when the Senate Military Affairs Committee took up military reform in earnest now that the war had ended. On October 30, the army presented its plan in testimony by Lt. Gen. Lawton Collins. The so-called Collins Plan combined the main elements of the Marshall and McNarney plans along with an element from the Richardson Committee report.

The Collins Plan created a powerful chief of staff of the armed forces, in direct command of the armed forces; a secretary of the armed forces, responsible for administration, mobilization, and research and development (R&D); and the US Chiefs of Staff, which was to be an advisory body in the areas of military policy, strategic planning, and budgets. There were no separate military departments. Collins averred that civilian-led military departments were unnecessary because "the military staffs can administer the military components."[24]

The navy opposed the Collins plan on the familiar grounds that it represented unnecessary overcentralization and accepted the questionable validity of what Marine Corps lieutenant general Victor Krulak later called "tri-elementalism"—the idea that everything involved with land warfare is in the army, everything that fights in the air is in the air force, and everything that fights at sea is in the navy. The naval services believed that, with the Collins Plan, the army was seeking to circumvent Congress by having the legislative branch concur with the general principle of unification, with the details to be resolved later within the executive branch.

They were especially concerned that a hostile secretary of defense could imperil the existence of naval aviation and the Marine Corps, a fear borne out by the tenure of Secretary of Defense Louis Johnson in 1949. A corollary concern of the naval services was that the Collins Plan proposed a unified budget that would be heavily influenced by the proposed armed forces chief of staff, eliminating the ability of the services to make their individual budgetary cases to Congress.

There were also concerns about the proposed role of a civilian secretary. Eberstadt argued that the proposed secretary should be empowered to "coordinate matters of common or conflicting interest between the three military departments . . . to integrate the budget, coordinate logistic and procurement matters, research programs, military intelligence, education and training, personnel policies, etc. . . . However, he should have no general or specific responsibility with respect to the administration of the three departments or any control over them."[25] In order to ensure that the secretary could not "undertake any detailed administration" of the three departments, Eberstadt gained approval of a limit on the number of individuals on the secretary's staff: "fifteen to twenty-five $10,000-a-year men and military officers."[26]

President Truman's position was very close to that of the Collins Plan. In a letter to Congress at the beginning of the unification debate, the president wrote:

> There should be a single Department of National Defense charged with full responsibility for national security. . . . The head of this Department should be a civilian, a member of the President's Cabinet. . . . There should be three coordinate branches of the Department of National Defense: one for the land force, one for the naval forces and one for the air forces, each under an Assistant Secretary. . . . There should be a Chief of Staff of the Department of National Defense [who along with] the commanders of the three coordinate branches of the Department should together constitute an advisory body to the Secretary of National Defense and to the President.[27]

He added: "Unification of the services must be looked on as a long-term job."[28] The meaning of these words became clear after passage of the National Security Act of 1947.

After two months, the committee hearings ended, but the debate had only begun. Over the next year and a half, the lines were drawn between two civil-military coalitions. On one side was grouped the army, its supporters in Congress and in the press, and President Truman. They supported the elimination of the Navy and War Departments and the creation of a unified defense establishment under a cabinet-level secretary; a separate air force; a single military budget; a JCS responsible for advising the president on overall military policy, strategy, and a unified budget; a chief of staff of the armed forces with direct access to the president and direct authority over the services, the theater commanders, and common supply and administrative issues; and limits on naval aviation and on the size and combatant functions of the Marine Corps. Ranged against them were the navy and marines, their congressional and press advocates, and the larger veterans' organizations, who opposed the creation of a single department of defense; supported the maintenance of cabinet-level military departments that would participate in the preparation of the defense budget; opposed the creation of a single military commander of chief of staff; supported the statutory establishment of the JCS; supported preservation of a balanced fleet, including carrier-based naval aviation and a Marine Corps combined-arms capability; and advocated creation of government mechanisms for coordinating economics, politics, intelligence, and mobilization.

Compromise Defense Plan

After coordinating with the army and the navy, the president transmitted a compromise plan to Congress on February 16, 1947. It did not please everyone. Some claimed that the new secretary of national defense would be too powerful; others charged the opposite. The army was displeased by the fact that it did not create a single commander of the armed forces. Supporters of the navy were disappointed that there was not adequate statutory protection for naval aviation and the Marine Corps. Nonetheless, the bill passed the Senate with only minor changes, a provision that clarified and limited the powers of the secretary of national defense and one ensuring the participation by each of the services in the budget process.

Although the bill faced challenges in the Senate, they were nothing compared to those it faced in the House. While the Senate Military Affairs Committee favored the army's unification plans, many House members were less well disposed. In addition, the Senate version of the defense unification bill was referred not to the House Military Affairs Committee but to the Committee on Expenditures in the Executive Department.

Both the army and navy witnesses supported the Senate bill, but the marine commandant, Gen. Alexander Vandegrift, insisted that Congress spell out the roles and mission of the services rather than leaving this issue to the executive branch. Vandegrift's fears were well grounded. Hearings before the House committee brought to light a series of documents known as the "JCS 1478 Papers," revealing the fact that the army intended to see the Marine Corps reduced to an inconsequential size. The Marine Corps issue nearly derailed the entire legislative program, but the final legislation supported the Marine Corps position on roles and missions.[29]

Legislative maneuvering continued, but the bill eventually passed the House. Following a series of compromises worked out during the House-Senate conference, the bill finally passed on July 24, 1947, becoming the National Security Act of 1947. The Act implemented the overall coordinating agencies of the Eberstadt Plan—the NSC and NSRB—and created a separate Department of the Air Force.

The act also rejected the concept of a single military officer superior to all others in uniform. While it created a single civilian secretary of defense, the act sharply circumscribed his authority, expressly granting the three service secretar-

Table 2.1: Service Roles and Missions and the National
Security Act of 1947

Army	Organized, trained, and equipped primarily for prompt and sustained combat incident to operations on land. The army shall be responsible for the preparation of land forces necessary for the effective prosecution of war except as otherwise assigned and, in accordance with integrated joint-mobilization plans, for the expansion of peacetime components of the army to meet the needs of war.
Navy	Organize, train, and equip primarily for prompt and sustained combat incident to operations at sea. The navy shall be responsible for the preparation of naval forces necessary for the effective prosecution of war except as otherwise assigned and, in accordance with integrated joint-mobilization plans, for the expansion of peacetime components of the navy to meet the needs of war.
Marine Corps	Organized, trained, and equipped to provide fleet marine forces of combined arms, together with supporting air components, for service with the fleet in the seizure or defense of advanced naval bases and for the conduct of such land operations as may be essential to the prosecution of a naval campaign. It shall be the duty of the Marine Corps to develop, in coordination with the army and the air force, those phases of amphibious operations that pertain to the tactics, technique, and equipment employed by landing forces. In addition, the Marine Corps shall provide detachments and organizations for service on armed vessels of the navy, shall provide security detachments for the protection of naval property at naval stations and bases, and shall perform such other duties as the president may direct, provided that such additional duties shall not detract from or interfere with the operations for which the Marine Corps is primarily organized.
Air Force	Organized, trained, and equipped primarily for prompt and sustained offensive and defensive air operations. The air force shall be responsible for the preparation of the air forces necessary for the effective prosecution of war except as otherwise assigned and, in accordance with integrated joint-mobilization plans, for the expansion of the peacetime components of the air force to meet the needs of war.

Source: National Security Act of 1947, Pub. L. 253, Chap. 343, 80th Cong., 1st Sess.,
S. 758.

ies access to the president. The law envisioned the secretary of defense as a coordinator of the military departments and not as having responsibility to direct the detailed administrative and planning activities of the military departments or the combatant commanders.

Finally, the act gave the JCS the clear authority, under the president and secretary of defense, to plan and execute the war-making functions of the national military establishment: "to prepare strategic plans and to provide for the strategic direction of the military forces" and "to establish unified commands in strategic areas."[30] The Key West Agreement of 1948 strengthened these functions, placing the JCS in the operational chain of command and declaring that "strategic direction of the military forces" was to include "general direction of all combat operations."[31]

Amendments, 1949–58

While no one was completely happy with the National Security Act of 1947, most believed that the compromise measure was acceptable and that it would prove capable of ensuring US national security in the postwar world. But two individuals in particular, President Truman and General Eisenhower, saw the 1947 act as merely the beginning of an evolutionary process leading to a more centralized organization in which one individual would dominate the defense budget process and the development of strategy.

Truman saw this individual as a strong secretary of defense. While still on active duty, Eisenhower saw this individual as a strong military chief, but once he became president he also came to support the idea of a strong civilian defense secretary. Over the next decade, first Truman and then Eisenhower came back to Congress again and again seeking to achieve a more centralized department of defense. The import of Truman's previously noted 1945 letter to Congress, in which he stated that unification must be seen as a long-term enterprise, became clear.

However, the campaign for greater defense-department centralization was aided by the changing position of those who had favored the compromise measure of 1947. The most prominent of these was James Forrestal, who, as secretary of the navy, had opposed the more centralized unification proposals but as the first secretary of defense now sought a substantial expansion of his authority. Following discussions between Truman and Forrestal, the president established the Committee on Organization of the Executive Branch, chaired by former president Herbert Hoover, which in turn created a Committee on National Security Organization (the Eberstadt Committee).

At the end of 1948, the Eberstadt Committee recommended a number of changes to the 1947 act, including expanding the authority of the secretary of defense over the military establishment and greater control over the defense budget; downgrading the secretaries of the military departments from cabinet level and, accordingly, denying them direct access to the president; and the creation of a chairman of the Joint Chiefs of Staff. All of these were included in the president's proposal submitted to Congress in March of 1949. Both chambers acceded to the president's plan, with the exception of the proposal that the secretary of defense be granted the authority to reassign, abolish, or consolidate the combatant functions of the several services, which was of particular concern to the Marine Corps and to naval aviation.

The amended law now designated the national military establishment as an executive department to be called the Department of Defense (DOD), which was created on August 10, 1949. The legislation provided for a cabinet-level secretary of defense with the authority to exercise full, rather than "general," direction of the department; created a chairman of the JCS, who "shall take precedence over all other officers of the Armed Forces" but—thanks to the resistance of Rep. Carl Vinson, a strong advocate of the navy's position on unification—"shall not exercise military command over the Joint Chiefs of Staff or over any of the military Services"; reduced the military departments from executive departments of the government to noncabinet military departments, denying the secretaries of the military departments their previous statutory right to present reports directly to the president and the Bureau of the Budget; and raised the limit on the size of the Joint Staff from 100 to 210.[32]

The Eisenhower administration then picked up the standard of defense unification, creating a committee on national security organization chaired by Nelson Rockefeller. In June 1953, President Eisenhower sent Congress a Defense Department reorganization plan based on the recommendations of the Rockefeller Committee. The plan proposed transferring the functions of the Munitions Board, the R&D Board, and other agencies to a military-civilian staff within the Office of the Secretary of Defense (OSD); the creation of six new assistant secretaries of defense; the proviso that the director of the Joint Staff be approved by the secretary of defense; and that the JCS chairman singly, rather than the chiefs in toto, manage the Joint Staff. The reorganization took effect on June 30, 1953.

As the eminent military historian Allan Millett once quipped, proposals to reform the way the American government makes and executes defense policy bloom along the Potomac with the same regularity as the cherry blossoms. And sure enough, only five years later, concerns about inefficiency and duplication of effort, growing out of interservice rivalry, generated new calls for defense reform. President Eisenhower recommended a further increase in the power of the secretary of defense; removing the JCS from the chain of command for combat operations, which under his plan would run from the president to the secretary and then to the unified theater commanders; lifting all restrictions on the secretary's authority to transfer, reassign, abolish, or consolidate the roles and functions of the services; and abolishing the requirement that the secretary of defense issue directives to the military departments through the service secretaries.

Congress expressed concern that to grant everything the president requested would constitute an abrogation of congressional authority. Members also noted a propensity for the executive branch to ask for new changes before the old ones had been given a chance to work. Nonetheless, the two houses of Congress gave the president most of what he requested. Public Law 85-599, the Department of Defense Reorganization Act of 1958, substantially strengthened the secretary of defense at the expense of the service secretaries and the JCS. Perhaps most significantly, the 1958 act excluded the JCS from any executive function in the assignment of military missions, making that the purview of the combatant commanders. No longer would the JCS be a warfighting organization, the purpose of which was to provide the strategic bridge between the operational commanders and the overall policymakers. Instead the JCS became an advisory committee that provided staff support to the secretary of defense, who by law was now the country's principal military executive.

These changes reflected ongoing concerns that the 1947 act might open the door to the creation of a powerful Prussian-style general staff, which in turn might lead to the erosion of civilian control of the military and possibly even lead to a replication of the militarism that had defined German and Japanese policies during the first half of the twentieth century. The 1958 legislation completed the process of dividing up military functions and preventing their concentration in the same hands. Those charged with training and equipping forces would have no control over how those forces were to be used. Those entrusted with planning and coordinating military operations—the Joint Staff—would not simultaneously be given power to execute, which was now vested separately in the hands of the combatant commanders, who directly reported to the secretary of defense. The combatant commanders, the "men in the field," however, could only request inputs—they could neither control procurement of equipment nor the training of personnel, functions that remained firmly under the purview of the services.

Critics of the 1958 act observed that when the defense unification debate began at the end of World War II, Congress was most concerned about the emergence of a "man on horseback," an all-powerful military man supported by something along the lines of a Prussian general staff. As General Krulak noted, what they got instead was a massive, self-nourishing civilian bureaucracy overseen by a very powerful secretary.[33]

After 1958

The 1958 act granted a great deal of discretionary authority to the secretary of defense, including authorization for him to undertake steps to improve the administration of the department, to centralize functions by creating, if necessary, new organizations within the department, and to establish unified and specified commands and determine their force structure. The first secretary of defense to fully embrace the new powers of the position was Robert McNamara, who extended his oversight to every aspect of military activity. He established three new agencies within the department—the Defense Intelligence Agency, the Defense Supply Agency, and the Defense Contract Audit Agency—and created three new assistant secretaries of defense.

The vast expansion of the OSD and the diminution of the JCS permitted McNamara to involve himself in every aspect of military planning—from the Bay of Pigs invasion and the Cuban Missile Crisis to the Vietnam War—without full consideration of the military perspective. As H. R. McMaster, one of McNamara's most vociferous critics, observes, the secretary essentially marginalized the JCS in the lead-up to the Vietnam War.

McNamara firmly believed that the centrality of nuclear weapons to the Cold War geopolitical environment rendered traditional military advice not only irrelevant but even dangerous. Thus, instead of counting on the JCS to provide broad military advice, McNamara relied instead on systems analysis as a way of justifying "graduated pressure" against the Vietnamese communists, an approach premised on the idea that decision makers could predict with great certainty the amount of force necessary to achieve the desired results. The evidence supports the contention that the chiefs knew that graduated pressure was flawed but went along anyway because McNamara was able to exploit the loyalty of the JCS members to their individual services.[34]

The effects of centralization extended beyond operational affairs. The disastrous TFX story illustrated OSD's foray into the development of weapon systems. Instead of permitting the air force to develop the TFX as a general-purpose, land-based fighter, OSD's director of defense research and engineering assumed control of the program to make the TFX a joint air force–navy airplane. After it was redesigned as the F-111, the navy eventually abandoned the airframe, while the air force ended up with a suboptimal weapon.

McNamara's tenure as secretary of defense during the Vietnam War confirmed the fears of those concerned about the impact of a marginalized JCS on strategy and policy. These fears would be revived some four decades later when another strong secretary of defense would essentially cut the JCS out of the strategy-policy loop.

But it was not only secretaries of defense who would ignore the military when it came to strategy. While some presidents consulted the chiefs, others, such as Lyndon Johnson and Jimmy Carter, did not. For instance, the planning for Operation Eagle Claw, the Iranian hostage rescue, was done almost completely in the absence of consultation with the chiefs; only the chairman of the JCS was included in the planning process. But although Carter's remoteness from his military advisers represents an extreme case, the fact is that no president since FDR has maintained a direct and routine relationship with the JCS.

Defense Reorganization Act of 1986

The genesis of what became the Goldwater-Nichols Defense Reorganization Act of 1986 can be traced to the end of the Carter administration and the Defense Organization Study of 1977–80, which suggested that the JCS and the service secretaries were "weak, ineffectual and sterile institutions" dominated by the service bureaucracies, and that the secretary of defense's influence over his department was only tenuous at best.[35]

In addition, Congress was roused to action by the confluence of three factors: (1) perceived military failures (or, at most, marginal successes) stretching from the Vietnam War to Operation Eagle Claw, the 1983 Beirut bombing, and the invasion of Grenada; (2) public criticism of the current defense structure by high-ranking officials (for instance, in 1982, outgoing CJCS Gen. David C. Jones severely criticized the JCS, claiming that the organization was not able to act in a timely or coherent manner); and (3) critiques by respected defense analysts and think tanks. Both houses of Congress began a process of investigations and hearings expected to culminate in legislation calling for substantial changes in the DOD.

Congress's central concern was the excessive power and influence of the separate military services. Archie Barrett, a retired air force colonel working on the House Armed Services Committee staff, argued that "the overwhelming influence of the four services was completely out of proportion to their legally assigned and limited formal responsibilities."[36] As a result, according to advocates of reform, it was difficult, if not impossible, to integrate the separate capabilities of service components into effective units capable of the sort of joint operations called for in modern war.

In the view of congressional reformers, service influence also accounted for the low quality of military advice because the "corporate" nature of the JCS prevented its chairman (the CJCS) from speaking in his own name. According to General Jones, "the corporate advice provided by the Joint Chiefs of Staff is not crisp, timely, very useful or very influential."[37] This view was reinforced by former secretary of defense James R. Schlesinger, who had served in the Nixon and Ford administrations and concluded: "The existing structure [of the JCS], if it does not preclude the best military advice, provides a substantial, though not insurmountable, barrier to such advice. . . . The unavoidable outcome is . . . log rolling, back-scratching, marriage agreements, and the like." He further noted that the plans and recommendations of the chiefs had to "pass through a screen designed to protect the institutional interests of each of the separate Services."[38]

Lengthy hearings on defense-reform proposals commenced with the House Armed Services Subcommittee on Investigations during the second session of the Ninety-Seventh Congress. These led to a far-reaching JCS reorganization bill that passed the House handily but died at the end of the Ninety-Seventh Congress when the Senate refused to act. When the Ninety-Eighth Congress convened, the House Armed Services Committee once again held hearings and reported out HR 3718, the Joint Chiefs of Staff Reorganization Act of 1983, which passed the House in October 1983.

The chairman of the Senate Armed Services Committee, John Tower, initiated his own hearings aimed at a comprehensive examination of the whole DOD organization. Accordingly the House bill was tacked as amendment onto the fiscal year 1985 defense authorization bill in May of 1984. During the Senate-House conference on the bill, some of the House provisions were adopted by the conferees: (1) the CJCS would now be able to select Joint Staff officers from a list of service nominees; (2) the CJCS could now force a decision on the chiefs; (3) the CJCS would now be able to act as spokesman for the commanders of the nine specified and unified commands on operational matters; and (4) restrictions on the tour length for the director of the Joint Staff were reduced.

Goldwater-Nichols Compromise

For the Ninety-Ninth Congress, the four House bills that would restructure the JCS—HR 2265 (Nichols), HR 2165 (Skelton), HR 2313 (Skelton), and HR 2710 (Aspin)—were consolidated as HR 3622 and sent to the House floor in late November 1985. A month earlier, the staff of the Senate Armed Services Committee (SASC) had produced a report titled *Defense Organization: The Need for Change*. This document, known informally as the Locher Report (after the SASC study director, James R. Locher), called for a number of revolutionary changes in the organization and decision-making process of the DOD.

Concerned that the changes Congress might impose on the DOD would be ill-advised, President Reagan appointed a Blue Ribbon Commission on Defense Management, which was chaired by David Packard, a deputy secretary of defense from 1969 to 1971. Its report, issued in June 1986, tempered many of the recommendations found in the Locher Report but still retained the call for a stronger CJCS. As the result of consultations between members of Congress and the Packard Commission, the subsequent legislation, named in honor of Sen. Barry Goldwater and Rep. Bill Nichols, two individuals who had led the reform effort, gained both bipartisan support in Congress and the president's imprimatur. It easily passed both houses of Congress and became law on October 1, 1986.

In passing Goldwater-Nichols, Congress sought to achieve eight objectives: (1) to reorganize the DOD and strengthen civilian authority within it; (2) to improve the military advice provided to the president, the National Security Council, and the secretary of defense; (3) to place clear responsibility on the commanders of the unified and specified combatant commands for the

Table 2.2: Functions of the Chairman, Joint Chiefs of Staff

Assist the president and the secretary of defense in providing for the strategic direction of the armed forces.

Prepare strategic, joint logistical, and mobility plans recommending the assignment of logistical and mobility responsibilities to the armed forces and perform net assessments to determine the capabilities of the armed forces of the United States and its allies as compared with those of their potential adversaries.

Provide for the preparation and review of contingency plans (to include logistics and mobility) that conform to policy guidance from the president and the secretary of defense. Establish and maintain a uniform system of evaluating the preparedness of each command to carry out missions assigned to the command.

Advise the secretary on critical deficiencies and strengths in force capabilities.

Advise the secretary on the extent to which the program recommendations and budget proposals of the military departments and other components of the Department of Defense for a fiscal year conform with the priorities established in strategic plans.

Develop doctrine and policies for the joint training and employment of the armed forces.

Source: Goldwater-Nichols Act of 1986, US Code, Title 10, Subtitle A, Part I, Chapter 5.

accomplishment of missions assigned to those commands; (4) to ensure that the authority of the commanders of the unified and specified combatant commands is fully commensurate with the responsibility of those commanders for the accomplishment of missions assigned to their commands; (5) to increase attention to the formulation of strategy and to contingency planning; (6) to provide for more efficient use of defense resources; (7) to improve joint officer-management policies; and (8) to enhance otherwise the effectiveness of military operations and improve the management and administration of the DOD.[39]

Each provision of the act addressed one or more of these elements of congressional intent. The first chairman after the law passed, Adm. William J. Crowe Jr., later wrote that "95 percent of the issues before the [service] chiefs are solved without the need for a 'strong' chairman. But two areas especially are divisive in interservice relationships. One is money. . . . The second is people. . . . Goldwater-Nichols empowered the Chairman to draw independent conclusions

. . . [and] was one of the legislation's more welcome advances."[40] Commenting on the importance of the chairman, former secretary of defense Robert Gates wrote: "One of his greatest strengths was his ability to bring the service chiefs together as a unified front when we had to deal with tough issues like the budget, thereby mostly avoiding internecine fighting among the services."[41] In addition to the chairman, the clear winners in the reforms were the combatant commands.

The Unified Command Plan

Issued every two years, the Unified Command Plan (UCP) is the overall blueprint for America's military commands.[42] First issued by President Truman in 1946, the UCP delineates geographic areas of responsibility and substantive areas of focus.[43] As of 2014, there are six geographic commands (European, Africa, Pacific, Northern, Southern, and Central) and three functional commands (Transportation, Special Operations, and Strategic).[44] The missions and responsibilities are defined in the UCP, but it is important to understand that US military forces are employed through these commands and not the military services located at the Pentagon. For example, the Chief of Naval Operations (CNO) does not direct naval operations. Instead, the CNO trains and equips naval forces that are employed by component commanders reporting directly to a joint combatant command responsible for all US military activities within a given region. The only exception to this is forces assigned to carry out organizational, recruiting, training, supplying, and other functions of the military departments assigned by law or assigned to multinational peacekeeping organizations. What is true for the navy is also true for the Marine Corps, army, and air force. Today the job of service chiefs is to train and equip military forces, which are then employed by combatant commands such as European Command or the relevant component commands such as Naval Forces Europe.

Since the UCP is written in the executive branch and approved under the president's commander-in-chief authority, it is relatively responsive to changes in the security environment and US national strategy. Prior to 2002, for example, no single command had responsibility for protecting the continental United States. But the 9/11 terrorist attacks gave rise to Northern Command, designed to fill in the homeland defense gap one year before Congress created the Department of Homeland Security. And in 2008, Africa Command was established to support the president's initiatives in Africa by providing focused security assistance. In contrast to the pre-2008 arrangement where three military commands engaged in Africa, the newest combatant command serves as a single point of entry for defense matters.[45] In 2010, the importance of cyberspace to the military was reflected in the UCP with formal assignment to Strategic Command.

In accordance with the UCP, each combatant commander is assigned missions and areas of responsibility. In addition to the general missions assigned, some geographic combatant commanders have specific responsibilities. For example, Southern Command is responsible for defending the Panama Canal and the surrounding area. Northern Command is responsible for homeland defense, supporting civil authorities, planning for responses to pandemics, and providing support to partner countries in the event of a catastrophic attack. And Africa Command is focused on building partners' operational and institutional capacity, with no emphasis placed on fighting wars in Africa. Evident in the assigned responsibilities and specific missions discussed above is that combatant commands do much more than fight wars. Instead, military commands support broader US government efforts during peacetime through security cooperation. Over the past two decades, the military has been incorporating new organizations, doctrine, and training to prioritize efforts to prevent war through security force assistance—in turn broadly defined to mean everything from training coast guards to providing educational and development assistance. This is a major effort and requires high levels of cooperation among the military services, US government departments, nongovernmental organizations, other governments, and international organizations.

However, this has also shifted the focus of the combatant commands away from confronting strong states via conventional means to weak states where subnational (e.g., gangs in Central America) and transnational security challenges (e.g., al-Qaeda) jeopardize sovereignty and regional stability.[46] It has also made the US military much more interested in questions of economics, trade, conflict resolution, and governance—things traditionally covered by the Department of State and the Agency for International Development—as necessary components for effective security assistance, leading to calls for greater coordination and collaboration between other organs of the US government and the DOD to address security challenges.[47]

This shift in focus has thus raised concerns about the "militarization of US foreign policy."[48] As more missions are defined as having relevance to security, earlier divisions between the missions of "defense," "development," and "diplomacy"—with each set of tasks assigned by statute to different departments and agencies and with established guidelines to prevent any trespass—become blurred. (In part, this is because, in the post–Cold War environment, clear distinctions between "peace" and "war" and between "peacemaking," "peacekeeping," and "peace enforcement" eroded.) Because the DOD has enjoyed a vast advantage in resources over other agencies of the US government—and Congress has been much more willing to appropriate funds for "defense" rather than "development" or "diplomacy"—generals and admirals have been incentivized to ask for funds for a wide variety of programs. In a perverse series of incentives, other agencies may then be quite prepared to back away from taking on missions normally within their purview because it is easier to let the Pentagon take over.

Table 2.3: Missions of a Combatant Command

Detecting, deterring, and preventing attacks against the United States and its territories, possessions, and bases. Employing appropriate force to defend the nation should deterrence fail.

Carrying out assigned missions and tasks. Planning for and executing military operations as directed.

Assigning tasks to, and directing coordination among, subordinate commands to ensure unified action.

Maintaining the security of the command and carrying out force-protection responsibilities for it, including assigned or attached commands, forces, and assets. The commander is also responsible for exercising force-protection responsibilities for all US military forces within the area of responsibility (AOR), except for DOD personnel for whom the chiefs of US diplomatic missions have security responsibilities by law or interagency agreement.

Certifying the readiness of assigned headquarters staffs designated to perform as a joint task force (JTF) or functional component headquarters staff.

Providing to other combatant commands, as directed, trained and ready joint forces.

Planning, conducting, and assessing security cooperation activities.

Planning and, as appropriate, conducting the evacuation and protection of US citizens, US nationals, and, in connection therewith, designated other persons in support of their evacuation from threatened areas. Reviewing such emergency action plans.

Providing US military representation to international and US national agencies unless otherwise directed.

Providing advice and assistance to chiefs of US diplomatic missions in negotiation of rights, authorizations, and facility arrangements required in support of US military operations.

Providing the single point of contact on military matters within the AOR.

Assuming combatant command of security assistance organizations in the event of war or an emergency that prevents control through normal channels or as directed.

When directed, commanding US forces conducting peace or humanitarian relief operations, whether as a unilateral US action or as part of a multinational organization. Supporting US forces that have been placed under the authority, direction, or control of a multinational organization.

Establishing and maintaining a standing joint-force headquarters core element.

Planning and conducting military support for security, stabilization, transition, and reconstruction (SSTR) operations, humanitarian assistance, and disaster relief, as directed.

Planning for, supporting, and conducting the recovery of astronauts, space vehicles, space payloads, and objects, as directed.

Source: Unified Command Plan 2008, signed October 3, 2008.

Assessing Goldwater-Nichols

Despite the ease with which the legislation was finally passed, Sen. Barry Goldwater remarked that the effort to reform the DOD was not easy: "Elements of the Pentagon fought us every inch of the way."[49] The navy's opposition, spearheaded by Secretary of the Navy John Lehman, was particularly robust.[50] Some of this opposition was bureaucratic in nature, reflecting concern about the prospective loss of "turf." But much was based on a real concern that the proposed legislation would have an adverse impact on the ability of the military to carry out its responsibilities under the Constitution.[51]

Thus thoughtful opponents of reform legislation warned of threats to civilian control of the military and the likelihood that a more powerful CJCS and a unified Joint Staff would tend to impose strategic monism on the US military establishment when the geographical position of the United States requires strategic pluralism.[52] Even the most vociferous defenders of the act recognize that all the promises of Goldwater-Nichols have not been fulfilled. In some cases, this is because Goldwater-Nichols has not been fully implemented. In others, it is because Congress's intent has not been realized due to loopholes in the law.

If problems with the act arose from these causes alone, it would be easy enough to rectify them through additional legislation. But far more serious is the fact that the legislation has given rise to unintended adverse consequences that may ultimately outweigh any positive aspects of the act. These are far more difficult to correct because they stem from the very philosophy underpinning Goldwater-Nichols.

Goldwater-Nichols can claim its greatest success in the area of increasing the authority of the combatant commanders to bring it into balance with their responsibilities. Although a major goal of the Department of Defense Reorganization Act of 1958 had been to create truly unified combatant commands "singly led and prepared to fight as one, regardless of service," this was a provision honored more in the breach than in the observance. In 1970, the Blue Ribbon Defense Panel found that "'unification' of either command or the forces is more cosmetic than substantive." Congress rectified this problem by specifying in detail the command authority of the combatant commanders and placing the bulk of US armed forces under their authority.

But while supporters of Goldwater-Nichols contrasted the failures and inefficiencies of operations before passage of the act (e.g., Vietnam, Lebanon, and Grenada) with the jewel in the Goldwater-Nichols crown, the Gulf War of 1991, postmortems of that conflict illustrate that even in Desert Storm, success was not unalloyed.[53]

For example, the combatant commander in the theater, Gen. H. Norman Schwarzkopf, did not adequately coordinate the plans of his marine and army component commanders. As a result, the overarching theater objective of the coalition, the entrapment and destruction of the Iraqi Republican Guard, was not achieved. This failure was exacerbated by the actions of the CJCS at the time, Gen. Colin Powell, who recommended cessation of military operations based on nonmilitary considerations, illustrating the perils of having one military officer, rather than the corporate body of the JCS, provide military advice to the president.

Some observers have also noted the extent to which the Air Staff in Washington infringed on the commander of Central Command's operational planning authority after Iraq's invasion of Kuwait. The Air Staff unilaterally developed a plan in response to the invasion without direction from General Schwarzkopf, the CJCS, or the National Command Authority.[54] And it is clear that many of the problems that arose during Operation Iraqi Freedom were the result of the marginalization of the JCS by Secretary of Defense Donald Rumsfeld.[55] But more important than these examples of military failures since Goldwater-Nichols has been the manifestation of some unintended consequences. The first of these has been an emphasis on the short term at the expense of the long term, a consequence of shifting power away from the services to the unified combatant commands. Critics of the pre-Goldwater-Nichols resource-allocation process expressed dismay over "wasteful interservice rivalry." Rivalry, of course, has not been eliminated by Goldwater-Nichols; however, it now occurs primarily among the combatant commands. But the unified commanders tend to be more concerned about the near term and less about the distant future, traditionally the perspective of the services. This is not to suggest that funding for readiness or operations and maintenance should be reduced but to observe that these categories have been funded largely at the expense of modernization and future force planning. The services see modernization and force planning as the primary means of implementing their aforementioned respective "strategic concepts." The shift in power from the services to the unified commands in the name of eliminating interservice rivalry merely ensures that the present and near future will be emphasized at the expense of potential future developments.

Not only has power shifted from the services to the combatant commands but also from the Services to the Joint Staff. This raises the very real possibility that a single strategic concept can come to dominate defense policy, the problem of "strategic monism."

The most intensely debated aspect of Goldwater-Nichols has been the expanded power of the CJCS. This debate centers on two main issues: First, is the quality of military advice now superior to that of the pre-Goldwater-Nichols era? Second, has a more powerful CJCS substantially increased the influence of the military in national affairs?

Not surprisingly, advocates of Goldwater-Nichols respond to the first query in the affirmative. Following Operation Desert Storm, Dick Cheney, who was the secretary of defense during that action, praised the advice he received from the chairman, considering it an advance over the "lowest common denominator of whatever the chiefs collectively could agree upon."[56]

But others have disagreed, claiming that the current advice is narrowly based on the chairman's own views, rather than reflecting the broad range of opinions available from the JCS as a whole. Additionally, Gen. Carl E. Mundy Jr., just before he retired as commandant of the Marine Corps, expressed concern about the decreasing service influence over joint issues. There can be no doubt that formal consultation between the chairman and the service chiefs has decreased. Once again, this has the potential to open the door to strategic monism.

In response to the second query, critics of Goldwater-Nichols contend that a more powerful CJCS has thrown American civil-military relations out of balance, claiming that the CJCS and Joint Staff are exerting undue influence on national decision makers. And there is always the potential danger that a powerful chairman and a centralized Joint Staff could impose a single view on the defense establishment.[57]

Another unintended consequence of the Goldwater-Nichols reforms has been the emergence of senior military officers, particularly the geographic combatant commanders (sometimes now labeled as "America's viceroys"), as policy entrepreneurs (as opposed to simply being "warfighters").[58] Generals such as Anthony Zinni and Wesley Clark epitomized the new breed of warrior-diplomat who directly engaged with foreign heads of state as emissaries of the president.[59] Far from rogue generals, these military leaders were directed by President Bill Clinton to engage with the world and promote security by assisting partners and assuring allies in a security environment freed from the Cold War dynamic. President George W. Bush and President Barack Obama have continued the practice of using the military to assist almost every government of the world. This raises concern that senior military officers may carry more weight in the policy process because combatant commanders and other senior military figures may have greater access to key US decision makers than diplomats or other civilian officials. Some have cited the "star power" of larger-than-life combatant commanders (such as David Petraeus) making them more attractive as interlocutors for foreign leaders with the president than dealing with "ordinary" bureaucrats who may not have access to the Oval Office.

Conclusion

Americans have great faith in the power of organizational charts. If a problem arises, the usual American response is to modify the organizational structure. This has certainly been true in the case of organizing for defense. As the

United States became a superpower during World War II, it abandoned its ad hoc approach to coordinating the activities of the army and navy during war and peace, moving ever closer to a large, centralized DOD. The American way of organizing for defense has evolved over the last sixty years, first in order to deal with the Soviet threat, then to serve as a guarantor of the present global system—with both missions seen as essential to ensuring the security of the United States. However, keeping the defense establishment firmly grounded in the constitutional parameters and political values of the Republic—with its historic distrust of concentrated power—has always remained a priority.

Four trends have shaped the organization of the American defense establishment since the end of World War II. First, the authority of the secretary of defense has increased at the expense of the service secretaries, the service chiefs, and the Joint Chiefs of Staff, especially with the growth of the Office of the Secretary of Defense. Second, the ties between the service secretaries and the service chiefs have been weakened. Third, the authority of the chairman of the JCS has increased at the expense of the JCS as a corporate body. Finally, the civilian and military bureaucracy of the Pentagon has exploded—and with it a plethora of new agencies and geographic and functional combatant commands. This has produced an American defense establishment with some unique characteristics.[60]

First, despite the enormous endowment of personnel and equipment, the use of the military instrument remains firmly under the control of the civilian political process. In contrast to other countries where civilian control is guaranteed because the military is kept small and/or underfunded in order to induce dependency on the state, the United States has gone through a number of substantial military buildups without running the risk of encouraging the military to disregard or even overthrow the established government. Indeed, unless civilian policymakers consciously abandon their prerogatives, the uniformed military, while certainly free to be forceful in providing advice and in advocating for courses of action, cannot nonetheless force policy choices.

Second, the bureaucratization of the military mission helps to ensure a degree of predictability. Because the moving parts of the DOD must be properly aligned in order to carry out any mission, there are sufficient checks in the system to guard against sudden, unexpected, or rash actions. Certainly no US geographic combatant commander today could ever emulate his tsarist counterparts in the nineteenth century who routinely "accidentally" seized and annexed khanates and emirates in Central Asia in the absence of, or sometimes in open defiance of, governmental edicts. Nor, given the way the military is structured, could an aspiring American Caesar or Napoleon be able to seize control of the governing apparatus.

Finally, the structure of the defense establishment has produced a global outlook. In contrast to many other countries whose militaries limit their scope of interest to the national territory and their nation's immediate environs, the US system of combatant commands covers every square inch of the world's surface as well as the global commons. At times this has led to dissatisfying performance, as former secretary of defense Gates lamented: "The very size and structure of the department assured ponderousness, if not paralysis, because so many different organizations had to be involved in even the smallest decisions."[61]

With many changes, culminating in Goldwater-Nichols, it is unclear if they have improved the performance of the US military in war and peace. There is no question that US military performance at the operational level is second to none. But it seems fair to ask how much of that improvement is attributable to changes in the US defense establishment. It is undeniable that the increased authority of combatant commanders has contributed to improvements in the ability of our armed forces to truly conduct joint operations. This is a major advance and is the major legacy of Goldwater-Nichols. But as the wars in Iraq and Afghanistan illustrate, the conduct of joint operations in and of itself does not ensure victory.

The problem was brutally summed up by Richard Kohn: "Nearly twenty years after the end of the Cold War, the American military, financed by more money than the entire rest of the world spends on its armed forces, failed to defeat insurgencies or fully suppress sectarian civil wars in two crucial countries, each with less than a tenth of the US population, after overthrowing those nations' governments in a matter of weeks."[62] Kohn attributes this lack of effectiveness to a decline in the US military's professional competence with regard to strategic planning. "In effect, in the most important area of professional expertise—the connecting of war to policy, of operations to achieving the objectives of the nation—the American military has been found wanting. The excellence of the American military in operations, logistics, tactics, weaponry, and battle has been manifest for a generation or more. Not so with strategy."[63] He echoes the claim of Colin Gray: "All too often, there is a black hole where American strategy ought to reside."[64]

What accounts for this strategic black hole? Ironically, it may be a consequence of the defense reorganizations that have occurred since World War II. There is no question that the US strategy during the Vietnam War was flawed. One of the reasons for this was the centralization of power in the Office of the Secretary of Defense and the concurrent marginalization of the JCS by Secretary of Defense McNamara. A similar marginalization of that body occurred during the tenure of Donald Rumsfeld, creating many of the same problems in Iraq and Afghanistan.

The Joint Chiefs of Staff are responsible for integrating theater strategy and national policy. But if they are marginalized—as has been the trend since the end of World War II—such integration does not occur. This institutional problem is illustrated by the case of Gen. Tommy Franks, the commander of US Central Command in the wake of 9/11, who, with the concurrence of Secretary Rumsfeld, simply bypassed the JCS. His justification is found in his memoirs, *An American Soldier*: "Operation Enduring Freedom in Afghanistan had been nitpicked by the Service Chiefs and the Joint Staff, and I did not intend to see a recurrence of such divisiveness in Iraq." He sent a message: "Keep Washington focused on policy and strategy. Leave me the hell alone to run the war."[65]

Explored in the next chapter, such an attitude is a dysfunctional consequence of the well-intentioned institutional arrangement created by Goldwater-Nichols, reinforcing the idea that there is an autonomous realm of military action within which civilians have no role. The result of such a disjunction between the military and political realms is that war plans may not be integrated with national policy and that strategy, despite lip service to its importance, in practice becomes an orphan. And in the absence of strategy, other factors rush to fill the void, resulting in strategic drift. This situation is likely to continue until the United States creates a defense establishment that focuses on strategy as the integrator of operations and national policy.[66]

Notes

1. James Madison, "Political Observations, Apr. 20, 1795," in *Letters and Other Writings of James Madison*, vol. 4 (1865) (Ithaca, NY: Cornell University Library, 2009), 491.

2. Alfred Thayer Mahan, *The Influence of Sea Power upon History, 1660–1783* (Boston: Little, Brown, 1898), 82.

3. Ibid.

4. "U.S. Navy Active Ship Force Levels, 1886–Present," Naval History and Heritage Command, available at www.history.navy.mil/branches/org9-4.htm.

5. Robert Farley, "The U.S. Navy: 1916 vs. 2012," *Diplomat*, October 17, 2012.

6. See, for example, Barton J. Bernstein, "The Quest for Security: American Foreign Policy and International Control of Atomic Energy, 1942–1946," *Journal of American History* 60, no. 4 (March 1974), esp. 1003, 1004, 1041.

7. William L. O'Neill, *A Democracy at War: America's Fight at Home and Abroad in World War II* (Cambridge, MA: Harvard University Press, 1993), 158.

8. Arthur A. Stein, "Domestic Constraints, Extended Deterrence, and the Incoherence of Grand Strategy: The United States, 1938–1950," in *Domestic Bases of Grand Strategy*, ed. Richard Rosecrance and Arthur Stein (Ithaca, NY: Cornell University Press, 1993), 113.

9. The full report is contained in Arthur Krock, *Memoirs: Sixty Years on the Firing Line* (New York: Funk & Wagnalls, 1968), 417–82.

10. Stein, "Domestic Constraints," 115–23.

11. Cf. Section VIII of NSC-68, archived at www.mtholyoke.edu/acad/intrel/nsc-68/nsc68-3.htm.

12. The address, delivered on January 17, 1961, is archived by the Eisenhower Presidential Library at www.eisenhower.archives.gov/research/online_documents/farewell_address.html.

13. Daniels's 1945 testimony on defense reorganization, quoted in Demetrious Caraley, *The Politics of Military Unification: A Study of Conflict and the Policy Process* (New York: Columbia University Press, 1966), 4.

14. The army had established an aviation unit in 1907 as part of the Signal Corps, and during World War I aviation was granted a separate organizational status within the army as the Army Air Service. But after World War I, aviators grew restive under War Department and army fiscal and operational control.

15. By 1933, most aviators had given up on the idea of a separate air force, settling on the more limited goal of establishing an air force within the War Department but independent of army ground corps commanders. Their goals included a separate budget, promotion list, and policy staff for the Air Corps. By 1935, the aviators had largely achieved what they had sought. Air units previously distributed to the army corps were centralized under a General Headquarters, Air Corps, commanded by a general who reported directly to the chief of staff of the army. In 1940, the chief of the Air Corps, Lt. Gen. Henry H. "Hap" Arnold, was designated deputy chief of staff of the army for air and then in 1941 appointed to the Joint Board, designated chief of the army air forces, and given a separate air staff and almost total control over army aviation. Caraley, *Politics of Military Unification*, 14.

16. Ibid., 15.

17. The only change in the composition of the JCS occurred in 1942. In April, Admiral Stark was replaced as chief of naval operations by Admiral King, who also continued in the position of CINCUSFLEET. In July, Adm. William Leahy was recalled from the inactive list to assume the position of "chief of staff to the commander in chief of the army and navy of the United States," the de facto chairman of the JCS. Interestingly, the JCS operated throughout the war without ever having been authorized in writing by the president.

18. Steven L. Rearden, *Council of War: A History of the Joint Chiefs of Staff, 1942–1991* (Washington, DC: National Defense University Press, 2012).

19. King testimony as recorded in *Department of Armed Forces, Department of Military Security*, hearings on S. 84 and S. 1482 before the Senate Committee on Military Affairs, 79th Cong., 1st sess. (1945) (hereafter cited as 1945 Hearings). Cited in Caraley, *Politics of Military Unification,* 19.

20. Samuel Huntington, "National Policy and the Transoceanic Navy," US Naval Institute *Proceedings*, May 1954, 488, 491–92.

21. Caraley, *Politics of Military Unification*, 35

22. Victor H. Krulak, *Organization for National Security* (Washington, DC: United States Strategic Institute, 1983), 17–20.

23. Samuel Huntington, *The Soldier and the State: The Theory and Politics of Civil-Military Relations* (Cambridge: Belknap Press at Harvard University Press, 1957), 418.

24. 1945 Hearings, 155 and following.

25. Ferdinand Eberstadt, letter to Hon. John McCloy, October 6, 1947. Cited in Krulak, *Organization for National Security,* 42.

26. Caraley, *Politics of Military Unification*, 150.

27. Harry S. Truman, "Letter to Congress: Special Message to the Congress Recommending the Establishment of a Department of National Defense," December 19, 1945, in *Public Papers of the Presidents: Harry S. Truman* (1945) (Washington, DC: Government Printing Office, 1961), 546–60.

28. Ibid., 550.

29. For an account of the role of the Marine Corps in the unification battle, see Victor Krulak, *First to Fight: An Inside View of the US Marine Corps* (Annapolis, MD: US Naval Institute Press, 1984), 17–66.

30. National Security Act 1947, Pub. L. 253, sec. 211B, 80th Congress.

31. Quoting from the memorandum "Functions of the Armed Forces and the Joint Chiefs of Staff," popularly known as the Key West Agreement, in Steven L. Rearden, *History of the Office of the Secretary of Defense: The Formative Years, 1947–1950* (Washington, DC: Government Printing Office, 1984), 136.

32. National Security Act of 1947, as amended by Pub. L. 216, 81st Cong., para. 101 (c) (1).

33. Krulak, *Organization for National Security*, 131.

34. H. R. McMaster, *Dereliction of Duty: Lyndon Johnson, Robert McNamara, the Joint Chiefs of Staff, and the Lies That Led to Vietnam* (New York: HarperCollins, 1997). Cf. Krulak, *Organization for National Security*, 82–102.

35. The most complete account of the reform efforts leading to the passage of the Goldwater-Nichols Defense Department Reorganization Act is James Locher, *Victory on the Potomac: The Goldwater-Nichols Act Unifies the Pentagon* (College Station: Texas A&M University Press, 2002).

36. Archie D. Barrett, *Reappraising Defense Organization* (Washington: National Defense University Press, 1983), 4.

37. Statement of David Jones, House Committee on Armed Services, Investigations Subcommittee, *Reorganization Proposals for the Joint Chiefs of Staff*, 97th Cong., 2nd sess., 1982, HASC no. 97-47, 54. Cf. Jones, "Why the Joint Chiefs of Staff Must Change," *Armed Forces Journal*, March 1982.

38. Statement of James Schlesinger, November, 2, 1983, before the Senate Armed Services Committee, S. Hrg. 98-275, *Organization, Structure and Decisionmaking Procedures of the Department of Defense*, part 5, 187.

39. James Locher, "Has It Worked? The Goldwater-Nichols Reorganization Act," *Naval War College Review* 14, no. 4 (Autumn 2001): 105–6.

40. William J. Crowe Jr., *The Line of Fire: From Washington to the Gulf, the Politics and Battles of the New Military* (New York: Simon & Schuster, 1993) 161.

41. Robert M. Gates, *Duty: Memoirs of a Secretary at War* (New York: Knopf, 2014), 101.

42. Title 10 of the US Code requires that the chairman of the Joint Chiefs of Staff, at intervals not to exceed two years, "review the missions, responsibilities (including geographic boundaries), and force structure of each combatant command" and make recommendations to the president, through the secretary of

defense, any changes that may be necessary. US Code, title 10, subtitle A, part I, chap. 6, sec. 161(b).

43. See William C. Story, *Military Changes to the Unified Command Plan: Background and Issues for Congress*, report Rl30245 (Washington, DC: Congressional Research Service, 1999).

44. Transportation Command is located at Scott Air Force Base, Illinois. Special Operations Command is located at McDill Air Force Base, Florida. Strategic Command is located at Offutt Air Force Base, Nebraska.

45. Africa Command is far from being a peculiarity of the Bush administration. Congress, led by Sen. Russ Feingold, directed the military to conduct a feasibility study for the command in 2006 legislation, which ultimately led to its creation a year later. It did so to meet the demands presidents place on it for cooperative-security missions. Further, it allows the three other geographic commands that had previous activities in Africa to focus on their core areas of Europe, the Middle East, and the Pacific.

46. Stephen D. Krasner and Carlos Pascual, "Addressing State Failure," *Foreign Affairs* 84, no. 4 (July/August 2005).

47. Donna L. Hopkins, *The Interagency Counterinsurgency Initiative*, Ruger Workshop proceedings (Newport, RI: US Naval War College, 2007), 281–85.

48. Gordon Adams and Shoon Murray, *Mission Creep: The Militarization of US Foreign Policy* (Washington, DC: Georgetown University Press, 2014).

49. Stephan Roberts, "Reorganization of the Military Command View as Certainty," *New York Times*, March 8, 1986.

50. John Lehman, "Is the Joint Staff a General Staff?," *Armed Forces Journal*, August 1995. Cf. Locher, *Victory on the Potomac*, passim.

51. Mackubin Thomas Owens, "The Hollow Promise of JCS Reform," *International Security* 10 (1985–86). But see the proreform article "The Case for JCS Reform" by William Lynn and Barry Posen in the same issue.

52. Richard Kohn, "The Crisis in Military-Civilian Relations," *National Interest*, Spring 1994; Mackubin T. Owens Jr., "Goldwater-Nichols: A Ten-Year Retrospective," *Marine Corps Gazette*, December 1996.

53. Michael Gordon and Bernard Trainor, *The Generals' War: The Inside Story of the Conflict in the Gulf* (Boston: Little, Brown, 1995).

54. Ibid., 75–122, 310–11.

55. Mackubin Thomas Owens, "Civil-Military Relations and the US Strategy Deficit," FPRI (Foreign Policy Research Institute) e-note, February, 2010, at http://www.fpri.org/articles/2010/02/civil-military-relations-and-us-strategy-deficit

56. "About Fighting and Winning Wars: An Interview with Dick Cheney," US Naval Institute *Proceedings*, May 1996, 33.

57. Kohn, "Crisis."

58. Derek S. Reveron, ed., *America's Viceroys: The U.S. Military and Foreign Policy* (New York: Palgrave Macmillan, 2004).

59. Dana Priest, *The Mission: Waging War and Keeping Peace with America's Military* (New York: Norton, 2004).

60. *Defense Organization: The Need for Change*, Staff Report to the Committee on Armed Services, United States Senate, 99th Cong., 1st sess., S. Prt. 99-86, 383–87.

61. Gates, *Duty*, 116.

62. Richard Kohn, "Tarnished Brass: Is the US Military Profession in Decline?," *World Affairs*, Spring 2009, 73.

63. Ibid., 76.

64. Colin S. Gray, *Another Bloody Century: Future Warfare* (London: Orion, 2005), 111.

65. Tommy R. Franks, *American Soldier* (New York: HarperCollins, 2004), 440.

66. Owens, "Civil-Military Relations."

3

The American Way of Civil-Military Relations

> Thirty-two years in the peacetime army had taught me to do my job, hold my tongue, and keep my name out of the papers.
>
> —Gen. Omar Bradley

No discussion of the US national security decision-making process is complete without a close look at the interrelationship between the civilian government and the military establishment. Given the military's legitimate monopoly on use of force, healthy civil-military relations can be characterized, at the institutional level, by the presence of "two hands on the sword."[1] The civil hand determines when to draw it from the scabbard and guides its use. The military's hand sharpens the sword for use and wields it in combat.[2]

Historically, in countries that were consciously charting a path to great-power status, there were always concerns that the military would seek to remove the "civil hand" from the sword or that the military power would, over time, seek to usurp the civilian power altogether. Indeed, America's founders were particularly worried about how the Roman Republic had degenerated into the Roman Empire—and the role played by the military in that transformation. Thus the founders were particularly concerned with setting the proper balance among the civilian authority, civilian population, and military power.[3] While the size, reach, and scale of the US military establishment today far exceeds what the founders might have envisioned, the balance they sought still rests on answering five questions that define the civil-military relationship: Who controls the military instrument? What is the appropriate level of military influence on society? What is the role of the military? What pattern of civil-military relations best ensures military success? Who serves?[4] Because these questions continue to be asked—even if the answers given have changed over time—the dialogue that they create has been an important reason why the United States has tended to remain an "incidental superpower" rather than developing a full-fledged "imperial class," which over time tended to define the politics of the great powers that preceded it.

Civil-Military Equilibrium

Throughout US history, certain circumstances—political, strategic, social, and technological—have changed the terms of the civil-military bargain. To restore the preexisting equilibrium, however, the parties engaged in an unequal dialogue—a dialogue in the sense that "both [the civilian and military] sides expressed their views bluntly, indeed, sometimes offensively, and not once but repeatedly—and unequal, in that the final authority of the civilian leader was unambiguous and unquestioned."[5] In the United States, the military, despite having a monopoly on coercive power, has generally accepted its position relative to the policy establishment; unlike other countries, officers have not exercised political control or sought economic influence.

As the idea of a periodic renegotiation of the civil-military bargain would suggest, there have been some fairly serious civil-military clashes throughout American history. They primarily reflected changes in the security environment but also have been driven to some degree by changing social and political factors, particularly the reality that during and after World War II, the military moved from being a peripheral institution to a central one within the United States.

Similarly the change in the security environment occasioned by the collapse of the Soviet Union led to a lack of consensus regarding what the US military was expected to do. Should the United States demobilize to generate a peace dividend, or could the military establishment set up to counter the Soviets be used for other tasks such as nation-building? The result was a period of drift that led to another renegotiation of the civil-military bargain. During this latter period, some observers worried that the US military had become more alienated from its civilian leadership than at any time in American history; that it had become politicized and partisan; that it had become resistant to civilian oversight; that officers had come to believe that they had the right to confront and resist civilian policy makers—to *insist* that civilian authorities heed their recommendations—and that the US military was becoming too influential in inappropriate areas of American society.[6]

Arguably another renegotiation of the civil-military bargain began to take shape after the 2001 terrorist attacks as the US military found itself fighting protracted irregular wars instead of the conventional wars it prefers. Illustrative of civil-military tensions were clashes between the uniformed services and President George W. Bush's first secretary of defense, Donald Rumsfeld, over efforts to "transform" the military from a Cold War force to one better able to respond to likely future contingencies and during the planning and conduct of US military operations in Afghanistan and Iraq. These tensions peaked with the so-called revolt of the generals in the spring of 2006, which saw a number of retired army and Marine Corps generals publicly and harshly criticize Secretary Rumsfeld for his conduct in office.[7] Former secretary of defense Robert Gates later commented that during this time, when it came to the conduct of the Iraq War (particularly the decision to undertake the 2007 "surge" that increased US troop strength there to carry out a new counterinsurgency strategy), there were often clear-cut divisions between the civilian and military leaders with the department.[8]

After Rumsfeld's departure and with the renewed focus on the tactical level of operations during the surge, some expressed hope that harmony might return to US civil-military relations. To be sure, Rumsfeld's successor, Robert Gates, undertook a tremendous effort to improve the civil-military climate in the last years of the Bush administration, but subsequent events—Gates fired two service secretaries and a service chief, recommended against renominating the chairman of the Joint Chiefs of Staff for a second term, and forced the retirement of a combatant commander—did not restore harmony. Civil-military tensions have continued in the Barack Obama administration. These include the very public disagreement on military strategy between President Obama and the commander in Afghanistan, Gen. Stanley McChrystal, McChrystal's subsequent relief, the departure of Gen. James Mattis from US Central Command, and disputes over the size of the defense budget making it clear that the state of US civil-military relations remains contentious at best.[9] It has also reignited the earlier debates as to whether the military is becoming more inclined to question the value of civilian oversight.

Nevertheless, the United States has over the last sixty years navigated its rise to superpower status (which included the creation of a large, powerful standing military force) without succumbing to militarism. Moreover, even though the size and influence of the military has grown exponentially, senior military officers have not translated that into political power, nor has the basic fabric of American representative democracy been shredded apart—notwithstanding some of the fears of the founders that a large military would inevitably threaten the foundations of a democratic republic. It seems the military's global focus and expeditionary culture insulate the military from conducting operations inside US borders.

Civil-Military Relations: More than Civilian Control

Most of the debate over American civil-military relations, especially since the 1990s, has been dominated by concerns about civilian control of the military establishment. But as noted above, control of the military—as important as it may be—is only one factor making up the American civil-military bargain—

and the myopic focus on civilian control has obscured other equally important elements of civil-military relations.[10]

A second factor is the appropriate degree of military influence in a liberal society such as the United States. What is the proper scope of military affairs? In today's environment, what constitutes military expertise? Does it go beyond what Samuel Huntington called in *The Soldier and the State* the "management of violence?"[11] For instance, to what extent should the military influence foreign policy? Has American foreign policy become "militarized"? Do combatant commanders exercise too much power? Have they become the new "viceroys" or "proconsuls," overshadowing or even displacing civilian ambassadors and other government officials?[12] What is the proper balance between the military and domestic politics—for instance, should active-duty officers be writing op-eds in support of particular programs or policies? Should retired officers get involved in partisan politics? What is the military's proper role in influencing how Congress allocates defense resources?

A third factor is the appropriate role of the military. Is the military establishment's purpose to fight and win the nation's wars against the formal militaries of other states or to engage in constabulary actions in support of partners who need assistance in coping with subnational and transnational actors? What kind of wars should the military prepare to fight? Should the focus of the military be on foreign challenges—as it has been since World War II—or on domestic security? The United States has answered this question differently at different times and under different circumstances. For example, throughout most of its history, the US Army was a constabulary force. It permanently oriented itself toward large-scale conflicts against foreign enemies only in the 1930s. The end of the Cold War and the attacks of 9/11 have suggested new approaches to conflict through counterinsurgency and counterterrorism, as well as an openness to the use of the military in domestic affairs—for example, disaster relief in response to emergencies such as Hurricane Katrina in 2005, domestic law enforcement during the Los Angeles riots in 1992, and ongoing border security operations.

A fourth factor addresses the pattern of civil-military relations that best ensures the effectiveness of the military instrument but without threatening the fundamentals of the constitutional order or negatively impacting civil liberties. This has raised the question as to whether the demands of military effectiveness require a military culture (rooted in a hierarchical, collectivist view) distinct in some ways from the larger society (which prizes an individual, entrepreneurial culture) it serves? What impact does societal structure have on military effectiveness? What impact does political structure exert? What impact does the pattern of civil-military relations have on the effectiveness of strategic decision-making processes?

The final factor answers the question: who serves? Is military service an obligation of citizenship or a volunteer calling that only a few need heed? How are enlisted members recruited and retained? How should military missions be balanced between the full-time, active-duty force and the reserves—and should service in the reserves impact a person's civilian life? These questions regarding military service have been answered differently by Americans at different times under different circumstances. Through most of its early history, the United States maintained a small regular peacetime establishment, staffed by volunteers. Only during wartime were the states responsible for raising soldiers for federal service, as either militiamen or volunteers—and citizens who did not want to serve, in some cases, could purchase exemption from service. While there was limited federal conscription during the Civil War and a more extensive draft during World War I, conscription only became the norm in the United States from the eve of World War II until the 1970s. Today the US military is once again a volunteer professional force. However, in recent years efforts have been undertaken to make the composition of the military more closely resemble the demographics of the US population and mirror the norms of civilian society.

In addition, the fact that liberal societies such as the United States often take civilian control for granted begs several further questions: Does civilian control refer simply to the dominance of civilians within the executive branch—the president or the secretary of defense? What is the role of the legislative branch in controlling the military instrument? Is the military establishment "unified"—that is, does it speak with anything like a single voice vis-à-vis the civil government?

Civilian Control: Executive Branch and the Congress

Constitutionally the US military has two civilian masters through the executive branch and Congress, with important implications for civil-military relations. For instance, while the president and secretary of defense control the military when it comes to the use of force, including strategy and rules of engagement, Congress controls the military directly with regard to force size, equipment, and organization, and indirectly regarding doctrine and personnel.

When it comes to questions as to how force is to be used, there remains a high degree of deference to the advice of the military. The military influences the decision on using force by defining force requirements (size), identifying risk to achieving political objectives through military force, and forecasting casualty rates for US and adversarial forces. However, once this has been provided, should military leaders "insist" that their advice be heeded? What courses of action are available to military leaders who believe the civilian authorities are making bad decisions? Is there a "calculus of dissent" that military leaders can invoke in cases where they believe civilian decisions are dangerous to the health of the country?

The US military accepts civilian control by both Congress and the president but is expected to provide its honest advice and assessment. This is in keeping with the instructions Maj. Gen. John J. Pershing provided to 1st Lt. George Patton in 1916: "You must remember that when we enter the army we do so with the full knowledge that our first duty is toward the government, entirely regardless of our own views under any given circumstances. We are at liberty to express our personal views only when called upon to do so or else confidentially to our friends, but always confidentially and with the complete understanding that they are in no sense to govern our actions."[13]

Generally US military officers implicitly agree to support presidential decisions on the budget and use of force regardless of their personal views (and notwithstanding their confidential comments to their friends), but they also must recognize an obligation to provide their considered professional opinion of any policy choice taken by the executive branch in response to direct queries from Congress. Military officers are obligated by statute to share their personal and professional views with Congress, even when their perspective goes against the preferences of the presidential administration.[14] While the short-term disagreements can be sharp and pointed, in the long run the ability of the uniformed military to provide their opinions to Congress has proven to be a source of strength, by helping to foster a general consensus for broad parameters of where and under what circumstances military action should be undertaken.

When the president and Congress are in agreement, the military complies no matter whether it agrees or disagrees with the choice. When the two branches are in disagreement, however, the military tends to side with the branch that most favors its own views but never to the point of direct disobedience to orders of the commander in chief. Yet Congress often exerts its control with less regard for military preferences than for the political considerations of individual members and committees. Thus congressional control of the military is strongly influenced by political considerations, or what Huntington called "structural" or domestic imperatives as opposed to strategic ones.[15]

Coups: The Canary in the Coal Mine of Civil-Military Relations

Unlike in many other countries, where a defense minister is usually a serving officer and where senior military officers occupy important political positions as a matter of course, serving US officers are barred from most political positions or are closely scrutinized if nominated.[16] Given these realities, therefore, the conventional wisdom has argued that the United States will never face the risk of a military coup d'état.

But if an outright coup—with senior military officials usurping the prerogatives of the civilian government—is not possible, a number of scholars, including Richard Kohn, Peter Feaver, Russell Weigley, Michael Desch, and Eliot Cohen, have argued that American civil-military relations have nonetheless deteriorated over the past two decades in a way that threatens the ability of civilian policymakers to exert effective control over the use of the military instrument.[17]

Their concern is that the American military "has grown in influence to the point of being able to impose its own perspective on many policies and decisions," which manifests itself in "repeated efforts on the part of the military to frustrate or evade civilian authority when the opposition seems likely to preclude outcomes the military dislikes." The result is an unhealthy civil-military pattern that "could alter the character of American government and undermine national defense."[18] In theory, Kohn argues, "civilians have the authority to issue virtually any order and organize the military in any fashion they choose":

> But in practice, the relationship is far more complex. Both sides frequently disagree among themselves. Further, the military can evade or circumscribe civilian authority by framing the alternatives or tailoring their advice or predicting nasty consequences; by leaking information or appealing to public opinion (through various indirect channels, like lobbying groups or retired generals and admirals); or by approaching friends in the Congress for support. They can even fail to implement decisions, or carry them out in such a way as to stymie their intent. . . . We are not talking about a coup here, or anything else demonstrably illegal; we are talking about who calls the tune in military affairs in the United States today.[19]

But this seems to support the contention that actual civil-military relations are the outcome of constant bargaining.

Kohn writes that balanced civil-military relations in the United States have traditionally rested on four foundations: the rule of law and reverence for the Constitution, a small force in peacetime, reliance on the citizen-soldier, and the military's own internalization of military subordination to civilian control. Yet he argues that current conditions are such that the threat of military insubordination is much greater than in the past. First, thanks to the Goldwater-Nichols Act of 1986, the military is united in an unprecedented way. Whereas in the past the armed services often were at odds over roles, missions, budgets, and weapon systems, today they can work together to shape, oppose, evade, or thwart the choices civilians make—and to mitigate the efforts of civilian policymakers to keep the military establishment divided and competing. (However, as noted in the previous chapter, civil-military disputes usually do not per se pit "civilians" against "the military" but involve one civil-military faction against another. As budgets decline, this is likely to be the main shape of civil-military discord for the foreseeable future—disagreements over how and where scare resources ought to be allocated, with new civil-military coalitions emerging to battle over budget allocations—eroding the concerns previously expressed by Kohn and others that, under conditions of "jointness," the military was in a stronger position to resist civilian management of the armed forces.)

Second, many of the issues in play today reach far beyond the narrowly military, not only to the wider realm of national security but also often to foreign relations more broadly (such as whether or not military officers ought to be engaged in diplomatic, development, or relief operations traditionally handled by civilians). In certain cases military affairs even affect the character and values of American society itself (for instance, in how military procedures ought to reflect or accommodate the growing diversity of practices and norms in American society). Kohn argues that this expanded role represents a significant encroachment on civilian control of the military because, in a sense, the military is becoming a self-contained entity that no longer needs to turn to the larger government (or even civil society) for needed capabilities.

Third, military advice and advocacy is now much more public than it once was. Serving military officers write op-eds, appear on television, and speak at conferences to explain strategy and policy (and are sometimes specifically tapped by civilian policymakers to do so) in a way that previous generations never did. Sometimes this more public face has occurred because civilian policymakers feel their own assessments will lack credibility because of their lack of military expertise and so seek the public validation of senior officers.

Fourth, these senior officers now lead a large, permanent peacetime military establishment that differs fundamentally from any of its predecessors. Kohn argues that this military is increasingly disconnected, even estranged, from civilian society while at the same time becoming a recognizable interest group, "larger, more bureaucratically active, more political, more partisan, more purposeful, and more influential than anything similar in American history."[20]

Kohn has concluded that the erosion of civilian control gives rise to "toxic" civil-military relations, which, he argues, damage national security in at least three ways: by paralyzing national security policy, by obstructing or even sabotaging the ability of the United States to intervene in foreign crises or to exercise international leadership, and by undermining the confidence of the military as an institution in their own uniformed leadership.[21]

The military has "pushed back" against civilian leadership on numerous occasions during the last two decades. This reaction has manifested itself (to use Feaver's formulation) in various forms of "shirking," "foot dragging," "slow rolling," and leaks to the press designed to undercut policy or individual policymakers.[22] Such actions were rampant during the Bill Clinton presidency and during the tenure of Secretary Rumsfeld. It continued in the Obama administration regarding strategy and force structure for Afghanistan and the use of force against Syria. Such pushback is based on the claim that civilians were making decisions without paying sufficient attention to the military point of view. This leads to the next principle of civil-military relations: Officers have an obligation to make their case as strongly as possible but do not have the right to "insist" that their advice be accepted.

The Nature of Military Advice

During the 1990s, some military officers explicitly adopted the view that soldiers have the right to a voice in making policy regarding the use of the military instrument, that indeed they have the right to insist that their views be adopted. Feaver has called those who advocate this position "professional supremacists." This position has been encouraged by a serious misreading of the very important book by H. R. McMaster, *Dereliction of Duty: Lyndon Johnson, Robert McNamara, the Joint Chiefs of Staff, and the Lies That Led to Vietnam.*[23]

The subject of *Dereliction of Duty* is the failure of the joint chiefs to challenge Secretary of Defense Robert McNamara adequately during the Vietnam War. Many serving officers believe the book effectively makes the case that the Joint Chiefs of Staff should have more openly opposed the Johnson administration's strategy of gradualism and then resigned rather than carry out the policy. But the book says no such thing. While McMaster convincingly argues that the chiefs failed to present their views frankly and forcefully to their civilian superiors, including members of Congress, he neither says nor implies that the chiefs should have obstructed President Lyndon Johnson's orders and policies by leaks, public statements, or resignation.

This misreading of *Dereliction of Duty* has dangerously reinforced the increasingly widespread belief among officers that they should be advocates of particular policies rather than simply serve in their traditional advisory role. For instance, according to a survey of officer and civilian attitudes and opinions undertaken by Ole Holsti for the Triangle Institute for Security Studies (TISS) in 1998–99, "many officers believe that they have the duty to force their own views on civilian decision makers when the United States is contemplating committing American forces abroad."[24]

The professional supremacists contend that (1) civilians are actively trying to suppress the military's opinion; (2) military opinion is right, or at least more right, than civilian opinion; and (3) the military should ensure not only that its voice is heard but also that it is heeded. They essentially blame the US failures in Iraq that predated the 2007 surge on the generals because they claim that the generals went along with civilian preferences rather than blocked them.[25]

The professional supremacist view is reflected in the TISS study cited above. When "asked whether military leaders should be neutral, advise, advocate, or insist on having their way in the decision" to use military force, 50 percent or more of the up-and-coming active-duty officers answered that leaders should "insist" regarding the following issues: "setting rules of engagement, ensuring that clear political and military goals exist, developing an 'exit strategy,'" and "deciding what kinds of military units will be used to accomplish all tasks." In the context of the questionnaire, "insist" definitely implied that officers should try to compel acceptance of the military's recommendations.[26] There is little to suggest that this view has changed.

On the other side of the debate are the "civilian supremacists," who argue that the uniformed military in the American system does not possess a veto over policy. Indeed, civilians even have the authority to make decisions in what would seem to be the realm of purely military affairs. This school of thought holds that "the primary problem of [wartime civil-military relations] is ensuring that well-informed civilian strategic guidance is authoritatively directing key decisions, even when the military disagrees with that direction."[27] And they add that the record illustrates that the judgment of the military is not necessarily superior to that of the civilian decision makers.

Consider some historical examples. During the Civil War, Abraham Lincoln constantly prodded Maj. Gen. George C. McClellan to take the offensive in Virginia in 1862. McClellan just as constantly whined about insufficient forces. Despite the image of civil-military comity during World War II, there were many differences between Franklin Roosevelt and his military advisers. George Marshall, the greatest soldier-statesman since Washington, opposed arms shipments to Great Britain in 1940 and argued for a cross-channel invasion before the United States was ready. History has vindicated Lincoln and Roosevelt.

Similarly many observers, especially those in the uniformed military, have been inclined to blame the US defeat in Vietnam on the civilians. But the US operational approach in Vietnam was the creature of the uniformed military. A growing number of historians argue that the operational strategy of Gen. William Westmoreland was counterproductive; it did not make sense to emphasize attrition of Peoples' Army of Vietnam forces in a "war of the big battalions"—that is, one involving sweeps through remote jungle areas in an effort to fix and destroy the enemy with superior firepower. By the time Westmoreland's successor could adopt a more fruitful approach, it was too late.[28]

Twenty years later, during the planning for Operation Desert Storm in late 1990 and early 1991, Gen. H. Norman Schwarzkopf, commander of Central Command (CENTCOM), presented a plan calling for a frontal assault against Iraqi positions in southern Kuwait followed by a drive toward Kuwait City. The problem was that this plan was unlikely to achieve the foremost military objective of the ground war: the destruction of the three divisions of Saddam's Republican Guard. The civilian leadership rejected the early war plan presented by CENTCOM and ordered a return to the drawing board. The revised plan was far more imaginative and effective and further indication that in wartime the military does not always know best.[29]

Dissent Is Not Disobedience: The "Calculus of Dissent"

This is not to suggest that the military has no option if military advice is not heeded. The minimalist position is articulated in *The Armed Forces Officer*, an official publication that lays out the moral-ethical aspects of officership and the question of military deference to civilian authority in very stark terms: "Having rendered their candid expert judgment, professionals are bound by oath to execute legal civilian decisions as effectively as possible—even those with which they fundamentally disagree—or they must request relief from their duties, or leave the service entirely, either by resignation or retirement."[30]

Many have argued that the choices provided by *The Armed Forces Officer* are too narrow. They contend that in terms of Albert Hirschman's classic study of responses to decline in firms, organizations, and states, *The Armed Forces Officer* offers officers only the choices of "loyalty" and "exit." But Hirschman argues that under certain circumstances, the institutionalization of greater "voice"— that is, dissent—can help stem massive exit.[31]

For instance, Leonard Wong and Douglas Lovelace write that there are alternatives "beyond blind obedience, resignation or retirement."[32] They propose a range of actions available to senior military leaders to give them Hirschman's "voice" when they are confronted with decisions by civilian leaders that military officers believe are flawed. They identify two variables: the degree of civilian resistance to military advice and the seriousness of the threat to national security that the policy embodies.

When the degree of civilian resistance to military advice is low and the magnitude of the threat is low, the options for the military are acquiescence or compromise. When resistance to military advice is low but the threat is high, options include frequent interaction between the uniformed military and the civilians, working to achieve consensus, or conducting cooperative analysis.

When the degree of civilian resistance to military advice is high and the magnitude of the threat is low, the options for military officers are declining advancement or assignment, requesting relief, waiting the civilians out, and retiring. When both civilian resistance to military advice and the level of the threat are high, the authors suggest options ranging from a public information campaign, writing articles, testifying before Congress, joining efforts with others, to resignation.[33]

Don Snider accepts the idea of broadening the choices available to uniformed officers when faced with what they believe to be flawed policy decisions by civilians but questions whether the two variables employed by Wong and Lovelace alone provide adequate guidance for a strategic leader of the American military profession who is considering dissent.[34] For Snider, the imperatives of military professionalism and the "trust" relationship between the military profession and other entities within American society and government also must play a role.

Snider suggests three trust relationships, which must be rated along a continuum ranging from "fully trusted"—the ideal—to "not trustworthy." The three relationships are: (1) that between the military profession and the American people; (2) that between the military profession and the peoples' elected representatives, both in the executive and legislative branches; and (3) that between the senior leaders of the military profession and their subordinate leaders.[35]

Having laid out the three trust relationships and the three responsibilities of professional military leaders, Snider addresses how the "other" in each trust relationship involving the military profession—the American people, civilian leaders, and junior leaders within the military profession itself—perceives and understands acts of dissent on the part of the military profession's senior leaders. Such a moral analysis, he argues, must address at least five considerations: the gravity of the issue to the nation, the strategic leader's expertise with regard to the issue that might impel dissent, the degree of sacrifice on the part of the dissenter, the timing of the act of dissent, and the consistency of the dissent.[36] Snider goes on to argue that a complete assessment on the part of the dissenter would require that he analyze the five considerations in the light of the three trust relationships.

Of course in practice, argues Snider, some factors are more salient than others. Like Wong and Lovelace, he believes that the gravity of the issue with regard to national security is most important: "Logically, the higher the stakes, the greater the temptation and justification will be for dissenters to speak out."[37] This is the case because the only reason to have a military is to ensure national security. The interpretation of acts of dissent is complicated, argues Snider, by the deeply polarized nature of American politics today and the perception on the part of some that the military as an institution has become too identified with the Republican Party.[38]

When determining the military's role in policy, part of the problem is that the meaning of professional military expertise has changed since Huntington's time when the military limited itself to the "management of violence." Today that description seems far too narrow. The fact is that today's military officer is really a "national security professional" whose expertise extends to the interconnected intellectual space of everything from strategic theory, strategic thinking, and strategy formation to diplomacy, nation-building, and homeland defense.[39] Thus, in practice, it is sometimes difficult to differentiate between what military and civilian national security professionals do.[40] And as historical examples cited earlier in this chapter illustrate, even when it comes to purely military affairs, the professional military officer is not necessarily more correct than the civilians.

In theory, US military officers accept the concept of civilian control and recognize the limits of dissent. But as the previous discussion illustrates, the actual practice of military subordination is complicated by a number of factors. The first of these is organizational and institutional: the separation of powers related to military affairs between the executive and legislative branches. But even more important is the tension between the loyalty and obedience of the military professional on the one hand and his military judgment and moral beliefs on the other.

This also raises the question as to whether the military has become more "political"—with the implication that the American way of civil-military relations requires officers to steer clear of politics. Yet it is important to recognize that there is a difference between being "political" and being "partisan." Military officers must be "political" in the sense of understanding the political environment, particularly the concerns of senior executive branch officials and members of Congress, and being able to navigate those currents. But they must be "non-partisan"—able to work with any administration or Congress duly elected by the American people. Moreover, the military, particularly the officer corps, must resist the temptation to become an adjunct of any particular political party and being reduced to being simply one among many different interest groups in the American political process.

Civil-Military Relations from Clinton to Obama

In the 1990s, a number of scholars and public policy experts claimed to have identified serious systemic problems affecting American civil-military relations. Some went so far as to contend that American civil-military relations were in crisis. These individuals argued, among other things, that:

- the US military had become more alienated from its civilian leadership than at any time in American history;
- there was a growing gap between the US military as an institution and civilian society at large;
- the US military had become politicized and partisan;
- the US military had become resistant to civilian oversight, as illustrated by the efforts to dictate when and under what circumstances it would be used to implement US policy;
- officers had come to believe that they had the right to confront and resist civilian policymakers, to *insist* that civilian authorities heed their recommendations; and
- the US military was becoming too influential in inappropriate areas of American society.[41]

The likely and very dangerous outcome of such trends, went the argument, was a large, semiautonomous military so different and estranged from society that it might become unaccountable to those whom it serves. Those who advanced this view worried about the expansion of the military's influence and were concerned about the possibility of a military contemptuous of American society and unresponsive to civilian authorities.

Most writers who took this line acknowledged that the crisis was not acute—it did not, for instance, involve tanks rumbling through the streets or soldiers surrounding the parliament building or the presidential palace. Instead, they said, it was subtle and subversive—like a lymphoma or termite infestation—destroying silently from within and appearing as mutual mistrust and misunderstanding, institutional failure, and strategic incapacitation.[42] If the problem had not yet reached the danger point, they contended, that time was not too far off if something was not done soon.

Not all scholars agreed with this assessment. Some argued that American civil-military relations were not in crisis but in transition, as a result of the Cold War's end and changes in American society.[43] Nonetheless, it was clear that when measured against the criteria of constitutional balance on the one hand and comity between civilian and military leaders on the other, the US civil-military relations record over the last two decades has been mixed.

During the Clinton administration, critics charged that the subordination of the military establishment to civilian control was under assault. For example, during the 1992 presidential campaign, Gen. Colin Powell, then chairman of the Joint Chiefs of Staff, published a piece in the *New York Times* warning about the dangers of intervening in Bosnia. Not long afterward, he followed up with an article in *Foreign Affairs*. Both articles were criticized as illegitimate attempts by the most senior military officer to preempt the foreign policy agenda of an incoming president. As such, they constituted a serious encroachment by the military on civilian "turf." Critics argued that it was unprecedented for the highest-ranking officer on active duty to go public with his disagreements with a potential president over foreign policy and the role of the military.

A second example of constitutional overreach was the military's purported resistance to involvement in constabulary missions. Critics contended that such instances were further examples of an illegitimate expansion of the military's influence into inappropriate areas. They argued that the uniformed defense establishment had succeeded in making military, not political, considerations paramount in the political-military decision-making process—dictating to civilians not only how its operations would be conducted, but also the circumstances under which the military instrument would be used.

This purported role reflected the post-Vietnam view dominant within the military that only professional military officers could be trusted to establish principles guiding the use of military force. Taking its bearings from the so-called Weinberger Doctrine, a set of rules for the use of force that had been drafted in the 1980s (named for Caspar Weinberger, defense secretary at the time), the US military did everything it could to avoid what came to be known—incorrectly—as "nontraditional missions": constabulary operations required for "imperial policing," such as peacekeeping and humanitarian missions.

The clearest example of a service's resistance to a mission occurred when the army, arguing that its proper focus was on preparing to fight conventional wars, insisted that the plans for US interventions in Bosnia, Kosovo, and elsewhere reflect the military's preference for "overwhelming force." As one contemporary source reported, the military greatly influenced the Dayton Agreement establishing an Implementation Force (IFOR) to enforce peace in Bosnia-Herzegovina. Many interpreted such hostility as just one more indication that the military had become too partisan (Republican) and politicized.[44]

Closely related to the influence of the uniformed military on the political decision to employ the military instrument was the issue of resources for defense and readiness. Here the target was not only the president but also Congress. By 1998, this issue had become so acrimonious that "the Joint Chiefs and US senators engaged in public accusations of dishonest testimony and lack of support."[45]

Comity or Harmony between Civilians and the Uniformed Military

The nadir of civil-military comity during this period was the unprecedented instances of downright hostility on the part of the uniformed military toward President Clinton.[46] Many of the most highly publicized disputes between the uniformed military and the Clinton administration reflected cultural tensions between the military as an institution and liberal civilian society, mostly having to do with women in combat and open homosexuals in the military. The catalog included the very public exchange on the issue of military service by open homosexuals between newly elected President Clinton on the one hand and the uniformed military and Congress on the other, the Tailhook scandal, air force lieutenant Kelly Flinn's adulterous affair, and the sexual harassment scandal at the Aberdeen Proving Ground in Maryland.[47]

However, civil-military disharmony did not disappear with the election of George W. Bush. Issues having to do with the "transformation" of the US military and the conduct of the Iraq War created serious tensions between the uniformed military and the Bush administration. This was illustrated by the fact that the instances of military officers undercutting Secretary of Defense Rumsfeld and his policies in pursuit of their own goals—what Feaver has called "shirking"—that had plagued the Clinton administration continued apace. In addition, public criticism by military officers of civilian leaders continued as well. For instance, in April of 2006, a number of retired army and Marine Corps generals publicly called for Rumsfeld's resignation. Much of the language they used was intemperate, indeed contemptuous. One described the actions of the Bush administration as ranging from "true dereliction, negligence, and irresponsibility" to "lying, incompetence, and corruption." Another called Rumsfeld "incompetent strategically, operationally, and tactically." The seemingly orchestrated character of these attacks suggested that civil-military disharmony had reached a new and dangerous level.[48]

Although the critics in this case were retired general and flag officers, observers of what the press called the "revolt of the generals" believed that these retired officers were speaking on behalf of not only themselves but many active-duty officers as well. As Richard Kohn has observed, retired general and flag officers are analogous to the cardinals of the Roman Catholic Church. While there are no legal restrictions that prevent retired members of the military—even recently retired members—from criticizing public policy or the individuals responsible for it, there are some important reasons to suggest that the public denunciation of civilian authority by soldiers, retired or not, undermines healthy civil-military relations.

Comity seemed to improve with President Bush's selection of Robert Gates to succeed Rumsfeld. On the one hand, civilian control seemed to have been reinstitutionalized within the US defense establishment. Not only did Gates fire the secretaries of the army and air force and the chief of staff of the air force, but he also signed a national defense strategy document over the objections of the Joint Chiefs of Staff.[49]

But there is evidence that the uniformed military continued to undermine civilian control after Rumsfeld's departure. For instance, according to Bob Woodward, the uniformed military not only opposed the Bush administration's Iraq War surge, *insisting* that its advice be followed, but it also subsequently worked to undermine the president once the decision had been made. In one respect, the actions taken by military opponents of the surge—the aforementioned foot dragging, slow rolling, and selective leaking—are all too characteristic of US civil-military relations during the last decade and a half. But the picture Woodward draws is far more troubling. Even after the surge policy had been laid down, many senior US military leaders—the chairman of the Joint Chiefs of Staff, Adm. Mike Mullen; the rest of the joint chiefs; and Gen. John Abizaid's successor as commander of CENTCOM, Adm. William Fallon—actively worked against the implementation of the president's policy.[50] Secretary Gates would later write: "I was struck in the meeting by the service chiefs' seeming detachment from the wars we were in and their focus on future contingencies and stress on the force. Not one uttered a single sentence on the need for us to win in Iraq."[51]

If Woodward's account is true, it means that not since General McClellan actively attempted to sabotage the war policy of Abraham Lincoln in 1862 has the military leadership so blatantly attempted to undermine a president in the pursuit of his constitutional authority. It should be obvious that such active opposition to a president's policy poses a threat to healthy and balanced civil-military relations, to America's ability to achieve military goals, and hence to America itself.

Writing before the 2008 election, Richard Kohn predicted "the new administration, like its predecessors, will wonder to what extent it can exercise civilian 'control.' If the historical pattern holds, the administration will do something clumsy or overreact, provoking even more distrust simply in the process of establishing its own authority."[52] After his election, Barack Obama sought to avoid the fate of Bill Clinton, choosing to duck any potential clashes with the military. First Lady Michelle Obama's first official visit outside Washington, DC, was to Fort Bragg, North Carolina. The president retained two holdovers from the Bush administration: Gates and Mullen. The president appeared to do this in order to show respect for the senior military leadership and to ensure continuity during difficult wartime conditions.

In addition, President Obama seemed to insulate himself from criticism with regard to military affairs by seeking out former high-ranking leaders for posts in his administration, including retired Marine Corps general James Jones (as national security adviser), retired army general Eric Shinseki (as secretary of veterans' affairs), and retired navy admiral Dennis Blair (as director of national intelligence). Richard Kohn observed that by selecting these individuals for his administration, the president "arranged it so that he [was] free to ignore the advice of his uniformed chiefs and field commanders because he [would] have cover of General Jones by his side and other senior military in his administration."[53]

But while attempting to demonstrate that he had been reaching out to the military and that he wanted to have the benefit of military judgment, President Obama, perhaps inadvertently, sowed the seeds of civil-military discord with his campaign rhetoric, which used Afghanistan as a club to beat the Republicans in general over the head about Iraq, in particular the party's presidential candidate, John McCain. In Obama's formulation, Afghanistan became the "good war" and "the central front on terror" from which we had been distracted by our misadventure in Iraq.

In keeping with his promise to reinvigorate the effort in Afghanistan, President Obama announced in March of 2010 a "comprehensive new strategy . . . to reverse the Taliban's gains and promote a more capable and accountable Afghan government," pledging to properly resource this "war of necessity."[54] The new operational strategy called for a counterinsurgency approach (like that of the surge in Iraq) and focused on the security of the population; it rejected the "counterterrorism" approach (which NATO had followed during the Bush years) that used special operations forces and air strikes launched from unmanned aircraft to hunt down and kill al-Qaeda terrorists. President Obama even replaced the US commander in Afghanistan, Gen. David McKiernan, with Gen. Stanley McChrystal, who had been General Petraeus's right-hand man in Iraq when a counterinsurgency strategy was successfully implemented.

But when McChrystal indicated in a confidential study that more troops would be needed to pursue the president's strategy, President Obama did nothing. Admiral Mullen, chairman of the Joint Chiefs, told Congress that more troops would be needed, and experts suggested that the number of additional soldiers and marines necessary to execute the new strategy was thirty to forty thousand. In contrast to George Bush in 2007, who pursued what he thought was the right approach in Iraq despite the unpopularity of his decision, President Obama apparently began to rethink his hard line in Afghanistan out of concern that his base did not support substantial troop increases.

News reports indicated that officers on General McChrystal's staff and elsewhere were frustrated by the president's failure to make a decision about how to proceed in Afghanistan and about perceived attempts to muzzle the general by cutting off his legitimate access to Congress. They wondered why, after having declared the conflict there a "war of necessity," the president had not provided the necessary means to fight it properly. They wondered why, having selected McChrystal to turn things around in Afghanistan, President Obama had not supported him the way that George Bush supported Petraeus in Iraq.[55]

It is easy to see the truth of Kohn's prediction that a misstep by the administration would sow distrust, thereby increasing civil-military tensions, but the steps taken by some in the military made the situation worse. First, someone leaked General McChrystal's strategic assessment to Bob Woodward of the *Washington Post*. Then an article published by the McClatchy Company quoted anonymous officers to the effect that McChrystal would resign if the president did not give him what he needed to implement the announced strategy.[56] Such actions on the part of the uniformed military are symptoms of a continuing civil-military relations problem: They reflect the widespread belief among military officers that they should be *advocates* of particular policies rather than simply serving in their traditional *advisory* role.[57]

This civil-military clash was a harbinger of things to come. In late June of 2010, a story published in *Rolling Stone* quoted officers on McChrystal's staff making disparaging remarks about the vice president, the national security adviser, and even the president.[58] General McChrystal was summoned to Washington, where he offered his resignation, which the president accepted.[59]

It seems clear that General McChrystal had no choice but to offer his resignation in the wake of the *Rolling Stone* story and that the president had no choice but to accept it. If nothing else, General McChrystal had created a command climate that did not discourage disrespectful speech on the part of the military for civilian authorities. Some saw this as a more sinister development. For instance, Andrew Bacevich saw this episode as an illustration of the fact that "long wars are antithetical to democracy. Protracted conflict introduces toxins that inexorably corrode the values of popular government. Not least among those values is a code of military conduct that honors the principle of civilian control while keeping the officer corps free from the taint of politics." The real problem, wrote Bacevich, is that in the past, "circumstances such as these have bred praetorianism," leading soldiers to become "enamored with their moral superiority and impatient with the failings of those they are charged to defend. The smug disdain for high-ranking civilians casually expressed by McChrystal and his chief lieutenants—along with the conviction that 'Team America,' as these officers style themselves, was bravely holding out against a sea of stupidity and corruption—suggests that the officer corps of the United States is not immune to this affliction."[60] But the worst was yet to come.

In December of 2012, it was announced that Gen. James Mattis would be leaving his post as commander of US Central Command in March, well short of what would be expected of a combatant commander. Most observers were stunned. There seemed to be no logical reason for his being replaced early. No general in recent times has represented the military side in the civil-military dialogue better than Mattis, who had presided over the most volatile region in the world since his appointment to the position.

During his time as commander, none of the symptoms of unhealthy civil-military relations, such as those that characterized the tenure of Donald Rumsfeld, manifested themselves. There were no leaks to the press over policy disagreements and no reports of "slow rolling" or "foot dragging" in General Mattis's implementation of the president's policy. He reiterated his commitment to civilian control during a talk at Johns Hopkins University's School of Advanced International Studies in late November of 2012, remarking, "We military leaders have a right and duty to be heard, to give our best military advice, but we were not elected to and we have no right to dictate." Yet Mattis retired early over perceived differences with the administration.[61]

Disagreements over Syria in 2013 revealed additional civil-military tensions. Leaked reports claimed that army general Martin Dempsey, chairman of the Joint Chiefs of Staff, clashed with Secretary of State John Kerry over proposals to use military force against Syria in response to the alleged employment of chemical weapons by the government against Syrian rebels. General Dempsey's advice was tempered by frustrations with Iraq and Afghanistan, while Secretary Kerry thought it was incumbent on the United States to lead an international intervention. It was not so much the policy disagreement per se that caused a rift in civil-military relations but the fact that it was leaked to the press.[62]

But the most troubling example of continuing civil-military tensions was an op-ed by retired army major general Robert Scales, former commandant of the Army War College, who purported to speak for the active-duty officer corps in criticizing President Obama's conduct of foreign policy related to Syria in 2013. Scales wrote: "After personal exchanges with dozens of active and retired soldiers in recent days, I feel confident that what follows represents the overwhelming opinion of serving professionals who have been intimate witnesses to the unfolding events that will lead the United States into its next war. They are embarrassed to be associated with the amateurism of the Obama administration's attempts to craft a plan that makes strategic sense. None of the White House staff has any experience in war or understands it."[63] This is a troubling example of praetorianism and a serious violation of the American tradition of civil-military relations.

General Scales was answered by retired army lieutenant general David Barno, who wrote: "Scales's argument implies that, in an era in which the nation's civilian leadership has less and less military experience, only the military has the expertise appropriate to judge the risks and rewards associated with going to war. But under the Constitution, it matters not one whit whether our civilian leadership has experienced war; Abraham Lincoln and Franklin Roosevelt were neophytes in warfare, and both were superb wartime leaders." He continued: "This breach of the proper civilian-military relationship is disruptive and potentially corrosive to our constitutional division of powers. It must be publicly rejected by our uniformed military leadership, who must reassert throughout the ranks the proper role of the military as faithful servants of the nation in the profession of arms."[64]

Barno is right. The US military is a profession only by virtue of its oath to serve the Republic. To the extent that the United States has taken on responsibility for maintenance of regional and global orders—including treaty obligations to defend dozens of allies from attack as well as commitments to ensure access to the global commons—then the maintenance of a healthy civil-military relationship that sustains a US national security establishment with adequate power-projection capabilities is critical for the security of the current international order.

Measuring Effectiveness

In essence, the ultimate test of a civil-military relations pattern is how well it contributes to the effectiveness of a state's military, especially at the level of strategic assessment and strategy making.[65] Chapter 2, "The American Way of Organizing for Defense," has addressed an important aspect of America's recent failure to integrate national policy and operational excellence, by pointing out some of the continuing discontinuities in the US national security system. Similarly the American pattern of civil-military relations further illustrates the incidental nature of America's superpower status, given the continuing reluctance to reconfigure the civil-military bargain to produce more effective strategic outcomes.

This failure of American civil-military relations to generate strategy can be attributed to the confluence of three factors. The first of these is the continued dominance within the American system of what Eliot Cohen has called the "normal" theory of civil-military relations: the belief that there is a clear line of demarcation between civilians who determine the goals of the war and the uniformed military who then conduct the actual fighting. Until President George W. Bush abandoned it when he overruled his commanders and embraced the surge in Iraq, the normal theory has been the default position of most presidents since the Vietnam War. Its longevity is based on the idea that the failure of President Johnson and Secretary of Defense McNamara to defer to an autonomous military realm was the cause of US defeat in Vietnam.

The normal theory can be traced to Huntington's *The Soldier and the State*, in which he sought a solution to the dilemma that lies at the heart of civil-military relations: how to guarantee civilian control of the military while still ensuring the ability of the uniformed military to provide security? His solution was a mechanism for creating and maintaining a professional, apolitical military establishment, which he called "objective control." Such a professional military would focus on defending the United States but avoid threatening civilian control.[66]

But as Cohen has pointed out, the normal theory of civil-military relations has rarely held. Indeed, storied democratic war leaders such as Winston Churchill and Abraham Lincoln "trespassed" upon the military's turf as a matter of course, influencing not only strategy and operations, but also tactics. The reason that civilian leaders cannot simply leave the military to its own devices during war is that war is an iterative process involving the interplay of active wills. What appears to be the case at the outset of the war may change as the war continues, modifying the relationship between political goals and military means. The fact remains that wars are not fought for their own purposes but to achieve policy goals set by the political leadership of the state.

The second factor, strongly reinforced by the normal theory of civil-military relations, is the influence of the uniformed services' organizational cultures. Each military service is built around a "strategic concept," which according to Huntington constitutes "the fundamental element of a military service," the basic "statement of [its] role . . . or purpose in implementing national policy."[67] A clear strategic concept is critical to the ability of a service to organize and employ the resources that Congress allocates to it. Carl Builder's book *The Masks of War* demonstrated the importance of the organizational cultures of the various military services in creating differing "personalities," identities, and behaviors. His point was that each service possesses a preferred way of fighting and that "the unique service identities . . . are likely to persist for a very long time."[68] The organizational culture of a service, in turn, exerts a strong influence on civil-military relations, frequently constraining what civilian leaders can do and often constituting an obstacle to change and innovation. The critical question here is this: Who decides whether the military instrument is effective—the civilian policymakers or the military itself?

An illuminating illustration of this phenomenon at work has been the recent attempt to institutionalize counterinsurgency doctrine within the US Army, a difficult task given the service's focus on the "operational level of war," which manifests itself as a preference for fighting large-scale conventional wars—despite the fact that throughout most of its existence, the US Army rarely engaged in large-scale conventional wars.

Beginning in the late 1970s, the army embraced the idea of the operational level of war as its central organizing concept. This made sense in light of that service's major warfighting concern of the time—defeating Warsaw Pact forces on the central plains of Europe—but as Hew Strachan has observed, "the operational level of war appeals to armies: it functions in a politics-free zone and it puts primacy on professional skills."[69] Brig. Justin Kelly and Michael James Brennan observe:

> Rather than meeting its original purpose of contributing to the attainment of campaign objectives laid down by strategy, operational art—practiced as a "level of war"—assumed responsibility for campaign planning. This reduced political leadership to the role of "strategic sponsors," quite specifically widening the gap between politics and warfare. The result has been a well-demonstrated ability to win battles that have not always contributed to strategic success, producing "a way of battle rather than a way of war."
>
> The political leadership of a country cannot simply set objectives for a war, provide the requisite materiel, then stand back and await victory. Nor should the nation or its military be seduced by this prospect. Politicians should be involved in the minute-to-minute conduct of war; as Clausewitz reminds us, political considerations are "influential in the planning of war, of the campaign, and often even of the battle."[70]

The task of strategy is to bring doctrine—concerned with fighting battles in support of campaigns—into line with national policy. But instead of strategy, we have Colin Gray's "black hole."[71]

The third factor contributing to the perseverance of the American strategic black hole is one that was, ironically, intended to improve US strategic planning: the Goldwater-Nichols Department of Defense Reorganization Act of 1986. As noted in chapter 2, the Joint Chiefs of Staff are responsible for integrating theater strategy and national policy. But if they are marginalized, as they were during much of the 2000s, such integration does not occur.

The result of such a disjunction between the military and political realms is that war plans may not be integrated with national policy and that strategy, despite lip service to its importance, in practice becomes an orphan. And in the absence of strategy, other factors rush to fill the void, resulting in strategic drift.

The current civil-military framework fails to provide strategic guidance for integrating the operational level of war and national policy. Rectifying this situation requires that both parties to the civil-military bargain adjust the way they do business. In the past, these divergences could be overlooked or failures accepted because negative consequences could be mitigated or because an over-abundance of resources helped to smooth over difficulties. In the twenty-first century, however, the maintenance of American global leadership in a time of resource constraints makes it imperative that this gap be bridged if American power is to be wielded more effectively.

Conclusion

Events during the administrations of Bill Clinton, George W. Bush, and Barack Obama suggest that the real civil-military danger facing the Republic is not a threat to civilian control of the military, but that the lack of trust between civilians and the military impacts how effectively American power can be wielded around the world. This has been a problem on both sides over the last three administrations. In the case of President Obama, news reports indicate that his civilian aides have been deeply suspicious of the military, accusing it of intentionally "boxing the president in" through a series of coordinated leaks to the media during the Afghanistan policy review.[72] For its part, many officers have seen the Obama administration setting up the military to take the blame should the American enterprise in Afghanistan fail.

Events over the last several years also point to the issue of *trust*: the mutual respect and understanding between civilian and military leaders and the exchange of candid views and perspectives between the two parties as part of the decision-making process. Establishing trust requires that both parties to the civil-military bargain reexamine their mutual relationship. On the one hand, the military must recover its voice in strategy making while realizing that politics permeates the conduct of war and that civilians have the final say, not only concerning the goals of the war but also how it is conducted. On the other, civilians must understand that to implement effective policy and strategy requires the proper military instrument and therefore must insist that soldiers present their views frankly and forcefully throughout the strategy-making and implementation processes. This is the key to healthy civil-military relations.

Notes

1. Vincent Brooks, Thomas Greenwood, Robert Parker, and Keith Wray, *Two Hands on the Sword: A Study of Political-Military Relations in National Security Policy* (Carlisle, PA: Army War College, 1999).

2. Frank G. Hoffman, "Dereliction of Duty *Redux*? Post-Iraq American Civil-Military Relations," *Orbis* 52, no. 2 (Spring 2008), 217–35.

3. Andrew Bacevich offered this formulation to an early version of Mackubin Owens's proposal for a book tentatively titled *Sword of Republican Empire: A History of U.S. Civil-Military Relations*.

4. For an in-depth discussion on these questions see Mackubin Thomas Owens, *U.S. Civil-Military Relations after 9/11: Renegotiating the Civil-Military Bargain* (New York: Continuum, 2011).

5. Eliot Cohen, *Supreme Command: Soldiers, Statesmen, and Leadership in Wartime* (New York: Anchor, 2002), 247.

6. Mackubin Thomas Owens, "Understanding Civil-Military Relations during the Clinton-Bush Era," in *Inside Defense: Understanding the 21st Century Military*, ed. Derek Reveron and Judith Hicks Stiehm (New York: Macmillan, 2008).

7. Mackubin Thomas Owens, "Renegotiating the Civil-Military Bargain after 9/11," in *Lessons for a Long War: How America Can Win on New Battlefields*, ed. Tom Donnelly (Washington, DC: American Enterprise Institute, 2010).

8. Robert M. Gates, *Duty: Memoirs of a Secretary at War* (New York: Knopf, 2014), 50.

9. Mackubin Thomas Owens, "The War on Terror and the Revolt of the Generals," *Wall Street Journal*, October 1, 2010, A19.

10. Mackubin Thomas Owens, "Civil-Military Relations and the Strategy Deficit," FPRI (Foreign Policy Research Institute) e-note, February, 2010, at http://www.fpri.org/articles/2010/02/civil-military-relations-and-us-strategy-deficit; Hoffman, "Dereliction of Duty *Redux*?"

11. Samuel Huntington, *The Soldier and the State: The Theory and Politics of Civil-Military Relations* (Cambridge: Harvard University Press, 1957).

12. Derek Reveron, ed., *America's Viceroys: The Military and U.S. Foreign Policy* (New York: Palgrave Macmillan, 2004).

13. Richard Kohn, "The Erosion of Civilian Control of the Military in the United States Today," *Naval War College Review* 55, no. 3 (Summer 2002): 19.

14. Charles A. Stevenson, *Warriors and Politicians: US Civil-Military Relations under Stress* (Abingdon, Oxon: Routledge, 2006), 207–8.

15. Samuel P. Huntington, *The Common Defense: Strategic Programs in National Politics* (New York: Columbia University Press, 1961), 4.

16. This was true in the cases of Gen. Colin Powell, who served as President Ronald Reagan's national security adviser, and Lt. Gen. Doug Lute, who served on the national security staff for Presidents George W. Bush and Barack Obama.

17. Kohn, "Erosion of Civilian Control"; Richard Kohn, "Out of Control: The Crisis in Civil-Military Relations," *National Interest* 35 (Spring 1994); Richard Kohn, "The Forgotten Fundamentals of Civilian Control of the Military in Democratic Government," John M. Olin Institute for Strategic Studies, Project on US Post–Cold War Civil-Military Relations, working paper 13, Harvard University, June 1997; Richard Kohn, "Coming Soon: A Crisis in Civil-Military Relations," *World Affairs*, Winter 2008, www.worldaffairsjournal.org/2008%20-%20Winter/full-civil-military.html; Peter Feaver, *Armed Servants: Agency, Oversight and Civil-Military Relations* (Cambridge, MA: Harvard University Press, 2003); Michael Desch, *Civilian Control of the Military: The Changing Security Environment* (Baltimore: Johns Hopkins University Press, 1999); Russell Weigley, "The American Military and the Principle of Civilian Control from McClellan to Powell," *Journal of Military History*, October, 1993; and Cohen, *Supreme Command*.

18. Kohn, "Erosion of Civilian Control," 9.

19. Ibid., 15–16.

20. Ibid., 21–22.

21. Ibid., p. 12.

22. See Feaver, *Armed Servants*.

23. H. R. McMaster, *Dereliction of Duty: Lyndon Johnson, Robert McNamara, the Joint Chiefs of Staff, and the Lies That Led to Vietnam* (New York: HarperCollins, 1997).

24. Ole Holsti, "Of Chasms and Convergences: Attitudes and Beliefs of Civilians and Military Elites at the Start of a New Millennium," in *Soldiers and Civilians: The Civil-Military Gap and American National Security*, ed. Peter D. Feaver and Richard H. Kohn (Cambridge, MA: MIT Press, 2001), 84, 489, and tables 1.27, 1.28.

25. Peter Feaver, "The Right to Be Right: Civil-Military Relations and the Iraq Surge Decision," *International Security*, Spring 2011, 94.

26. Holsti, "Of Chasms," 84, 489, and tables 1.27, 1.28.

27. Feaver, "Right to Be Right," 89–90.

28. See Lewis Sorley, *A Better War: The Unexamined Victories and Final Tragedy of America's Last Years in Vietnam* (New York: HBJ/Harvest Books, 2000).

29. See Michael Gordon and Bernard Trainor, *The Generals' War: The Inside Story of the Conflict in the Gulf* (Boston: Little, Brown, 1995).

30. Department of Defense, *The Armed Forces Officer* (Washington, DC: Department of Defense, 2006), 27.

31. Albert O. Hirschman, *Exit, Voice, Loyalty: Responses to Decline in Firms, Organizations, and States* (Cambridge, MA: Harvard University Press, 1970).

32. Leonard Wong and Douglas Lovelace, "Knowing When to Salute," *Orbis* 52, no. 2 (Spring 2008), 284.

33. Ibid., 284–87.

34. Don Snider, "Dissent and Strategic Leadership of the Military Profession," *Orbis* 52, no. 2 (Spring 2008), 256–77.

35. Ibid., 266.

36. Ibid., 269.

37. Ibid., 269.

38. Andrew Bacevich and Richard Kohn, "Grand Army of the Republicans: Has the U.S. Military Become a Partisan Force?," *New Republic*, December 8, 1997, 22–25.

39. Harry Yarger, *Strategy and the National Security Professional: Strategic Thinking and Strategy Formulation in the 21st Century* (Westport, CT: Praeger, 2008). Cf. George W. Bush, Executive Order 13434 of May 17, 2007, "National Security Professional Development," www.fas.org/irp/offdocs/eo/eo-13434.htm.

40. On the difficulty of defining the content and boundaries of the military profession, see Richard Lacquement, "Mapping Army Professional Expertise and Clarifying Jurisdictions of Practice," in *The Future of the Army Profession*, 2nd ed., ed. Don Snider and Gayle Watkins (New York: McGraw-Hill, 2005). On the negative consequences of defining the military profession too narrowly, see Richard Lacquement and Nadia Schadlow, "Winning Wars, Not Just Battles: Expanding the Military Profession to Incorporate Stability Operations," in *American Civil-Military Relations: The Soldier and the State in a New Era*, ed. Suzanne Nielsen and Don M. Snider (Baltimore: Johns Hopkins University Press, 2009), 112–32.

41. Cf. Kohn, "Erosion of Civilian Control"; Weigley, "American Military"; Edward Luttwak, "Washington's Biggest Scandal," *Commentary* 97, no. 5 (May 1994); Charles Dunlap, "The Origins of the Coup of 2012," *Parameters*, Winter 1992–93; Charles Dunlap, "Welcome to the Junta: The Erosion of Civilian Control of the Military," *Wake Forest Law Review*, Summer 1994; Gregory Foster, "Confronting the Crisis in Civil-Military Relations," *The Washington Quarterly* 20, no. 4 (Autumn 1997); Bacevich and Kohn, "Grand Army," 22–25; and Holsti, "Of Chasms."

42. Foster, "Confronting the Crisis," 15.

43. See, for instance, Douglas Johnson and Steven Metz, "American Civil-Military Relations: A Review of the Recent Literature," in *US Civil Military Relations: In Crisis or Transition?*, ed. Don M. Snider and Miranda A. Carlton-Carew (Washington, DC: Center for Strategic and International Studies, 1995), 201, and Desch, *Civilian Control of the Military*, 141.

44. According to Clinton administration officials, the agreement "was carefully crafted to reflect demands from the military. . . . Rather than be ignored . . . the military, as a price for its support, has basically gotten anything it wanted. Warren Strobel, "This Time Clinton Is Set to Heed Advice from Military," *Washington Times*, December 1, 1995, 1. But military resistance to Clinton's foreign policy predated Bosnia. See, for example, Richard A. Serrano and Art Pine, "Many in Military Angry over Clinton's Policies," *Los Angeles Times*, October, 19, 1993, 1.

45. Kohn, "Erosion of Civilian Control," 21n5. Cf. Eric Schmitt, "Joint Chiefs Accuse Congress of Weakening US Defense, *New York Times*, September, 30, 1998, 1; and Elaine Grossman, "Congressional Aide Finds Spending on 'Core Readiness' in Decline," *Inside the Pentagon*, June, 28, 2001, 1.

46. For examples of the hostility of the uniformed military toward President Clinton, see John Lancaster, "Accused of Ridiculing Clinton, General Faces Air Force Probe," *Washington Post*, June 8, 1993, 21; "A Military Breach?," *Seattle Post-Intelligencer*, June 11, 1993, 10; David H. Hackworth, "Rancor in the Ranks: The Troops vs. the President," *Newsweek*, June 28, 1993; Rowan Scarborough, "Marine Officer Probed for Blasting Clinton," *Washington Times*, November 11, 1998, 1, and "Major Gets Punished for Criticizing President," *Washington Times*, December 7, 1998; C. J. Chivers, "Troops Obey Clinton despite Disdain," *USA Today*, November 18, 1998; and Jane Perlez, "For 8 Years, a Strained Relationship with the Military," *New York Times*, December 28, 2000, A13.

47. Cragg Hines, "Clinton's Vow to Lift Gay Ban Is Reaffirmed," *Houston Chronicle*, November 12, 1992, A1; Barton Gellman, "Clinton Says He'll 'Consult' on Allowing Gays in Military," *Washington Post*, November 13, 192, A1; US Department of Defense, Office of the Inspector General, *The Tailhook Report: The Official Inquiry into the Events of Tailhook '91* (New York: St. Martin's, 1993); William McMichael, *The Mother of All Hooks* (New Brunswick, NJ: Transaction Publishers, 1997); Elaine Sciolino, "B-52 Pilot Requests Discharge That Is Honorable," *New York Times*, May 18, 1997, A1; Bradley Graham, "Army Leaders Feared Aberdeen Coverup Allegations," *Washington Post*, November 11, 1996, A1.

48. Greg Newbold, "Why Iraq Was a Mistake," *Time*, April 17, 2006, 42–43; David S. Cloud and Eric Schmitt, "More Retired Generals Call for Rumsfeld Resignation," *New York Times*, April 14, 2006, A1.

49. Thom Shanker, "2 Leaders Ousted from Air Force in Atomic Errors," *New York Times*, June 6, 2008, www.nytimes.com/2008/06/06/washington/06 military.html?_r=1&adxnnl=1&ref=todayspaper&adxnnlx=1212735795-6qf VDvbLA5+MI1/c0v7/bg&oref=slogin; "Gates Approves New Defense Strategy over Objections of Service Chiefs," *The Insider from Inside Defense*, June 12, 2008, http://insidedefense.com/secure/insider_display.asp?f=defense_2002 .ask&docid=6122008_june12d.

50. See Bob Woodward, *The War Within: A Secret White House History, 2006-2008* (New York: Simon & Schuster, 2008), 340, 342–43, 348–49.

51. Gates, *Duty*, 39.

52. Kohn, "Coming Soon."

53. Quoted in Will King, "Panel Discusses Civil-Military Relations at Fort Leavenworth," *Leavenworth Lamp*, March 27, 2009, www.army.mil/ article/18852/panel-discusses-civil-military-relations-at-fort-leavenworth/.

54. President Barack Obama, "Remarks on a Strategy for Afghanistan and Pakistan," March 27, 2009, archived at www.cfr.org/publication/18952#.

55. See Nancy A. Youssef, "Military Growing Impatient with Obama on Afghanistan," McClatchy Washington Bureau, September 18, 2009, www .mcclatchydc.com/227/v-print/story/75702.html.

56. See Bob Woodward, "McChrystal: More Forces or 'Mission Failure,'" *Washington Post*, September 21, 2009, www.washingtonpost.com/wp-dyn/

content/article/2009/09/20/AR2009092002920.html?referrer=emailarticle; Youssef, "Military Growing Impatient."

57. For the fullest account of this episode to date, see Bob Woodward, *Obama's Wars* (New York: Simon & Schuster, 2010).

58. Michael Hastings, "The Runaway General," *Rolling Stone*, June 22, 2010, www.rollingstone.com/politics/news/17390/119236.

59. Scott Wilson and Michael D. Shear, "Gen. McChrystal Is Dismissed as Top US Commander in Afghanistan," *Washington Post*, June 24, 2010, www.washingtonpost.com/wp-dyn/content/article/2010/06/23/AR20100623 00689.html.

60. Andrew Bacevich, "Endless War: A Recipe for Four Star Arrogance," *Washington Post*, June 27, 2010, B1.

61. According to an authoritative source, Mattis became persona non grata primarily "because he pushed the civilians so hard on considering the second- and third-order consequences of military action against Iran. Some of those questions apparently were uncomfortable. For example, what do you do with Iran once the nuclear issue is resolved and it remains a foe? What do you do if Iran then develops conventional capabilities that could make it hazardous for US Navy ships to operate in the Persian Gulf? He kept saying, 'And then what?'" See Tom Ricks, "The Obama Administration's Inexplicable Mishandling of Marine Gen. James Mattis," *The Best Defense* (blog), *Foreign Policy* online, January 18, 2013, at http://ricks.foreignpolicy.com/posts/2013/01/18/the_obama_ administration_s_inexplicable_mishandling_of_marine_gen_james_mattis.

62. "Top US General, Diplomat Clash over Syria," Agence France-Presse, June 19, 2013, www.google.com/hostednews/afp/article/ALeqM5iunl_yhD0w9gHE eJVUupkmfncPSA?docId=CNG.ec7aa72604f6be3611f0879e975d9e8e.221.

63. Robert Scales, "A War the Pentagon Doesn't Want," *Washington Post*, September 5, 2013.

64. David Barno, "U.S. War Decisions Rightfully Belong to Elected Civilian Leaders, Not the Military," *Washington Post*, September 12, 2013.

65. On the relationship between patterns of civil-military relations and strategic assessment, see Risa Brooks, *Shaping Strategy: The Civil-Military Politics of Strategic Assessment* (Princeton, NJ: Princeton University Press, 2008). Chapter 7 of her book addresses in detail the impact of the pattern of civil-military relations during Donald Rumsfeld's tenure as secretary of defense on the planning and execution of the presurge phase of the Iraq War.

66. Huntington, *Soldier and the State*, 83–84.

67. Samuel Huntington, "National Policy and the Transoceanic Navy," US Naval Institute *Proceedings*, May 1954, 483.

68. Carl Builder, *The Masks of War: American Military Styles in Strategy and Analysis* (Baltimore: Johns Hopkins University Press, 1989), 39.

69. Hew Strachan, "Making Strategy after Iraq," *Survival* 48, no. 3 (Autumn 2006): 60.

70. Justin Kelly and Michael James Brennan, *Alien: How Operational Art Devoured Strategy* (Carlisle, PA: US Army War College, Strategic Studies

Institute, 2009), viii, www.strategicstudiesinstitute.army.mil/pubs/display.cfm
?pubID=939.

71. Colin S. Gray, *The Navy in the Post-Cold War World: The Uses and Value
of Strategic Sea Power* (University Park: Penn State University Press, 2005).

72. Evan Thomas, "McChrystal's War," *Newsweek*, October 5, 2009.

4

Drivers, Continuities, and Challenges of US Foreign Policy

> For generations, the United States of America has played a unique role as an anchor of global security and as an advocate for human freedom.
>
> —Barack Obama, March 28, 2011

Even though incendiary language at election time might suggest otherwise, there is a fairly broad and durable bipartisan consensus about America's role in the world—including the need to use military force, if necessary, to defend key interests and values that have endured for several decades.[1] Politics, it seems, stops at the water's edge where both major political parties accept a global political, economic, and security role for the United States. Henry Kissinger summed up the main arguments in favor of American global leadership: "Without our commitment to international security, there can be no stable peace. Without our constructive participation in the world economy, there can be no hope for economic progress. Without our dedication to human liberty, the prospect of freedom in the world is dim indeed."[2]

Every president since Franklin Roosevelt has accepted the outline sketched out by Kissinger as operative for US foreign policy, a consensus labeled by Chris Brose under the rubric of "pragmatic internationalism."[3] Simply put, presidents remain committed to using US power—as well as enlisting the support of allies and partners—in "managing and successfully harnessing the forces of globalization towards stability and prosperity."[4] This idea is continuous in US history, beginning with the founding of the Massachusetts Bay Colony in 1630 when its governor, John Winthrop, charged his fellow colonists to tell the world "that we shall be as a city upon a hill—the eyes of all people are upon us." Whether the leader was John F. Kennedy, Ronald Reagan, or Secretary of State Madeleine Albright, the United States was seen as the indispensable nation.

Presidential candidates have disagreed, sometimes quite vociferously during election campaigns, over their priorities, in what they choose to emphasize, and how they might respond to specific challenges. But continuity in US foreign policy demonstrates that there is less fundamental disagreement about overall objectives—especially maintaining global leadership—"but rather, on the goals, strategies and tactics that should be employed in implementing that role."[5] For example, despite Barack Obama's election commitments to pursue change in US foreign policy—and a set of interagency reviews in 2009 to reexamine US policy direction—the United States nonetheless continues to follow (and execute) President John F. Kennedy's Cuba policy, President Richard M. Nixon's China policy, President Jimmy Carter's Middle East policy (especially the Carter Doctrine, which commits the United States to the defense of the Persian Gulf to safeguard global energy supplies), President Ronald Reagan's democracy-promotion policy, President George H. W. Bush's free-trade policy, President Bill Clinton's anti-genocide policy, and President George W. Bush's counterterrorism policy. Indeed, a striking feature of the US system is that one president may start a process that another one, even from the rival party, will complete—such as a comprehensive arms-control treaty or the creation of a new international regulatory regime. For example, the North American Free Trade Agreement was launched under President Reagan, the main negotiations were held under the auspices of the George H. W. Bush administration, but the agreement was ratified and brought into existence by the president who defeated Bush for reelection, Clinton.

What usually occurs in the transition between US presidential administrations is the shift in the "thematic priorities" of different presidents—in how they rank particular challenges, in their preference for using different tools of statecraft, or in what they decide to give priority to—rather than major and systematic changes in the direction and focus of US foreign and security policy.[6] There is a noticeable adjustment in perspective when the successful presidential candidate shifts from "campaign mode" to governing, including the realization that sudden changes in policy are difficult to successfully execute. Often a president is willing to accept continuity on a whole host of national security policies with the previous administration in order to retain the freedom to make significant changes on those questions he deems to be most important—for example, President Obama tended to downplay some aspects of his predecessor's missile defense programs in an attempt to improve relations with Russia. Continuity both reflects enduring US national interests, as well as the stability of the national security establishment, and highlights the limits of presidential power.[7]

Limits of Presidential Power

The essential continuity in US foreign policy was especially dramatized in the aftermath of the 2008 presidential elections. The election of Barack Obama had generated wide-ranging expectations "about the possibility of substantive change in US foreign and domestic policy"—especially with regard to some of the strategies of the George W. Bush administration that had not been well received in a number of countries around the world.[8] The Obama administration did make alterations to the policies pursued by its predecessors, canceled some programs, and announced a change in geopolitical focus (a "pivot" away from the Middle East toward the Asia-Pacific region)—but it did not halt or reverse many of the steps taken by the previous team.[9] Indeed, a series of policy reviews undertaken in 2009—which created the appearance that dramatic changes in US foreign policy were in the works—tended to recommend alterations to Bush-era policies rather than their complete abolishment.[10]

The Obama administration might have dropped the Bush nomenclature of the "global war on terror" and called for the closure of the Guantanamo Bay detention facility, but it was surprisingly amenable to continuing to use the strategies and methods of its predecessor, including counterterrorism strikes and widespread electronic surveillance.[11] In part, continuity of personnel between administrations—both at the political-appointee level and also within the senior executive service—can also be an important factor to consider. The retention of a number of Bush administration officials (with Defense Secretary Robert Gates only the most prominent example) into the first term of the Obama administration worked in favor of continuity over change. This led observers to note that "the degree of continuity is noteworthy—and comes [as] a surprise (and sometimes a disappointment) [to those] who expected more change, and a vindication to those who predicted that much of the Bush Administration's foreign policy [would] be proven to be both necessary and effective."[12] Despite all the talk of change, the assessment is that Obama, as president, pursued a foreign policy approach that was broadly in sync with what previous administrations had done, "even if he disagreed with certain strategies or rhetorical terms adopted by his predecessor."[13]

In the end, while presidents often change the tone or focus of the policies of their predecessors or tinker at the margins, it is rare for them to reverse wholesale the major decisions taken by previous presidents. David Brooks argues that one of the "myths" about the power of any president to institute change is that "we can begin the world anew. In fact, all problems and policies have already been worked by a thousand hands and the clay is mostly dry. Presidents are compelled to work with the material they have before them."[14] Presidential historian Richard Neustadt diagnosed the limits of the White House, noting "presidential power is the power to persuade."[15] As a result, while some of the "details of U.S. foreign policy have differed from administration to administration," the United States, for the past seven decades, has pursued a consistent grand strategy in its approach to the world.[16] US leadership, free trade, and democracy promotion are its tenets.

This is due in part to the fact that while administrations may change, fundamental US interests have not, including the need for securing access to reliable sources of energy, protecting the US homeland from catastrophic attack, sustaining a global system marked by open lines of communication to facilitate commerce, and preserving regional balances of power to prevent powers hostile to the United States from being able to dominate important areas of the world or destructive regional conflicts from impinging on US prosperity and security. Combined with this is an enduring idealistic vision of spreading the benefits of democracy to other parts of the globe, with a corresponding assumption that democracies will be friendly to the United States and supportive of its global agenda.[17] All of these interests require the United States to "play an active leadership role in world affairs."[18] This consensus guarantees that the United States is not likely to retreat from global engagement back to a "Fortress North America" because Americans are well aware, as Kissinger noted, that "upheavals thousands of miles away can threaten American lives or jeopardize American prosperity."[19]

This consensus on foreign policy also dominates within Congress as members *generally* defer to the executive branch in how a president will shape and execute US foreign and defense policy. This includes a greater willingness to allow the president to send US forces into combat situations if it is seen to be in defense of US interests.[20] Often encapsulated by the remark of Sen. Arthur Vandenberg when he became chairman of the Senate Foreign Relations Committee in 1947 that "partisan politics [ends] at the water's edge," this approach takes the position that the legislature—particularly the opposition party—ought not to dictate how the president conducts national security affairs as long as it falls within the broad parameters of this internationalist paradigm. Yet the Vandenberg proviso does not mean extending a blank check. If members of Congress believe that the executive branch is ignoring an issue they deem is vital to US national security, they are prepared to use their abilities to pass legislation as a way to push for change and to constrain the executive branch. Congressional foreign policy entrepreneurship occurs when members use their position to lobby a presidential administration for a policy change, use their "bully pulpits" to alert the public as to a looming danger and/or a possible solution, and marshal support among their colleagues for legislative action—even over the objections of the president and his national security team.[21]

Foreign Policy Interests

Individual presidents may have had their preferences and their pet projects, but there is a common set of core US interests that no chief executive can ignore or repudiate. As a result, while different administrations may make "course alterations" or emphasize different priorities, there is agreement about the core elements.[22] This is the basis of a "bipartisan foreign policy consensus" on a number of issues, which translates into a number of policies.[23] These include a continuing commitment to the health and stability of the North Atlantic Treaty Organization (NATO) and of other bilateral alliances; denuclearizing states that are seen as threats to the United States or the current global order (such as North Korea and the Islamic Republic of Iran); supporting longtime ally Israel; reducing the impact of a resurgent Russia, a rising China, and other emerging powers; muting the challenges posed by nonstate actors to preserve existing international arrangements (especially American preeminence); and sustaining a global economic system that permits the ready flow of energy, resources, and goods to the United States while enhancing the ability of other countries to purchase American goods and services. All of these elements are part of the ultimate end state: a security community where members do not use force against each other, do not engage in military competition that could destabilize their regions or threaten US predominance, and have a stake in shared prosperity and stability.[24]

The creation of such a security community requires the active use of American power to sustain it. For much of the US foreign policy establishment, there is no faith that a balance of power could emerge to provide an orderly international environment if the United States were to cease its engagement. Critics of retrenchment point to the United States withdrawal from Afghanistan-Pakistan in 1989, with the assumption that regional powers would, in pursuing their own interests, stabilize the region. Instead of bringing stability to Central Asia, however, the ensuing instability in Afghanistan provided the means for al-Qaeda to find a sanctuary.[25]

At the global level, the fear is that the vacuum caused by a possible US withdrawal from the world means that there would be "no single government or alliance of governments with the political and economic muscle to drive an international agenda."[26] Forward engagement also rests on the assumption that, as then senator Barack Obama told the Chicago Council on Global Affairs in 2007, "in today's globalized world, the security of the American people is inextricably linked to the security of all people."[27] One of the lessons that policymakers drew from the 9/11 attacks was that problems in distant regions of the world with no apparent or immediate connection to the United States could become incubators for threats that, left unchecked and unaddressed, would grow in strength to pose a real challenge to American security. This buttressed the drive to continue to expand the zone of security and prosperity by extending alliances and bringing new members into US-led international organizations.[28]

Part of the concern about American withdrawal rises from the assessment that an active American presence is required to buttress regional security arrangements and prevent conflicts from developing or from spiraling out of control, particularly in Europe and East Asia. A forward-deployed American presence also allows for the chance to strike at "ill-intentioned forces" before they can reach critical mass to pose a threat to the US homeland.[29]

The core interests are translated into concrete policies depending on specific situational factors. In theory, fundamental changes in the international strategic environment should lead to a recalibration of the US global posture and of specific courses of action.[30] For instance, the US interest in a stable energy flow—usually considered to be one of the top core interests of the United States—led to the creation of the Fourth Fleet during World War II to safeguard oil tankers traversing the Caribbean and made Latin America a region of heightened importance for US security. During the 1970s and 1980s, Jimmy Carter and Ronald Reagan took steps to secure access to the Persian Gulf, first by designating the region to be one of vital interest for American security (via the Carter Doctrine and the Reagan Corollary committing the United States to maintain the security of Persian Gulf states against both external and internal threats) and then through the creation of US Central Command (CENTCOM) in 1983. Beginning in the 1990s, the US government strongly supported alternative routes for Eurasian pipelines that would link Central Asian energy sources to Western markets without having to pass through Russia or Iran.

Forward Engagement

America's posture in the world is usually categorized under the rubric of forward engagement—utilizing "a global network of alliances and partnerships" as well as US instruments of power (including overseas military deployments) "to secure American interests in critical regions."[31] Forward engagement translates American power "into the global capacity to manage security affairs in multiple regions."[32] In the past the argument has been raised that guaranteeing the security and prosperity of the United States did not require active engagement with the rest of the world and certainly not the forward deployment of US instruments of national power—given America's size as a continental power with a massive resource endowment, its large internal market, and the belief that its favorable geographic position provided "immunity from attack."[33]

Yet autarkic isolationism was never a realistic option for the United States at any point in its history, given its reliance on foreign trade and investment, but especially not under current conditions. American businesses have widely invested "in overseas presence" because of the economic benefits that are accrued; one estimate is that US economic integration with the rest of the world leads to a 12 percent increase in US per capita income.[34] Yet these favorable conditions cannot exist in a security vacuum. In the 1990s, the chief of naval operations, Adm. Jay Johnson, and the commandant of the Marine Corps, Gen. Charles Krulak, spoke of US engagement as a "peace insurance dividend" meant to preserve this positive state of affairs.[35] The alternative is the risk that, in the absence of a power willing to guarantee the stability of the international order, the global economic system would unravel, as occurred in the 1920s and 1930s, with disastrous consequences.[36]

Forward engagement seeks to, at minimum, apply prophylactic measures to isolate problems before they metastasize into larger threats but, whenever possible, to actively intervene to solve them, under the assumption that "it is much better—and cheaper—to resolve a crisis before it burns out of control."[37] A guiding principle is encapsulated in the so-called Adolf Hitler analogy arising out of the assessment that if Hitler had been stopped earlier in his career, the world could have avoided the devastation of the Second World War.[38] It takes the perspective that "no adverse development anywhere in the world is entirely irrelevant to the security and well-being of the United States"—even if there is no immediate threat to core US interests.[39] In the late 1990s, the Serbian counterinsurgency campaign to retake control of the province of Kosovo did not directly imperil the United States or even its allies, but the Clinton adminis-tration justified its involvement, first by trying to broker a diplomatic settlement and then by engaging in a military campaign, on the grounds that this problem might ignite "a powder keg at the heart of Europe" and lead to a much wider war that would negatively impact American equities.[40] A similar rationale was articulated by President Barack Obama in justifying American involvement in the Libyan Civil War in 2011. Further, the intense US involvement in trying to settle the civil war between the North and the South in Sudan—in essence, serving as the key facilitator for trying to broker an end to a conflict that on its face did not threaten the United States—was justified in terms of ensuring stability on the African continent, which would enhance the US fight against international terrorism.[41]

Thus, for the past sixty years, there has been convergence between the strate-gic logic of America's strategy of forward deployment and the economic imper-ative of securing the nation's prosperity. Opposition from naturally isolationist tendencies of the American body politic has been overcome, in part, by the argument that prosperity at home could only be secured by guaranteeing access to markets and resources abroad. By the 1990s, this approach had reached its apex in the emergence of a truly global system of trade, defined by "just-in-time" supply networks, containerized shipping, and the outsourcing of many of the stages of manufacturing away from the US homeland. American politicians could no longer argue against the US global presence by claiming that prob-lems abroad had no impact on domestic prosperity. With oil flowing from West Africa and the Persian Gulf, high-technology components shipped in from East Asia and Europe, and a veritable flood of low-cost consumer goods flowing from China and other low-wage centers around the world, American strategists could easily educate the general public about how US global engagement affected the prosperity and well-being of ordinary Americans.[42] The idea that America has to take the lead in protecting, patrolling, and defending the "global commons"—

domains that lie outside the control of any one state, such as the high seas or space—because US prosperity is at stake has become the accepted wisdom in both of America's major political parties.[43]

Regional Challenges

The United States is a global power, but particular regions rise and fall in importance over time. For instance, when problems began in Kosovo in 1981, there was neither the need nor the opportunity for the United States to become involved in trying to settle the conflict. The reality of the Cold War still was that "nuclear tension suppressed nationalism and ethnic tensions," meaning that the risk the conflict might escalate was kept in check by the larger geopolitical realities.[44] Eighteen years later, with the threat of escalation removed, there was in contrast a real concern that "key U.S. allies could be drawn into a wider conflict, a war we would be forced to confront later, only at far greater risk and greater cost."[45]

Periodically the United States may review its global posture "to determine how to make it more strategically sound, operationally resilient and politically sustainable," which may result in areas once deemed to be of critical importance being demoted or having resources and attention shift to other, more pressing concerns.[46] For instance, as the Cold War drew to a close, some US forces were withdrawn from Europe, while detachments that remained—which previously were intended to deter a Soviet invasion—were now tasked to be able to respond to a variety of noncombat missions over a wider geographic area, including being sent to Africa or the Middle East.[47] Or in the case of Africa, the continent was largely irrelevant to the United States in the 1970s and 1980s. But beginning with President George W. Bush's ambitious public health program in 2003 and later President Obama's electrification program in 2013, Africa assumed an important role in US foreign policy.

At the same time, there are enduring, long-standing commitments that no US administration will lightly abandon—starting with the NATO alliance and the security treaties with Japan, the Philippines, Thailand, South Korea, and Australia. The "sustained U.S. military presence" in Europe and in East Asia "has reaped decades of peace and prosperity for the United States."[48] The rationale for forging deep and enduring commitments first grew out of a Cold War necessity "to prevent the encroachment of Soviet power into regions containing the world's wealthiest, potentially most powerful, and most resource-rich states." After the collapse of the Soviet Union, the United States did not withdraw from these areas but shifted its "aim . . . to make these same core regions more secure, and so make the world safer for the United States" by allowing Washington "to shape the security environment" in a way that would best serve US interests.[49] The structure of US policy is not a result of post–Cold War inertia but is based on the assessment that a sudden and precipitous withdrawal from these core regions "would be detrimental to U.S. national security and economic recovery."[50]

Forces for Continuity

This bipartisan consensus was not formed by the long-lasting dominance in the United States of one political party, which then imposed its perspective on the political system. In contrast to countries where single parties were able to imprint a lasting stamp on foreign and defense policies—such as Japan, where the Liberal Democratic Party controlled the government from 1955 to 1993 and again from 1994 to 2009, and India, where the Congress Party held power continuously for thirty years (from 1947 to 1977)—there has been considerable political discontinuity in the United States; no one party has been able to shape the country's orientation. Since World War II, the presidency has regularly rotated between the Republicans (who in recent years won the 1980, 1984, 1988, 2000, and 2004 elections) and the Democrats (who were victorious in 1992, 1996, 2008, and 2012). Particularly in the post–Cold War period, control of Congress has also shifted between the two parties. The Republicans held the Senate from 1981 until 1987, retook control in 1995, temporarily lost it in 2001, regained it following the 2002 elections, and then lost the majority in that chamber to the Democrats after the 2006 elections. The Democrats controlled the House of Representatives until being swept from the majority in the 1994 elections, regained control in 2007, but lost it once again in 2011. In spite of the absence of one long-lived dominant governing party, there are identifiable factors to account for continuity in US foreign and defense policy decision making.

First, an "incoming president will inherit the foreign policy commitments of his predecessor."[51] Should those commitments have been spelled out in a binding treaty ratified by the Senate or in enabling legislation passed by Congress and given force of law, a new president would have no legal standing to unilaterally change or abrogate them.[52] For example, the 1949 Treaty of Washington, which created NATO, and the 1960 Treaty of Mutual Cooperation and Security between the United States and Japan commit the United States to defend these allies as a matter of US law, not of personal presidential preference. US sanctions against countries such as Iran and Cuba are codified by congressional statute; when such matters are regulated by law, the president cannot unilaterally dispense with them upon taking office.[53] To the extent that US security policy has been so institutionalized, this produces "limited room for maneuver available to an incoming administration" to break new ground in foreign and defense policy.[54] Second, while the ongoing transitions from Congress to Congress and administration to administration may give the impression of continuous flux, in reality there is a high degree of institutional cohesion buttressed by stability of cadres, not simply in terms of executing day-to-day policies of the United States but even at the highest planning and decision-making echelons of the US government. While the charge that a president's wishes and preferences are largely ignored by the bureaucracy may be overblown, it is also true that "agency willingness to follow an administration's agenda is not always a given."[55] There is a certain degree of ballast in the policy process that corrects against sudden changes. The active role of civil servants in drafting policy helps to create the parameters in which presidential wishes will be interpreted, particularly in how policy options are formulated and presented to the president. The president has flexibility to make choices within a larger overarching grand strategy—but at the same time, may find his freedom of maneuver to radically innovate restricted.[56] Radical shifts in US policy are unlikely, therefore, because policy becomes "institutionalized and embedded with the institutions, practices and material interests of American society and politics."[57] This highlights an observation by Andrew Stigler, a professor in the National Security Affairs Department of the Naval War College: "Inertia is often a governing force."[58] Bureaucracies are locked into policies that have become standard operating procedures. Presidents and their advisers discover that making significant policy changes disturbs important stakeholders, and any new administration can only pay attention to a limited number of issues, often trading the ability to dramatically alter a few key programs in return for guaranteeing continuity on a whole host of issues that are of less importance.[59]

Moreover, it is very possible for officials, even political appointees at the subcabinet level, to have been able to serve consistently in foreign and defense policy positions through different administrations, providing a degree of continuity that transcends the electoral cycle.[60] For instance, R. Nicholas Burns served as George H. W. Bush's director for Soviet/Russian affairs at the National Security Council, starting in 1990 as the USSR began to implode; he retained that portfolio for Bill Clinton until 1995. He then served as the spokesman for the Department of State from 1995 to 1997. After serving out the rest of the Clinton administration as ambassador to Greece, he was appointed by George W. Bush as US permanent representative to NATO (2001–5), and concluded his career as undersecretary of state for political affairs. Burns's immediate successor as ambassador to NATO, Victoria Nuland, had served in the Clinton administration as the chief of staff to Deputy Secretary of State Strobe Talbott, who had overarching responsibility for post-Soviet affairs, and in the Bush administration was the principal deputy foreign policy adviser for Vice President Dick Cheney before taking up the NATO appointment. In the Obama administration, she was tasked to serve as the special envoy for the Treaty on Conventional Armed Forces in Europe talks, became the State Department spokesperson, and was then chosen by Obama to become assistant secretary of state for European and

Eurasian affairs. Thus, Burns and Nuland served in senior positions in four administrations—two Democratic and two Republican—over a two-decade period, shaping and executing US policy toward Europe and Eurasia according to a general consensus that carried over from one administration to the next. This example reflects how a broad conceptualization of US strategy serves to "provide focus and coherence to the institutions of US foreign policy."[61]

The Idealistic Component

Forward engagement, as a strategy, is driven by an assessment of core US interests, but Americans for the most part are deeply uncomfortable with a purely realpolitik approach to foreign affairs.[62] That is, Americans provide assistance to countries in need not for trade preferences but out of moral obligation. Defending and promoting American values are also seen as desirable policy objectives. Indeed, "for generations, American leaders have emphasized the promotion of democracy abroad as a key element of America's international role."[63]

Presidential rhetoric often appeals to this American sense of global mission. Woodrow Wilson's Second Inaugural Address in 1917 referred to Americans as "citizens of the world" and declared that "we shall be more American if we but remain true to the principles in which we have been bred . . . the principles of a liberated mankind." In George W. Bush's Second Inaugural Address, delivered eighty-seven years later, he amplified Wilson's declaration, stating, "Across the generations we have proclaimed the imperative of self-government, because no one is fit to be a master, and no one deserves to be a slave. Advancing these ideals is the mission that created our Nation. It is the honorable achievement of our fathers. Now it is the urgent requirement of our Nation's security, and the calling of our time. So it is the policy of the United States to seek and support the growth of democratic movements and institutions in every nation and culture, with the ultimate goal of ending tyranny in our world."[64]

Indeed, most Americans believe that their "political ideals and principles are in theory universally applicable," and US officials believe it is a legitimate consideration to be "concerned with—and judgmental about—the domestic order in other countries."[65] The desire to spread liberal-democratic forms of governance—and particularly to transform autocratic regimes into more open societies—does not simply arise out of a sense of altruism. Instead, US government officials make the case that "durable stability" in the global order "flows from a domestic politics built on consensus and peaceful competition, which more often than not promotes similar international conduct for governments."[66] This is based on an assessment that the character of a regime has an impact on its foreign policies; thus the effort to create a more stable and secure community of nations rests on the extent to which countries share common political values.[67] Linked to this is the expectation that mature democracies do not go to war with each other (the so-called democratic peace thesis). The use of US power to assist the spread of democratic forms of governance around the world, therefore, is not seen as an altruistic measure but a useful strategy to ensure peace and US security and, since the 1990s, has been incorporated into US strategic documents.[68]

American idealism, of course, is not the sole driver of US foreign policy, and the desire to promote democracy and human rights occurs within an understanding of foreign policy rooted in pragmatism rather than strict adherence to ideological formulations.[69] A clear example of this is the decades-old US support for authoritarian Saudi Arabia due to its role in global energy markets and its opposition to Iran. Where divergence occurs from administration to administration is not whether the United States should promote values, but the extent to which it ought to actively attempt to shape political developments overseas. The debate often focuses on whether US policy should be to simply create conditions for democracy to emerge over time (the "exemplar" approach that recalls America as "the city on a hill") or whether the United States "should step in and give history a push" through much more active measures.[70] Both of the major US political parties, however, affirm a "determination to renew America's commitment to advancing democracy" as part of their foreign policy platforms, even if there is disagreement on tactics and implementation.[71]

This means that there is constant pressure on the US government to, at minimum, raise these questions as part of America's bilateral relations with other countries—even when it may conflict with or complicate the pursuit of vital strategic interests.[72] Sometimes "countervailing interests, both security-related and economic," will override or even sublimate democracy-promotion aims—one of the criticisms often raised when the US security relationship with such states as Saudi Arabia and Bahrainis is examined.[73] Yet even those within the US foreign policy establishment most inclined to hold a long-term, evolutionary view on democracy promotion cannot ignore human rights issues in how the United States conducts its relations with other countries. In fact, Congress requires the Department of State to publish annual reports on human rights and religious intolerance.

At the same time, the United States itself may impose conditions on its aid based on human rights considerations. Since 1997, for instance, based upon legislation introduced by Sen. Patrick Leahy, the United States cannot provide security assistance or training to units of a foreign military or security service that, according to credible evidence, has committed human rights abuses.[74] How states conduct their internal affairs and treat their citizens becomes a factor, even if not the predominant one, in how the United States considers its relationships and weighs the prospect of closer security and economic ties—it does not take place only on a cold assessment of vital interests. Even merely "raising" these questions can have negative impacts on security interests—such as when Uzbekistan ejected the United States from military facilities being used to prosecute the campaign in Afghanistan in the aftermath of US criticism of how the regime of Islam Karimov had used force against antigovernment opponents in 2005.

The Cost Factor

If the United States cannot pursue a strategy of forward engagement founded solely on strategic calculation, it is also constrained by the unwillingness of the US public, contrary to John F. Kennedy's stirring pronouncements to "pay any price" and "bear any burden" to defend and promote American values around the world. There is a very clear aversion on the part of Americans to "risk casualties in undertakings that may be vital to the security of allies or the preservation of the global order" in the absence of any direct, existential threat to the United States homeland.[75] Americans are not opposed, in theory, to an activist policy of forward engagement—until the costs are perceived to outweigh any clear and immediate benefits.[76] Initial enthusiasm for intervention, particularly on humanitarian grounds, fades once casualties or other losses become apparent in cases where missions are not seen as successful and where political leaders have not made a compelling case for the necessity for accepting these losses, as occurred during the course of the operations in Somalia in 1992–93.[77] Long-term commitments that exact rising costs in blood and treasure not only lose public support—as occurred as the Korean, Vietnam, Afghanistan, and Iraq wars continued—but can also make the American public far less interested in "embarking on such ventures again" for a period of time afterward.[78] Particularly since the end of the Cold War, the preference of the American public has been to pursue limited ends in dealing with global and regional challenges and thus to deploy limited means—and to avoid, as much as possible, large-scale interventions in complex situations.[79] This does not mean that the United States eschews major efforts in the global system, but it explains the political calculus to either adopt a low-cost scenario for US action (such as relying primarily on airpower rather than ground forces in the Kosovo and Libya campaigns) or to at least promise that US action can be cost-effective (the promises in 2003 that military action against Iraq would be swift, would not require large amounts of US forces, and that reconstruction of the country would be funded primarily from Iraq's own oil revenues). The lingering, long-term negative aftereffects of the Afghan and Iraq interventions, as well as the perception that the 2011 air campaign against Libya had not enhanced US security or promoted American values, constrained the Obama administration's ability to convince the US public and a majority in Congress to authorize military strikes against Syria in 2013 in response to the alleged use of chemical weapons by the government against the opposition—a

Table 4.1: Free-Trade Agreements

Agreement	Countries
North American Free Trade Agreement (NAFTA)	Canada and Mexico
Central American Free Trade Agreement / Dominican Republic (CAFTA/DR)	Costa Rica, Dominican Republic, El Salvador, Guatemala, Honduras, Nicaragua
Other Free Trade Agreements	Australia, Bahrain, Chile, Colombia, Israel, Jordan, South Korea, Morocco, Oman, Panama, Peru, Singapore

Source: International Trade Association, http://trade.gov/fta/.

rare occasion where an unusual "liberal-libertarian" coalition overrode the traditional bipartisan consensus in favor of decisive US action.[80]

There is also a growing skepticism about the value to the United States of committing to multilateral treaties and joining rules-based international organizations that would appear to constrain its freedom of action on the global stage. This is especially the case when, in contrast to very specific and limited provisions, a treaty seems to create "open-ended delegations of law-making authority over a significant range of issues" away from the United States.[81] The belief that the pacts the United States concludes with other states seem to impose more costs on it than on other partners is also a factor. US officials regularly complain that treaty allies in Europe and East Asia engage in "free riding"—benefiting from US security guarantees without assuming a fair share of the burden. Arguments from those sectors of the US foreign policy community who maintain that "U.S. alliances constitute a massive wealth transfer from U.S. taxpayers (and their Chinese creditors) to bloated European welfare states and technologically-advanced Asian nations" have achieved greater salience in recent years.[82] At the same time, free-trade agreements, which in the past have been an important way of binding partners to Washington, have now become much harder to pass in Congress, as questions are raised about whether the costs to American businesses outweigh any potential benefits.[83]

Presidents, of course, have a good deal of latitude to act, but given the nature of electoral politics, they cannot completely ignore popular concerns about the costs of US international engagement. At the same time, other countries prefer binding treaties with the United States rather than informal agreements—yet such pacts require Senate ratification and congressional support for funding any commitments undertaken.[84] Assessing what sort of agreements or guarantees could receive congressional approbation is an important driver to consider.[85] In recent years, concerns about costs (both in dollar amounts and in terms of US commitments) have begun to dominate the discussion about whether or not a particular course of action is worth choosing.

A proposal that might, on its merits, seem strategically sound may be politically infeasible to implement. Significantly, even those officials who are the strongest proponents of an activist stance for the United States nonetheless feel it necessary to reassure the American public that "forward engagement . . . does not mean policing the world or letting other countries free-ride on U.S. security guarantees" nor does it mandate "relinquishing American sovereignty to regional and international institutions."[86] From the domestic side, therefore, concern about costs and obligations means that US foreign policy "remains a balancing act between a number of often opposing forces: a volatile domestic public opinion versus hard international realities; short-term political gains versus long-term national interests; a populist impulse towards isolationism versus a missionary zealotry and a tendency to overreach; militarism versus the need for constructive engagement abroad in an age of increased interdependence and, ultimately, between (liberal) values and (realist) interests."[87]

At the same time, however, America's ability to sustain a policy of sustained, deep forward engagement is eroding. Traditionally America's dominant economic position helped to fund its global infrastructure, but the US share of the global economy has steadily been decreasing. In 1999, the US share of the world's gross domestic product (GDP) as measured in purchasing power parity was 23.78 percent; by 2016, this is expected to decline to 17.7 percent.[88] Moreover, the military engagements in Iraq and Afghanistan have presented a formidable bill to the Treasury, with some estimates that the total cost of both overseas contingency operations could reach $6 trillion.[89] As a result, "the United States lacks the resources to continue as the primary provider of global public goods" across the entire globe, even if it retains formidable military capabilities.[90]

In the course of this decade, "America's defense budget is set to decline by every metric: in real terms, as a percentage of the federal budget, and relative to the size of our economy."[91] The defense strategic guidance released in January 2012 calls for a rebalancing of US deployments in favor of the Asia-Pacific region, a continuation of the strategic presence in the Middle East, an evolution of the US posture in Europe, and an emphasis on low-cost partnerships to secure US interests in Latin America and Africa—an approach that was validated by the 2014 Quadrennial Defense Review (QDR), given its projection about the still-uncertain security environment.[92] While the United States will still enjoy a formidable defense advantage over all other countries, gaps will begin to open up in Asia where the United States can project power, since "even with . . . a pledge to hold U.S. capabilities steady in Asia while cutting force structure else-where, . . . [the] planned cuts means hollowing out other commands' assets in ways that will ultimately force cannibalizing of [Pacific Command] assets when crises hit the Middle East or elsewhere."[93] Yet if there is an ongoing crisis in the Pacific, the alternative would be to ignore problems elsewhere if assets could not be diverted.

Nor can the United States swap greater economic engagement to com-pensate for a smaller military footprint. The same forces propelling cuts in the defense budget also mean that the nation is also no longer in any position to launch major new foreign aid initiatives. If the Marshall Plan is calculated in current dollars to have cost $740 billion, the United States, the other members of the Group of Eight, and the Gulf Arab monarchies combined came up with an aid package of only $70 billion to assist in the transitions following the Arab Awakening.[94] The United States still remains the world's leading power, but, after the events of the past decade, it is an "exhausted nation" that needs to reevaluate its level of commitments around the world.[95]

In the past the United States could maintain its architecture of forward engagement because of its partnerships with other states. They allowed Wash-ington to "sustain a role in the world that would not be bearable if America had to rely on its own resources alone."[96] The 2012 defense strategic guidance and the 2014 QDR repeatedly invoke the assistance that allied and partner nations are expected to provide to help achieve its objectives. The reality, how-ever, is that other countries are not stepping forward to close the gaps that are emerging from the decision to reduce the level of US defense and aid spending. NATO countries taken together spend less than 2 percent of their GDP on defense; Japan is at 1 percent; South Korea under 3 percent. The other major European powers—France and Britain—are cutting back rather than increas-ing spending to make up the difference and to be in position to assume more responsibilities as the United States pivots to Asia. In fact, the United States now finances 75 percent of NATO's military spending—an increase from the 63 percent in 2001.[97] Rising powers such as Brazil, China, and India "are claiming international standing" due to the growth of their economies, but their "ability to effectively lead on a global level is limited as they do not yet provide enough global public goods."[98] Given the significant internal challenges such as poverty and limited infrastructure, it is unlikely these countries can invest much more than criticisms of the international system. Not all rising powers share America's vision of the global order, moreover, and no other country is prepared to take on the burden of sustaining America's commitments in their current fashion and configuration.

Table 4.2: NATO Defense Expenditures, 2011

Country	Percentage of GDP
Albania	1.5
Belgium	1.1
Bulgaria	1.4
Canada	1.4
Croatia	1.5
Czech Republic	1.1
Denmark	1.4
Estonia	1.7
France	1.9
Germany	1.4
Greece	2.1
Hungary	1
Italy	1.4
Latvia	1
Lithuania	0.8
Luxembourg	0.5
Netherlands	1.3
Norway	1.5
Poland	1.7
Portugal	1.5
Romania	1.3
Slovak Republic	1.1
Slovenia	1.3
Spain	0.9
Turkey	1.9
United Kingdom	2.6
United States	4.8

Source: Financial and Economic Data Relating to NATO Defence, April 13, 2012, www.nato.int/nato_static/assets/pdf/ pdf_2012_04/20120413_PR_CP_2012_047_rev1.pdf.

Conclusion

Faced as it is with rising costs and burdens not evenly shared, one might expect a US administration to embrace wholesale retrenchment or even isolationism. Speaking at the United Nations in September 2013, however, President Obama forcefully declared that "disengagement would be a mistake."[99] The 2014 QDR backs up the president's assertion by laying out a strategy that endeavors to sustain "America's global leadership role" even in light of budget cuts and a more challenging international security environment.[100] Of necessity, the "quantity" of America's global engagement will give way in favor of a lighter footprint and by a greater propensity to accept risks.[101] In place of an earlier propensity to throw resources at challenges, the United States will be guided in the future by a so-called smart interventionism, the emerging outlines of which are contained in the 2014 QDR. However, before we address this in greater detail, it is first important to understand America's cause for going to war.

Notes

1. Robert Kagan, "Bipartisan Spring," *Foreign Policy*, March 3, 2010, at www.foreignpolicy.com/articles/2010/03/03/bipartisan_spring?page=full.

2. Henry Kissinger, "Continuity and Change in American Foreign Policy," *Society* 35, no. 2 (January/February 1998): 185.

3. Christian Brose, "The Making of George W. Obama," *Foreign Policy* (January/February 2009), at www.foreignpolicy.com/story/cms.php?story_id=4588.

4. Dimitris Keridis, "US Foreign Policy: Continuity and Change in an Increasingly Complex World," *International Politics in Times of Change*, ed. N. Tzifakis (Athens: Konstantinos Karamanlis Institute for Democracy, 2012), 18.

5. Ole R. Holsti, "Continuity and Change in the Domestic and Foreign Policy Beliefs of American Opinion Leaders," paper prepared for the 1997 Annual Meeting of the American Political Science Association, August 28–31, 1997, Washington, DC, 1–2.

6. Nik Hynek, "Continuity and Change in the U.S. Foreign and Security Policy with the Accession of President Obama," policy paper, Institute of International Relations, Prague, August 2009, 16; Stephen M. Walt, "Beyond bin Laden: Reshaping U.S. Foreign Policy," *International Security* 26, no. 3 (Winter 2001–2): 64.

7. The president, in the words of the Supreme Court decision in the 1936 Curtiss-Wright Export Corporation decision, is the "sole organ of the federal government in the field of international relations," but Congress can shape and influence what the chief executive does through its control of the purse strings, its ability to investigate government activity and to have officials testify, and, for the Senate, its constitutional prerogative to "consent" to treaties and presidential appointees.

8. Richard Jackson, "Culture, Identity and Hegemony: Continuity and (the Lack of) Change in US Counterterrorism Policy from Bush to Obama," *International Politics* 48, no. 2/3 (2011): 390.

9. A striking example of the divergence between campaign promises of change versus continuity once in office was seen in the drawdown of forces in Iraq. In September 2008, Sen. Barack Obama, the Democratic nominee for president, harshly criticized the proposals put forward by the sitting president, George W. Bush, for the gradual withdrawal of US forces from Iraq. Bush's plan was formally enshrined in the strategic framework document that accompanied the status-of-forces agreement negotiated with Iraq and ratified by the Iraqi parliament in November 2008. Candidate Obama, who earlier in February had categorically pledged to "bring this [Iraq] war to a close" and that "in 2009, I will bring our troops home," reiterated his strong opposition to this approach, argued that his Republican rival, Sen. John McCain, if elected, would carry out the Bush approach and pledged to withdraw a brigade from Iraq every month once he took office. Voters had every right to expect that, if elected, Obama would initiate a major change in US Iraq policy. Right after taking office on January 20, 2009, he directed the Pentagon to examine options for a "responsible military drawdown" in Iraq. In the weeks that followed, the Obama national security team began to abandon the position on Iraq developed by the campaign. Instead of implementing his pledge to begin immediate withdrawals, Obama announced a strategy at Camp Lejeune, North Carolina, in February 2009 that called for the US "combat mission" in Iraq to end by August 31, 2010, and with fifty thousand troops to remain in Iraq to engage in training and counterterrorism missions until the end of 2011. Indeed, the administration even attempted to negotiate with Iraq to permit a residual US military force to remain in that country after the original December 2011 deadline for withdrawal expired; it was the Iraqi government's unwillingness to grant legal immunity to US personnel from prosecution in Iraqi courts that prevented any extension of the US military presence. Ironically it was Obama, not McCain, who upon becoming president adhered to the Bush approach, implementing the withdrawal plan that he inherited from his predecessor.

10. Nikolas K. Gvosdev, "Barack W. Obama Revisited," *World Politics Review*, January 8, 2010, at www.worldpoliticsreview.com/articles/4912/the-realist-prism-barack-w-obama-revisited. For instance, the Obama team canceled the Bush administration's plan to deploy a land-based theater-missile-defense system in Poland and the Czech Republic but did not repudiate the concept altogether. Instead, it replaced it with a sea-based system that will have some land components, notably in Romania.

11. John B. Bellinger III, "More Continuity than Change," *New York Times*, February 14, 2010, at www.nytimes.com/2010/02/15/opinion/15iht-edbellinger .html?_r=0.

12. Harry Harding, "Change and Continuity in the Obama Administration's Foreign Policy," *Thinking about Asia*, July 4, 2009, at http://thinkingaboutasia .blogspot.com/2009/07/change-and-continuity-in-obama.html.

13. Jackson, "Culture," 401.

14. David Brooks, "The Analytic Mode," *New York Times*, December 4, 2009, A35, at www.nytimes.com/2009/12/04/opinion/04brooks.html?_r=3&em&.

15. Richard E. Neustadt, *Presidential Power and the Modern Presidents: The Politics of Leadership from Roosevelt to Reagan* (New York: Free Press, 1991), 28.

16. Stephen G. Brooks, G. John Ikenberry, and William C. Wohlforth, "Lean Forward," *Foreign Affairs* 92, no. 1 (January/February 2013), at www.foreign affairs.com/articles/138468/stephen-g-brooks-g-john-ikenberry-and-william-c-wohlforth/lean-forward.

17. Robert J. Art, "A Defensible Defense: America's Grand Strategy after the Cold War," *International* Security 15, no. 4 (Spring 1991): 9; Walt, "Beyond Bin Laden," 64.

18. Holsti, "Continuity and Change," 1.

19. Kissinger, "Continuity and Change," 185.

20. Despite some vocal opposition, Congress took no efforts to prevent President Obama from deploying US military assets during the 2011 Libyan campaign. Whether Congress would have blocked the administration's plan to strike Syria in 2013 is open to debate; the decision first to seek congressional approval and then to forgo armed action prior to any vote being taken was made unilaterally by the president.

21. Ralph G. Carter and James M. Scott, *Choosing to Lead: Understanding Congressional Foreign Policy Entrepreneurs* (Durham, NC: Duke University Press, 2009), 30. One such example of congressional activism was the "Soviet Nuclear Threat Reduction Act of 1991." As the Soviet Union began to unravel, defense experts became worried about the threat to US national security of a possible loss of control over the Soviet nuclear arsenal, including the prospect of uncontrolled proliferation of nuclear weapons. They recommended that the United States create a comprehensive program of assistance so that the Soviet nuclear legacy—not only weapons but also the factories and scientists who had created them—could be safeguarded. However, this proposal did not initially attract much support from within the George H. W. Bush administration. Government agencies were not eager to divert funds from their own preferred programs, particularly at a time when there were growing calls to reduce defense expenditures. In addition, some members of the president's national security team, viewing the USSR as the main threat to the United States, were not inclined to provide US financial assistance to help an avowed foe secure a nuclear weapons establishment still perceived as an existential threat to the country. President Bush and Secretary of Defense Dick Cheney both expressed skepticism about the value of and need for a massive American program to secure Soviet "loose nukes."

The experts, including former US government officials who were back in the academic and think tank worlds, found a more receptive audience with senior members of Congress who had extensive experience in international affairs and arms control issues, such as Sen. Richard Lugar, Sen. Sam Nunn, and Rep. Les Aspin, who were also concerned by the threat posed by the Soviet nuclear arsenal and who were prepared to act if the administration would not. Nunn's own sense of urgency was heightened by a meeting he had with Soviet president Mikhail

Gorbachev after the failed coup attempt in August 1991, in which doubts were raised about the reliability of control over the Soviet nuclear arsenal.

An initial effort by Nunn and Aspin to promote amendments to the fiscal year 1992 defense authorization bill to provide for US aid to assist the Soviet Union in securing and dismantling weapons of mass destruction failed, and the Bush administration was not enthusiastic about congressional efforts to mandate a binding spending requirement, rather than having this be an advisory recommendation on the part of Congress.

Nunn and Lugar changed tactics. They brought a team of experts that had been assembled under the aegis of Harvard University's Kennedy School of Government to brief members of Congress and lobbied their colleagues for support, including accepting a series of benchmarks for the disbursement of aid proposed by the chairman of the Senate Foreign Relations Committee, Jesse Helms. The ongoing collapse of the Soviet state also helped to focus attention on the problem, as well as an op-ed penned by Nunn and Lugar for the *Washington Post* on November 21, which cast the issue not as a handout to the Soviets but as an investment in long-term US national security. The campaign worked: The Soviet Nuclear Threat Reduction Act of 1991 passed with 86 votes in the Senate on November 26 and by acclamation in the House of Representatives the next day. After reconciliation, President Bush signed the measure into law on December 12.

The legislation, which was crafted without significant input from the executive branch, created the Cooperative Threat Reduction (CTR) Program. This mission was handed over to the Department of Defense, and the program was charged with the mandate to secure and dismantle weapons of mass destruction and their associated infrastructure in the states of the former Soviet Union. For two decades, the CTR program was one of the centerpieces of the US-Russian relationship, and it played a critical role in preventing a nightmare scenario—the uncontrollable proliferation of Soviet nuclear components to rogue states and nonstate actors.

22. Stephen G. Brooks, G. John Ikenberry, and William C. Wohlforth, "Don't Come Home, America: The Case against Retrenchment," *International Security* 37, no. 3 (Winter 2012–13): 13.

23. Nikolas K. Gvosdev, "Introduction: Change and Continuity in U.S. Foreign Policy," in *Case Studies in Policy Making*, ed. Hayat Alvi and Nikolas K. Gvosdev (Newport, RI: Naval War College, 2010), 3. A bipartisan consensus can be said to exist when it is based on a shared worldview that persists even when there are changes in government from one party to the next. Ellen C. Collier, *Bipartisanship and the Making of Foreign Policy: A Historical Survey* (Bloomington, IN: Xlibris, 2011), 9.

24. See, for instance, Henry Nau, *At Home Abroad: Identity and Power in American Foreign Policy* (Ithaca, NY: Cornell University Press, 2002), 34; Keridis, "US Foreign Policy," 21; Mayang A. Rahawestri, "Obama's Foreign Policy in Asia: More Continuity than Change," *Security Challenges* 6, no. 1 (Autumn 2010) 109.

25. Michael Ignatieff, "Barbarians at the Gate," *New York Review of Books*, February 25, 2002, 5.

26. Ian Bremmer, "Welcome to the G-Zero Era," *Huffington Post*, June 14, 2012, at www.huffingtonpost.com/ian-bremmer/international-trade-asia-states_b_1515310.html.

27. "Remarks of Senator Barack Obama to the Chicago Council on Global Affairs," April 23, 2007, Council on Foreign Relations, www.cfr.org/elections/remarks-senator-barack-obama-chicago-council-global-affairs/p13172.

28. Ignatieff, "Barbarians at the Gate," 5.

29. Michael Mandelbaum, *The Case for Goliath: How America Acts as the World's Government in the 21st Century* (New York: PublicAffairs, 2005), 39–40, 56–57.

30. Michele Flournoy and Janine Davidson, "Obama's New Global Posture," *Foreign Affairs* 91, no. 4 (July/August 2012): 57.

31. Ibid., 54–55.

32. Brooks, Ikenberry, and Wohlforth,"Don't Come Home," 13.

33. Michael Sherry, *In the Shadow of War: The United States since the 1930s* (New Haven, CT: Yale University Press, 1995), 4.

34. Jay L. Johnson and Charles Krulak, "Forward Presence Essential to U.S. Interests," *Defense Issues* 11, no. 100 (1996): 1; Jeffrey A. Frankel, "Globalization of the Economy," *National Bureau of Economic Research*, working paper 7858 (2000), 27, at www.nber.org/papers/w7858.

35. Johnson and Krulak, "Forward Presence Essential," 2.

36. Frankel, "Globalization of the Economy," 7.

37. Johnson and Krulak, "Forward Presence Essential," 1.

38. William A. Dorman and Steven Livingston, "News and Historical Content: The Establishing Phase of the Persian Gulf Policy Debate," in *Taken by Storm: The Media, Public Opinion, and U.S. Foreign Policy in the Gulf War*, ed. W. Lance Bennett and David L. Paletz (Chicago: University of Chicago Press, 1994), 69–75.

39. Ted Galen Carpenter, "How Good Was the Good War?" *American Conservative*, July 14, 2008, 13.

40. See President Bill Clinton's speech on Kosovo delivered March 24, 1999, and archived at Miller Center, University of Virginia, http://millercenter.org/president/speeches/detail/3932.

41. Kelly Machinchick, "U.S. Involvement in Sudan Peace Process Keeps Both Sides at Table," *ReliefWeb*, May 2, 2003, at http://reliefweb.int/report/sudan/us-involvement-sudan-peace-process-keeps-both-sides-table.

42. Nikolas Gvosdev, "Energy Independence a Game-Changer for U.S. Defense Posture," *World Politics Review*, February 22, 2013, at www.worldpoliticsreview.com/articles/12737/the-realist-prism-energy-independence-a-game-changer-for-u-s-defense-posture.

43. Definition of "global commons" from the Division of Environmental Law and Conventions of the United Nations Environment Programme, located at www.unep.org/delc/GlobalCommons/tabid/54404/Default.aspx.

44. Johnson and Krulak, "Forward Presence Essential," 1.

45. See Clinton's speech on Kosovo, March 24, 1999.

46. Flournoy and Davidson, "Obama's New Global Posture," 58.

47. See, for instance, "U.S. Military Presence in Europe: Issues Related to the Drawdown," statement of Joseph E. Kelley, director in charge, International Affairs Issues, National Security and International Affairs Division of the General Accounting Office, in testimony before the Subcommittee on Readiness, Committee on Armed Services, House of Representatives, April 27, 1993.

48. Flournoy and Davidson, "Obama's New Global Posture," 58.

49. Brooks, Ikenberry, and Wohlforth, "Don't Come Home," 11.

50. Flournoy and Davidson, "Obama's New Global Posture," 58.

51. Wyn Rees, "Securing the Homelands: Transatlantic Co-operation after Bush," *British Journal of Politics and International Relations* 11, no. 1 (2009): 117.

52. See, for instance, Lance T. LeLoup and Steven A. Shull, *The President and Congress: Collaboration and Combat in National Policymaking* (New York: Longman, 1990), 124–25.

53. See, for instance, the remarks of Rep. Doug Bereuter on the floor of the House of Representatives, *Congressional Record*, November 12, 1997, H10568.

54. Rees, "Securing the Homelands," 117.

55. See, for instance, Richard Perle, "Ambushed on the Potomac," *National Interest* 99 (January/February 2009): 35; Gordon Adams, "The Office of Management and Budget: The President's Policy Tool," in *The National Security Enterprise: Navigating the Labyrinth*, ed. Roger Z. George and Harvey Rishikoff (Washington, DC: Georgetown University Press, 2011), 61.

56. Comments of Colin Dueck, "U.S. Grand Strategy: Intended and Actual Outcomes," Current Strategy Forum of the Naval War College, June 18, 2013. See, for instance, the discussion about US-Indian policy in the first term of the George W. Bush administration, in Robert D. Blackwill, "The India Imperative," *National Interest* 80 (Summer 2005): 9–17.

57. Jackson, "Culture," 395.

58. Andrew Stigler, interview by authors, November 7, 2013, Newport, RI.

59. Gvosdev, "Introduction: Change and Continuity," 3.

60. Amb. Robert E. Hunter, interview by Charles Stuart Kennedy for the Association for Diplomatic Studies and Training Foreign Affairs Oral Project, August 10, 2004, 60, at www.adst.org/OH%20TOCs/Hunter,%20Robert%20E .toc.pdf.

61. Jackson, "Culture," 395.

62. James Traub, "The Combative Consigliere," *Foreign Policy*, June 6, 2013, at www.foreignpolicy.com/articles/2013/06/06/the_combative_consigliere?page=full.

63. Thomas Carothers, *Aiding Democracy Abroad: The Learning Curve* (Washington, DC: Carnegie Endowment for International Peace, 1999), 3.

64. George W. Bush, Second Inaugural Address, January 20, 2005, www .inaugural.senate.gov/swearing-in/address/address-by-george-w-bush-2005.

65. Gideon Rose, "Democracy Promotion and American Foreign Policy: A Review Essay," *International Security* 25, no. 3 (Winter 2000–1): 186.

66. Mark P. Lagon, "Promoting Democracy: The Whys and Hows for the United States and the International Community," *Markets and Democracy Brief*, Feb-

ruary 2011, Council on Foreign Relations, at www.cfr.org/democracy-promotion/promoting-democracy-whys-hows-united-states-international-community/p24090.

67. See, for instance, the comments of the then undersecretary of state Paula Dobriansky, "The Core of U.S. Foreign Policy," *Foreign Affairs* 82, no. 3 (May/June 2003): 141–44.

68. See, for instance, John M. Owen, "How Liberalism Produces Democratic Peace," *International Security* 19, no. 2 (Fall 1994): 87–125.

69. David Milne, "Pragmatism or What? The Future of US Foreign Policy," *International Affairs* 88, no. 5 (2012): 951.

70. Rose, "Democracy Promotion," 187.

71. Thomas Carothers, "Repairing Democracy Promotion," *Washington Post*, September 14, 2007, at www.washingtonpost.com/wp-dyn/content/article/2007/09/13/AR2007091302241.html.

72. Dobriansky, "Core of U.S. Foreign Policy," 141.

73. Carothers, *Aiding Democracy*, 3; see, for instance, Kenneth Roth, "Dump These Unsavory Allies," *Foreign Policy*, January 2, 2013, at www.foreignpolicy.com/articles/2013/01/02/the_second_coming?page=0,4.

74. See the discussion with former US diplomats and military officers on this question in Joshua Kucera, "What Military Equipment Should the U.S. Give Uzbekistan?," *Eurasianet*, March 10, 2013, at www.eurasianet.org/node/66667.

75. Holsti, "Continuity and Change," 10–11.

76. See comments of Grover Norquist at the Center for the National Interest, "Taxes and U.S. Foreign Policy," August 13, 2012. A video of the presentation was broadcast by C-SPAN and is available at www.c-span.org/Events/Grover-Norquist-Discusses-Role-of-Taxes-in-National-Security/10737433053/.

77. See Peter D. Feaver and Christopher Gelpi, *Choosing Your Battles: American Civil-Military Relations and the Use of Force* (Princeton, NJ: Princeton University Press, 2004), 134–36.

78. John Mueller, "The Iraq Syndrome," *Foreign Affairs* 84 (November/December 2005): 44–54.

79. See, for instance, Eric V. Larson, *Casualties and Consensus: The Historical Role of Casualties in Domestic Support for U.S. Military Operations* (Santa Monica, CA: RAND Corp., 1996).

80. Ronald Brownstein, "Americans Overwhelmingly Oppose Syria Strike, Want Obama to Back Down," *National Journal*, September 9, 2013, at www.nationaljournal.com/congressional-connection/coverage/americans-overwhelmingly-oppose-syria-strike-want-obama-to-back-down-20130909.

81. Paul B. Stephan, "International Governance and American Democracy," *Chicago Journal of International Law* 1, no. 237 (2000): 257.

82. Christopher J. Preble, "Your Tax Dollars at Work: Subsidizing the Security of Wealthy Allies," *Cato at Liberty*, April 15, 2013, at www.cato.org/blog/tax-dollars-work-subsidizing-security-wealthy-allies.

83. See the discussion on the politics of such agreements in Peter Cowhey, "Crafting Trade Strategy in the Great Recession: The Obama Administration and

the Changing Political Economy of the United States," in *Politics in the New Hard Times: The Great Recession in Comparative Perspective*, ed. Miles Kahler and David A. Lake (Ithaca, NY: Cornell University Press, 2013), 216–22. See also Nikolas K. Gvosdev, "Selling U.S. Diplomacy to Congress," *World Politics Review*, December 21, 2012, at www.worldpoliticsreview.com/articles/12588/the-realist-prism-selling-u-s-diplomacy-to-congress.

84. Lisa J. Martin, "US Military Commitments: Multilateralism and Treaties," in *Multilateralism and Security Institutions in an Era of Globalization*, ed. Dimitris Bourantonis, Kostas Ifantis, and Panayotis Tsakonas (New York: Routledge, 2008), 76; Cowhey, "Crafting Trade Strategy," 213.

85. See, for instance, the comments of Sen. Jeanne Shaheen about the unlikelihood that Russia could receive legally binding assurances about missile defense because it would be nearly impossible to secure the votes in the Senate for such an agreement: "The Future of U.S.-Russia Relations: Beyond 2012: Keynote Address," Carnegie Endowment for International Peace, November 28, 2012, archived at http://carnegieendowment.org/2012/11/28/future-of-u.s.-russia-relations-beyond-2012/eiwi.

86. Flournoy and Davidson, "Obama's New Global Posture," 60.

87. Keridis, "US Foreign Policy," 18.

88. Marina Watson Peláez, "America in Decline? It Could Take China Just Five Years to Surpass the U.S. Economy," *Time*, April 27, 2011, at http://newsfeed.time.com/2011/04/27/america-super-power-in-decline/#ixzz2XWLn8vU5.

89. Alan Zarembo, "Cost of Iraq, Afghanistan Wars Will Keep Mounting," *Los Angeles Times*, March 29, 2013, at http://articles.latimes.com/2013/mar/29/nation/la-na-0329-war-costs-20130329.

90. Ian Bremmer and Nouriel Roubini, "A G-Zero World," *Foreign Affairs* 90, no. 2 (March/April 2011): 4.

91. Mackenzie Eaglen, quoted in "Up for Debate: Defense Budget?," The FAS Blog (Federation of American Scientists), November 12, 2012, at www.fas.org/policy/debates/20121115_defense_budget.html#eaglen.

92. Department of Defense, *Sustaining U.S. Global Leadership: Priorities for 21st Century Defense* (Washington, DC: Department of Defense, 2012), 2-3, at www.defense.gov/news/Defense_Strategic_Guidance.pdf. For commentary on the 2014 QDR, see Patrick N. Cronin, "Three Hidden Time Bombs in the US-Japan Alliance," *Diplomat*, February 28, 2014, at http://thediplomat.com/2014/02/three-hidden-time-bombs-in-the-us-japan-alliance/.

93. Michael J. Green, "Rethinking U.S. Military Presence in Asia and the Pacific," in *2012 Global Forecast: Risk, Opportunity and the Next Administration*, ed. Craig Cohen and Josiane Gabel (Washington, DC: Center for Strategic and International Studies, 2010, 18–19.

94. "Arab Spring Needs a Mini-Marshall Plan," *Bloomberg*, January 13, 2013, at www.bloomberg.com/news/2013-01-13/arab-spring-needs-a-mini-marshall-plan.html.

95. Gregor Peter Schmitz, "Global Leadership Vacuum: Europe Incapable, America Unwilling," *Der Spiegel*, February 1, 2013, at www.spiegel.de/international/

world/the-global-leadership-vacuum-europe-incapable-america-unwilling-a-880945.html.

96. Nau, *At Home Abroad*, 86.

97. Steven Erlanger, "Shrinking Europe Military Spending Stirs Concern," *New York Times*, April 23, 2013, A3; Ted Galen Carpenter, "Rational and Reckless Alliances," *National Interest*, May 9, 2013, at http://nationalinterest.org/commentary/rational-reckless-alliances-8448.

98. Robert Kappel, *The Decline of Europe and the US: Shifts in the World Economy and in Global Politics*, German Institute of Global and Area Studies (GIGA) Focus, no. 1 (Hamburg: GIGA, 2011), 1.

99. "Remarks by President Obama in Address to the United Nations General Assembly," September 24, 2013, United Nations, New York, archived by the White House at www.whitehouse.gov/the-press-office/2013/09/24/remarks-president-obama-address-united-nations-general-assembly.

100. *Quadrennial Defense Review 2014* (Washington, DC: Department of Defense, March 2014), iii.

101. See, for instance, the comments of Acting Deputy Secretary of Defense Christine H. Fox at the 2014 AFCEA West Conference, February 11, 2014. A transcript of her remarks is available at www.defense.gov/Transcripts/Transcript .aspx?TranscriptID=5369.

5

The American Way of Warfare

A persisting problem with the American way of war has been not so much how well Americans fight, but rather how well or poorly that combat and sacrifice have served the country's political goals.

—Colin Gray

Prior to the Spanish-American War, the American military rarely deployed for conflict away from the homeland. Instead the military primarily supported westward expansion in North America by building forts to create footholds for further expansion, fighting native populations, and repelling occasional raids from Mexico. In the late nineteenth century, this changed as American predominance solidified in North America, and the military gradually developed a small expeditionary capability to send constabulary forces into other countries in the Western Hemisphere in the early twentieth century.

When the world wars compelled the United States to intervene in Europe and Asia, massive efforts were necessary to conscript and train people for war and mobilize the economy to build military hardware. Once hostilities concluded, the process was reversed through massive demobilization. This pattern of mobilization followed by demobilization started to change when the United States, reluctantly at first, accepted the need after the Korean War for a permanent military establishment with forces deployed outside of North America. The occupation forces for Germany and Japan provided the basis for this change.

In contrast to its European allies, which had a territorial defensive orientation, US forces became expeditionary forces capable of traveling to and fighting in any part of the globe. Indeed, since 1945, the United States has deployed military forces to a different area of the world every four years. Some deployments were high-intensity conflicts, such as Korea in 1950–53 and Iraq in 1990–91. Other deployments were long-term efforts to defeat insurgencies and build functioning states, such as Vietnam from 1959 to 1975 and Afghanistan

Table 5.1: Significant American Military Operations, 1946–2014

Operation	Year(s)
Greece	1947
Germany (Berlin Airlift)	1948
Korea	1950–53
Vietnam	1961–73
Dominican Republic	1965
Iran Hostage Rescue Attempt	1980
Lebanon	1982–84
Grenada	1983
Libya	1986
Panama	1989
Iraq	1990–91
Somalia	1992–93
Haiti	1994
Bosnia-Herzegovina	1995–2004
Kosovo	1999–Present
Afghanistan	2001–Present
Iraq	2003–11
Libya	2011
Iraq-Syria	2014

Note: Excluded from this list are humanitarian interventions such as in Japan after the tsunami in 2011 and in Pakistan after a major earthquake in 2005.

from 2001 to 2014. In contrast to many traditional European wars—which were fought either to defend or to seize territory—every American military intervention during the Cold War period was not to address a looming, immediate military threat to the US homeland but instead was driven by a particular strategic narrative such as "containment." Post–Cold War interventions have been driven by narratives such as the "global war on terrorism" or the "responsibility to protect." In other words, US military intervention supported a particular internationalist strategy rather than being directly connected to homeland defense. Underlying these narratives, there is a distinctive American way of warfare that is multidomain, technologically biased, joint, comprehensive, and internationalized.

Way of War or Warfare?

It is not unusual for planners to claim that the new technologies that enable military interventions have changed "the very nature of war"—a particularly seductive claim for an American culture always looking for the "better mousetrap" and in particular enamored of finding a technological solution that will allow for low-cost, no-casualty wars. But it seems clear that the nature of war—as best described by the Prussian "philosopher of war" Carl von Clausewitz—remains constant. War is the use of violence to achieve political ends, and it is fought with uncertainty. Clausewitz reminds us that war is a violent clash between opposing wills, each seeking to prevail over the other. Clausewitz also identified the enduring characteristics of war: the persistence of "general friction" as a structural component of combat, the seeming impossibility of eliminating uncertainty from war (regardless of technology), and the critical importance of the "moral factors" in war.[1]

On the other hand, the "character" of warfare is infinite. Warfare is the manner in which conflict is waged, and as Sir Michael Howard warns, "to abstract war from the environment in which it is fought and study its technique as one would those of a game is to ignore a dimension essential to understanding, not simply of the wars themselves but of the societies which fought them."[2] Simply, the security environment and culture matter in warfare.

Russell Frank Weigley's seminal work *The American Way of War: A History of United States Military Strategy and Policy* charted key characteristics of how the United States organized and fought from the founding through Vietnam. With a strong resource base and large population, "the strategy of annihilation became characteristically the American way in war."[3] While arguing there are flaws in Weigley's argument, Antulio Echevarria agrees with the overall finding that "Americans saw the primary object of war as the destruction of an opponent's armed might rather than as the furtherance of political objectives through violent means—so much as they qualify it."[4]

There is an inherently punitive dimension to how the United States employs military force, but Brian Linn offers four main objections to Weigley's thesis of annihilation and notes that "American soldiers have been forced to adapt, to overcome tactical, logistical, personnel, and other constraints, in order to practice a 'way of war' better suited to their specific circumstances."[5] Far from simply annihilating the adversary, the US military builds as much as it destroys. This was evident during conflict in Iraq (2003–11) where generating electricity for Iraqi civilians was considered essential. And it is evident after conflict when unconditional surrenders in Germany and Japan led to massive reconstruction efforts leading to those countries' economic successes. To be explored in the next chapter, this was a departure from the tradition of *vae victis* (woe to the vanquished) and in deep contrast to the Soviet approach in East Germany, where machinery and factories were shipped to the Soviet Union.

Colin Gray sees "the American defense debate is severely hampered by the popular conflation of war with warfare and, by extension, the confusion of principles of war with principles of warfare."[6] In this case, war is waged to achieve political objectives, whereas warfare is the way a military fights. The distinction is important to make sense of battlefield victories in Vietnam, Iraq, and Afghanistan yet the strategic failures there.

Echevarria has done much to advance the important distinction between a way of war and a way of warfare. Noting the debate is not new, he sees it rooted in the late nineteenth century and draws the connection to the Elder Helmuth von Moltke, Chief of the Prusso-German General Staff from 1857–88, "who equated grand strategy with policy—which he considered the discrete province of statesmen—and insisted that, while policy had the right to establish the goals of a conflict, even changing them when it saw fit, it had no right to interfere with the conduct of military operations."[7] This tends to be the dominant view today, and it is easy to identify a gap between those who decide to take the country to war and those who go to war.

While an important gap, the arrangement between statesman and general does appeal to the military professional who wants the exclusive right to employ military force according to one's professional military judgment rather than enabling politicians who could micromanage conflict from afar. This tendency, explored in a civil-military relations context in chapter 3, creates a gap between the military's ability to wage warfare and the national security establishment's ability to translate battlefield success into strategic victory. However, Grant Hammond offers a more humble interpretation of battlefield success and sees these military victories skewing interpretation of American success since they were "achieved against the small, weak, or incompetent. From Panama to Operation Iraqi Freedom in Iraq, the United States has not faced a truly formidable foe."[8] Had the United States fought wars against more capable adversaries, the debate might be more focused on how wars are waged rather than the gap between war and warfare (this might explain why air-sea battle dominates thinking about the US role in Asia rather than a plausible rationale for explaining why the United States would wage war against its second largest trading partner, China).

In any event, "the American way of war tends to shy away from thinking about the complicated process of turning military triumphs, whether on the scale of major campaigns or small-unit actions, into strategic successes."[9] The Vietnam, Iraq, and Afghan wars reinforce this point. In a contemporary context, Harlan Ullman sees "the Bush administration's plans for the postwar period simply failed. On the basis of the last war [1990–91], the administration expected huge refugee problems, catastrophic damage to oil facilities, and (through the use of weapons of mass destruction) the threat of famine and lack of water. Instead, the problems turned out to be political, social, and economic:

to rebuild the country and provide enough proof of better lives so as to rally public support."[10] While the military embraced the nonmilitary challenges in Iraq, it highlighted the gap between the country's ability to wage war to achieve political objectives and the military's ability to wage warfare to achieve military objectives, which proved to be of little relevance.

Echevarria expands on this point and sees a significant hazard in thinking about war: "Its underlying concepts—a polyglot of information-centric theories such as network-centric warfare, rapid decisive operations, and shock and awe—center on 'taking down' an opponent quickly, rather than finding ways to apply military force in the pursuit of broader political aims. Moreover, the characteristics of the US style of warfare—speed, jointness, knowledge, and precision—are better suited for strike operations than for translating such operations into strategic successes."[11] This is an outcome of technological advances as well as Americans' predilections for technology to solve operational problems and policymakers using the military for punitive action.

To be sure, American culture, as already noted in the chapter on civil-military relations, matters deeply to this debate. Samuel Huntington argues, "The United States is a big, lumbering, pluralistic, affluent, liberal, democratic, individualistic, materialistic (if not hedonistic), technologically supremely sophisticated society. Our military strategy should and, indeed, must be built upon these facts. The way we fight necessarily will reflect the way we live."[12] Brian Linn contends that military officers' perceptions of war and their lessons shape the concept of war that influences procurement, organization and training, doctrine, and planning for future conflicts.[13] This appears on the battlefield and was explained by Maj. Gen Robert Scales, who writes that "so many soldiers recall that their first instinct in a firefight is disbelief that someone unknown really wants to kill him. The positive side of this social affection is a congenital predisposition for American soldiers to befriend strangers, even enemies."[14] Vice Adm. Arthur Cebrowski adds a temporal dimension and sees that "war cannot be divorced from the era in which it takes place. . . . So the way of war reflects the way a society creates, measures, and disposes of power and wealth."[15] As explored further in the American way of peace chapter, this sentiment underlies postconflict activities that eschew retribution and offers focus on reconciliation.

With no clear victories since World War II—in part because this was the last "total war" carried out between traditional great powers—the military tends to cling to a narrow view of its role in national security where it limits itself to advising civilian policymakers and planning for the tactical operations needed to secure success in the precombat and combat phases of a campaign. Consistently this leads to an assessment of postwar US engagements as a series of victorious engagements with the overall peace being lost. This leads Echevarria to conclude that "Americans—not unlike many of their European counterparts—considered war an *alternative* to bargaining, rather than part of an ongoing bargaining process, as in the Clausewitzian view. Their concept of war rarely extended beyond the winning of battles and campaigns to the gritty work of turning military victory into strategic success, and hence was more a way of *battle* than an actual way of war. Unfortunately, the American way of battle has not yet matured into a way of war."[16] With this as backdrop, the rest of the chapter examines the American way of warfare and operational principles for waging warfare.

American Way of Warfare

Colin Gray identifies twelve characteristics of the American way of war(fare). It tends to be apolitical, astrategic, ahistorical, problem-solving/optimistic, culturally ignorant, technologically dependent, firepower focused, large-scale, profoundly regular, impatient, logistically excellent, and sensitive to casualties.[17] To the list Ralph Peters adds, perhaps unnecessarily, "moral," contending that the US military is "'principled' to the extreme, arguing over a checklist of campaign rules inherited from Napoleon's disciples, while concerned about hurting our enemy's feelings."[18] Peters agrees with Gray that the American way of warfare should be firepower focused and that "campaigns must be not only swift but also devastating" to ensure there is a lasting psychological impact on the adversary.[19] Along these lines, had the American invasion of Iraq been slower and more destructive, the ensuing insurgency might have been less lethal.

The American way of warfare largely persisted during the Cold War but was profoundly affected by changes in technology, international law, and the imperatives of limited wars. As the United States professionalized its force, thereby reducing the number of people in the military, it came to rely on technology, coalitions, and interservice cooperation to make up for large numbers of conscripts. In Europe in the 1980s, for example, AirLand Battle doctrine united the three military services, which would combine to repel an invading Soviet army. This concept relied on an extensive logistical capability and expeditionary orientation to reach the supposed battlefields of Europe. While never executed against the Soviets, the joint way of warfare epitomized by AirLand Battle created a lasting impact on how the United States would fight in the Middle East and Central Asia in subsequent campaigns.

At the same time, a modern media providing real-time coverage of the battlefield as well as advances in human rights law undercut the traditional American way of warfare that targeted civilian populations until adversarial surrender, particularly once the human costs of such tactics could be broadcast to the American public (and to the world) in real time. Technological advances aided this new American way of warfare, which emphasized precision targeting and smaller munitions. Capturing these changes, Fred Kagan writes in *Finding the Target*, "the reforms of the 1970s affected every aspect of the U.S. military and marked a true watershed in the history of the military art."[20] Thomas Mahnken in *Technology and the American Way of War* later writes, "Although technology has in some cases shaped the services, particularly the development of nuclear weapons and long-range ballistic missiles, more often the services have molded technology to suit their purposes."[21]

To be sure, Americans in general, and the defense establishment in particular, maintain a predilection for technology. Yet the American way of warfare was also tempered by the realities of frustrated stability operations in the Balkans of the 1990s and stubborn counterinsurgency operations of Iraq and Afghanistan in the 2000s, where low-tech methods utilized by irregular forces and opponents could mitigate American hi-tech advantages. There technological superiority had little relevance to achieving national goals of security and stability. John Lynn captures the essence of American warfare by indentifying "three related tendencies: (1) abhorrence of U.S. casualties, (2) confidence in military technology to minimize U.S. losses, and (3) concern with exit strategies."[22] Later H. H. Gaffney describes the American way of warfare as "deliberate, sometimes agonizing, decision-making, careful planning, assembly and movement of overwhelming forces, the use of a combination of air and ground forces, joint and combined, applied with precision, especially by professional, well-trained military personnel."[23] Evidenced by conflict over the last decade, long-duration operations required ways to broaden the cost-sharing base by including international partners at all levels of war.

To reconcile the historical tradition of attrition, the importance of technology, and operational experiences, this chapter identifies the new American way of warfare, which can be characterized as comprehensive, multidomain, joint, and internationalized, requiring the US military to be postured to operate in all domains from cyberspace to outer space and to perform a full spectrum of missions from major combat operations to humanitarian assistance. In this new American way of warfare, combat operations do not cease when the adversarial government falls. Rather, the American way of warfare seeks to remove preconditions of insecurity and support economic development, build institutions, and professionalize former foes through security force assistance. The main principles underlying this approach are reducing the "drivers" of conflict and strengthening indigenous institutions. Before developing this, however, it is necessary to consider three competing schools within defense circles that define the American way of warfare.

The Three Schools

There is substantial debate on the proper roles and missions within the military.[24] Sam Sarkesian's analysis of the Army officer corps in Vietnam provides a useful structure to understand broader military culture. Sarkesian saw three types of officers: traditionalists, transitionalists, and modernists.[25] The traditionalists were largely World War II veterans who were frustrated by the failure to apply conventional warfare practices of large-scale maneuver in order to achieve victory in Southeast Asia. For example, Gen. William Westmoreland, the overall US commander in Vietnam from 1964 to 1968, contended that "the United States failed in Vietnam because it did not use its military power to maximum advantage."[26]

The transitionalists cut their teeth in the 1950s and envisioned technology as the major way to assure success in conventional warfare. Many of these officers argued in particular that the surest means to victory was the application of strategic airpower in order to neutralize strategic or operational "centers of gravity" or key nodes. Through well-planned targeting, precision weapons, and other technology, the United States could liberate itself from attrition warfare. This was also congruent with doctrine developed to employ nuclear weapons, which became an "ace in the hole" for the United States.

Finally, the modernists, largely affected by their Vietnam experience, believed that conventional militaries were somewhat irrelevant to insurgencies and other limited wars. For them, economy of violence, small-unit tactics, and civil-military cooperation were essential to securing the population from insurgents. This group attempted to place military conflict in Clausewitizian terms: For war to achieve political ends—the reason for which wars are presumably fought—the military must develop capabilities for the types of wars presidents direct. For this group, Westmoreland's experience in Vietnam is illustrative; it is possible to win every battle but fail to achieve the political objectives of the war.

Sarkesian's typology is historically important, but in today's environment the debate is focused on two core questions. First, what went wrong after major combat concluded in Iraq and Afghanistan? For some, the Iraq and Afghanistan wars have been a rude awakening to the military's shortcomings.[27] Second, what are the implications of these lessons for how the military trains and equips? Andrew Bacevich sees answers emanating from two basic camps, which he labels "crusaders" and "conservatives."[28] The basic division is right, but if the question of military strategy is expanded beyond counterinsurgency to include all aspects of the American way of warfare, there is an important faction of conservatives called "modernists." Modernists are the heirs of the transitionalists: devout followers of military transformation and effects-based operations. Modernists see a natural trade-off between personnel and technology, which supports Americans' cultural predilections for technology. The remainder of this section examines three schools affecting the American way of war: traditionalist, modernist, and irregular.

Traditionalist School

The traditionalist school sees challenges in potential peer competitors, requiring preparation for high-end warfare reminiscent of World War II operations such as D-Day and the Battle of Midway. For former army chief of staff Gen. George Casey, traditionalists see that "lethality is our core competency."[29] In the colloquial, the military is good at killing people and breaking things. This emphasis began in the 1970s after failed counterinsurgency operations in Vietnam, significant budget cuts, and a desire to professionalize the force given challenges of conscription. To guide change, AirLand Battle doctrine emerged in 1982, focusing on the importance of the swift movement of information and the striking power of precision-guided munitions. Since the United States could not match the Soviet Union on weapons production, the traditionalist school sought other ways to prepare for war. Instead of matching US tank against Soviet tank, the United States employed advanced technology, fielding better attack aircraft, surface-to-surface missiles, and tanks.

The traditionalists cling to the military's historic role as defender of the state with deterring or waging combat as its sole purpose. Traditionalists see major war against another military power as the greatest potential threat to national security. For example, Colin Gray argues that great power politics, regional nuclear wars, and traditional conflict will return.[30] In general, the Defense Department develops a military in line with Gray's predictions, and it is more interested in preparations for major war than peacetime engagement or stability operations.[31]

Traditionalists object to soft uses of the military and worry these "feel good" operations undermine the military's warfighting ethos. Dissuading, deterring, and defeating existential threats should be the object of the American way of war. For example, John Hillen writes, "To maintain the skills necessary to execute this [warfighting] function requires strategy, doctrine, training, and force structure focused on deterrence and war fighting, not on peacekeeping missions."[32] Dunlap advises to "forget the lessons of Iraq" and reject the idea that soldiers should be social workers, engineers, schoolteachers, nurses, and Boy Scouts.[33] The army's own 2008 strategy echoed this point: "We have focused our training and leader development almost exclusively on counter-insurgency operations (COIN) to the detriment of major combat operations."[34] Finally, former chairman of the Joint Chiefs of Staff Adm. Mike Mullen erected a signpost: "We've converted from a conventional force to focus on counterinsurgency. That said, I think we've got to broaden our training and readiness with respect to full spectrum conflicts, put in balance the counterinsurgency requirement, which is very much in evidence in Iraq and Afghanistan, and preserve the capability to prosecute a conventional war."[35] Fundamentally, traditionalists fight to protect the military being transformed from a warfighting organization into a police organization that is ill-suited for major combat.

For the army perspective of this view, Gian Gentile reaches back to doctrine from his formative years that saw military operations involving "fundamental decisions about when and where to fight and whether to accept or decline battle."[36] Gentile has become the "traditionalists' traditionalist," arguing that "the Army has been steamrolled by a process that proposes its use as an instrument of nation building in the most unstable parts of the world."[37] For Gentile and other traditionalists, shifting capabilities away from traditional warfare tempts "the fate of many past states and their militaries that thought they had become smarter than war and had divined its future, only to find out they were wrong after squandering much blood and treasure."[38] Traditionalists draw from recent nation-building experiences in Iraq and Afghanistan to illustrate significant costs of transforming societies.

Modernist School

The modernist school is a subset of the traditional school. It sees preparing for and prevailing in major war the military's sole purpose, but the key difference is the role of technology. For the traditionalist, mass (i.e., the preponderance of numbers), matters; indeed it is a principle of war. For the modernist, however, technology replaces mass and emphasizes the effects of an operation. For example, to neutralize an air defense network, targeting should focus on radar installations and communications rather than destroying the missiles. Without a brain, the missiles are rendered useless.

The modernist school also assumes its technological prowess will dissuade or prevent challenges to US dominance, establishing what economists would call a "barrier to entry" by potential competitors.[39] But Echevarria sees this "new grammar of the early 2000s—which focuses on achieving rapid military victories—as a recipe for winning only battles, not wars.[40] This technology-centric approach began during the Cold War but really took off during the information technology revolution. During the 1990s, the military services became transfixed by technology under a program called "transformation," which was defined as "a process that shapes the changing nature of military competition and cooperation through new combinations of concepts, capabilities, people, and organizations that exploit our nation's advantages and protect against our asymmetric vulnerabilities to sustain our strategic position."[41]

Scholars and practitioners debated transformation and the existence of a "Revolution in Military Affairs," by which information technology propelled a new type of warfare.[42] Moving beyond the American way of attrition warfare, the new method "eschews the bloody slogging matches of old. It seeks a quick victory . . . its hallmarks are speed, maneuver, flexibility, and surprise."[43] Future military operations should emphasize "stand-off firepower over physical movement, software over hardware, and extensive deployment of light infantry as well as special forces over armored or mechanized forces."[44]

A key advocate of transformation was the late Admiral Cebrowski, who argued that through networked sensors, dominant battlespace awareness, and precision weapons, "you can achieve your initial military ends without the wholesale slaughter" endemic to traditional warfare.[45] Former vice chairman of the Joint Chiefs of Staff Adm. William Owens contended technology could eliminate the fog and friction inherent in warfare, which would reduce overall risk to using the military.[46] The meaning of this was clear for Cebrowski:

> We are entering a new era of military operations and capabilities. The very character of warfare is changing to account for the massive implications of the information age. It embodies the new decision logic with attributes we will become increasingly familiar with and comfortable. We can already see its effects in current operations. The last time we witnessed change of this magnitude was with the advent of the industrial age and the levee en masse (the mobilization of entire societies for war). Both of these events are rapidly receding into the past. A new American way of war has emerged—network centric operations.[47]

During the 1990s, the technologists prevailed in defense debates; overall personnel numbers declined, but investments in technology continued. The rationale was clear: Technology could make warfighting more efficient, which coincided with shrinking defense budgets that saw deep personnel cuts. As opposed to mass as a principle of war, network-centric war espoused "de-massed" forces that substituted information and effects obviating the need to concentrate physical forces.[48] General Dunlap argued that in the future, "air strikes to demolish enemy capabilities complemented by short-term, air assisted raids and high-tech Air Force surveillance" would be needed and not "colossal, boots on the ground efforts."[49] The chief of staff of the air force at the time, Gen. Ronald R. Fogelman, echoed this view, saying, "In the first part of the 21st century, you will be able to find, fix or track, and target—in near real-time—anything of consequence that moves or is located on the face of the Earth. Quite frankly, I can tell you we can do most of that today. We just can't do it in real-time."[50] There was an echo of this during the 1990s in the war with Yugoslavia when the head of the air campaign, US Air Force lieutenant general Michael Short advocated a swift defeat of Belgrade. Disappointed that the operation was restrained, Short later said the United States has unique capabilities and needs to "use shock, lethality, and as much power as we could bring to bear as rapidly as possible" to achieve victory.[51]

Those who make this argument are essentially arguing that the classic Clausewitzian trinity of primordial violence, chance, and probability and the subordination of war to policy have been superseded by a new technological trinity: intelligence, surveillance, and reconnaissance (ISR) technologies; advanced command, control, communications, and computer (C^4) systems, and precision-strike munitions.[52] In accordance with the new trinity, planners assumed future wars would be short and stressed such concepts as "rapid halt," "rapid, decisive operations," and "shock and awe."

Overall, modernists argue that US military strength rests on the foundation of technological superiority (not raw numbers or mass), and the early part of the war in Afghanistan was the test case for the modernist way of war.[53] In 2001, a very small US force supporting anti-Taliban Afghan groups, including the Northern Alliance, and linked through technology to US airpower captured much of the country in fewer than two months.[54] Likewise the 2003 combat operations in Iraq were also seen as validation of the modernist way of war. After all, Baghdad was captured in just three weeks. Max Boot wrote in 2003 that the US victory in Iraq "must rank as one of the signal achievements in military history."[55] Ralph Peters wrote: "The basic lessons that governments and militaries around the world just learned was this: Don't fight the United States. Period. This stunning war did more to foster peace than a hundred treaties could begin to do."[56]

For Boot and others at the time, Gen. Tommy Franks was in the pantheon of military leaders. Yet in both wars what happened after major combat is what mattered most. The lack of preparation for postcombat and counterinsurgency exposed the limits of a high-tech military that sacrifices manpower for technology. Neutralizing key nodes may have won battles but left ammunition depots and large numbers of former troops available for an insurgency. Echevarria wrote: "The new American way of war did show a marked tendency to focus on the act of fighting more than on its follow-through, what is now commonly referred to as war's aftermath. There were clearly plans drawn up for Phase 4, but the plan that was chosen was one that fit the politics of the day rather than the practical situation."[57]

Critics seized on lessons like these and attempted to reshape the American way of warfare. Marine lieutenant general Paul Van Riper pointed out that "once you understand how you're going to fight, then you bring the technology to it. If you lead with the technology, I think you're bound to make mistakes."[58] Another transformation critic, Maj. Gen. Robert Scales, argued that "net-centric warriors are best able to make their arguments in big wars against enemies who depend on the electromagnetic spectrum and uncluttered mediums such as air, sea, and space."[59] In other words, the United States military is well prepared to fight itself rather than competitors in the real world.

Maj. Gen. H. R. McMaster saw a "wide disparity between prewar military thought and the reality of those conflicts that also helps explain why the over-extension and strain on US land forces was described as a temporary 'spike,' why senior military and defense officials resisted reinforcing forces that were clearly overtasked, and why leaders repeatedly denied the need to expand the size of the Army and Marine Corps despite the strain on these forces."[60] And Tom Ricks could write: "Pentagon officials like to talk about 'rapid decisive operations.' The technocratic notion behind it was that U.S. forces, taking advantage of advances in sensors, communications, computer technology, and long-range weaponry and precision logistics, all areas in which it excelled, would fight so quickly and adeptly that the enemy would never have a chance to catch up and understand what was happening. Blinded, confused, and overwhelmed, the enemy's will would break, U.S. forces would triumph, and everyone would live happily ever after."[61] Tempered by operational experiences with shortcomings highlighted by critics, the irregular warfare school gained popularity to explain why and how the military should think about warfare.

The Irregular School

As Philip Bobbitt has observed, for five centuries it has taken the resources of a state to destroy another state. Only states could muster the huge revenues, conscript vast armies, and equip the divisions required to threaten the survival of other states. Indeed, meeting such threats *created* the modern state. In the past every state knew that its enemy would be drawn from a small class of nearby potential adversaries with local interests. But because of globalization, global reach, advances in international telecommunications, rapid computation and methods of mass destruction, this is no longer true.[62] A weaker adversary can adopt various modalities of war to engage and defeat a stronger power. Success in war has traditionally gone to the most adaptive side that can bear the costs of the conflict relative to what Clausewitz called "the value of the object." Accordingly the record shows that the materially weaker side has prevailed in a conflict a surprisingly large number of times.

The irregular school attempts to make sense of this phenomenon and a security environment dominated by weak states and nonstate actors, which necessitates a military optimized for small wars. In irregular warfare, it is better to address underlying conditions or confront local crises before they become regional ones. Retired army lieutenant colonel John Nagl holds the view that instability creates alienated populations and ungoverned spaces that can become incubators for international security challenges that range from anti-Americanism to terrorism. In his influential 2002 book *Learning to Eat Soup with a Knife: Counterinsurgency Lessons from Malaya and Vietnam*, Nagl identified the military implications of this. The US military should not just be able to dominate land, sea, and air domains, but "change entire societies." For Nagl, "the Army today is out of balance, but not just because of a stressful operational tempo and certainly not because of a long-overdue increase in counterinsurgency training and education. Rather, it is because the Army, along with the broader defense establishment it is a part of, remains rooted in an organizational culture that continues to prioritize the requirements for a hypothetical future big war over the irregular conflicts the force is currently fighting."[63] This is consistent with Thomas Hammes's ideas about "fourth-generation warfare" (4GW), which focuses on nonstate actors waging political and social warfare against states.[64] Given the insurgencies that arose after major combat concluded in Afghanistan and Iraq, 4GW theorists gained currency. Tim Benbow sees the concept of fourth-generation warfare as a useful corrective for the military's tendency to focus on interstate warfare.[65]

According to its advocates, the goal of 4GW is to convince the enemy that its strategic objectives are unachievable at acceptable cost. The methodology of 4GW is to use all available networks—political, economic, social, and military—to directly attack the will of the enemy. Hammes contends that 4GW has been the most successful form of warfare during the previous half century, defeating the United States three times (Vietnam, Lebanon, and Somalia), the Soviet Union / Russia twice (Afghanistan and Chechnya), and France twice (Indochina and Algeria). Indeed, only 4GW, he argues, has succeeded against superpowers. Despite this, discussion of what Hammes calls 4GW has been largely absent from the debate within the Department of Defense (DOD) in spite of US military history.

According to the army field manual on stability operations, "contrary to popular belief, the military history of the United States is one characterized by stability operations, interrupted by distinct episodes of major combat."[66] The last major American sea battle was Leyte Gulf in 1944, and the last serious air-to-air engagement was Linebacker II in 1972.[67] Thus the army in particular, and the military in general, need the capabilities and capacity for stability operations. Nagl and others have argued that "rather than rethinking and improving its counterinsurgency doctrine after Vietnam, the Army sought to bury it, largely banishing it from its key field manuals and the curriculum of its schoolhouses."[68] The irregular warfare school is fighting today to ensure history is not repeated yet faces a tough battle given unease with the outcomes in Iraq and Afghanistan. Secretary of Defense Robert Gates saw this directly and wrote, "All the services regarded the counterinsurgency wars in Iraq and Afghanistan as unwelcome military aberrations, the kind of conflict we would never fight again—just the way they felt after Vietnam."[69]

The irregular warfare school highlights the dangers of ignoring history and the historic change that is reflected in the lessons of the 2000s. Nagl reminds us that "inadequate contingency planning by both civilian leaders and military commanders to secure the peace contributed to the chaotic conditions that enabled insurgent groups to establish themselves. With some notable lower level exceptions, the institutional Army did not adapt to these conditions until it was perilously close to losing these wars."[70] David Galula argues that due to the centrality of politics to this type of warfare, counterinsurgent forces must craft a political and nonwarfighting strategy that is sensitive to the needs of the population; seeks to secure their loyalty to the government; mobilizes the community to identify, expel, or fight the insurgent; and extends the authority and reach of the central government.[71] For Galula, "politics becomes an active instrument of operation," and every military move has to be weighed with regard to its political effects and vice versa."[72] As Lawrence Freedman has observed, "in irregular warfare, superiority in the physical environment is of little value unless it can be translated into an advantage in the information environment. . . . Our enemies have skillfully adapted to fighting wars in today's media age, but for the most part we, our country, our government, has not."[73]

Hybrid Wars

In spite of the three schools' attempts to define three unique wars of the future, there is an emerging consensus that future war will have elements of all three or be hybrid wars. A hybrid war, according to Frank Hoffman, has the "lethality of state conflict with the fanatical and protracted fervor of irregular warfare."[74] While the term did not gain currency until 2008, modern hybrid wars trace their roots to Marine Corps general Charles Krulak's "three-block war." Influenced by his experience in Somalia in the early 1990s, Krulak wrote: "At one point in time, one block, they've got a child in their hands, they're wrapping that child in swaddling clothes, they're feeding it, and it's called humanitarian assistance. The next moment, they're keeping two factions apart— that's called peacekeeping. And what you're seeing is the third block, every once in a while coming into the second, and the third block in the three-block war is what we call mid-intensity, highly lethal conflict."[75]

In other words, war and peace are not easily divisible. The institutional military attempted to run away from a three-block war depiction of the future. The 1990s are instructive. In Somalia it was able to hand off relief operations to the United Nations. In Rwanda it was simply able to avoid conflict and peacekeeping altogether. And in the Balkans, North Atlantic Treaty Organization (NATO) and US National Guard and Reserve units primarily conducted the stabilization operations after the high-intensity air campaign concluded. Active forces largely remained in reserve for potential war with Iraq or North Korea. But for Krulak and others like him, this was a mistake. Speaking of future war, he said, "It is not going to be the son of Desert Storm. It's going to be the stepchild of Chechnya."[76] But the Pentagon ignored this prediction, yet in Dominic Tierney's formulation, Americans are addicted to regime change and allergic to nation-building.[77]

A hybrid world exhibits a number of characteristics that currently affect the American way of warfare—and will most likely continue to do so in the future. These include such phenomena as expanded global interdependence, which although seen as a boon to globalization, also permits terrorists and other violent ideologues to inflict damage at a very low cost and risk to themselves. In the words of Shamil Basayev, a Chechen commander and mastermind of the 2004 massacre in Beslan, Russia, "we are not bound by any circumstances, or to anybody, and will continue to fight as convenient and advantageous to us and by our rules."[78] John Robb observes that "this new method of warfare . . . offers guerrillas the means to bring a modern nation's economy to its knees and thereby undermine the legitimacy of the state sworn to protect it. Furthermore, it can derail the key drivers of economic globalization: the flow of resources, investment, people, and security." Those who adopt this form of warfare, says Robb, are not really terrorists, but *global guerrillas*, who represent "a broad-based threat that far exceeds that offered by terrorists or the guerrillas of the past."[79]

Such global guerrillas are able to exploit the dissonance caused by uneven economic development and urbanization, the diffusion of and impact of technology, and the dislocation caused by globalization and demographic bulges. They are able to effect "systems disruption" in advanced economies by causing "cascading" failures in the system. "If attackers can disrupt the operations of the hubs of a scale-free infrastructure network, the entire network can collapse in a cascade of failure."[80] Because of interdependence, failures within a single network can cause the failure of others. In a tightly interconnected infrastructure, not only do the transportation network, the water network, and the fuel network depend on the electricity network, but also the electricity network depends on the fuel and transportation. "Global guerrillas have proven to be increasingly adept at using these interconnections to cause cross-networks of failure," according to Robb.[81]

In a hybrid world, "Microsoft coexists with machetes, and stealth is met by suicide bombers."[82] Hybrid war, like almost all wars in history, can be chaotic. It is not only defined by fog and friction, but it is also fraught with ambiguity of objective. Preparation for hybrid war underlies significant change in the military. Former secretary of defense Gates told an audience at the Air War College in 2009 that we "need to think about future conflicts in a different way. To recognize that the black and white distinction between irregular war and conventional war is an outdated model."[83] Chairman of the Joint Chiefs Adm. Mike Mullen echoed this that same year: "In every operational situation, the joint force commander will have to develop a concept of operations that integrates—and reconciles the frequently competing demands of—combat, security, engagement, and relief and reconstruction as they apply."[84] Or, as army special operations commander Lt. Gen. Charles T. Cleveland pointed out, he envisions preparing his soldiers for two broad missions. "When I am at war, I have to campaign to win," he said. "When I am not at war, I am campaigning to either shape the environment or I am campaigning to prevent war."[85] In short, the military can no longer disaggregate war and assign certain responsibilities to particular forces or agencies. The transition between major combat and stability operations is abrupt, and end states ebb and flow. Instead of chasing the specialization illusion, all military personnel need the capability to adapt to a variety of missions, recalling Krulak's three-block war or Frank Hoffman's hybrid war orientation.

The New Adversary?

An example of a prototype hybrid actor is Hezbollah. During its 2006 war with Israel, Hezbollah exhibited both state-like capabilities—long-range missiles, antiship cruise missiles, sophisticated antiarmor systems, armed unmanned aerial vehicles, and signals intelligence—while still skillfully executing guerrilla warfare. Hezbollah was able to stand up to the Israel Defense Force (IDF) because it was able to skillfully adapt to the particular circumstances that it faced. For instance, unlike US forces, which must be prepared to fight in a variety of environments and under various conditions, Hezbollah was able to tailor its forces specifically to counter the IDF. Since Hezbollah did not have to organize for offensive operations, it was able to concentrate on defense in depth.

Hezbollah exhibited flexibility by fielding modular units and adopting mission-type orders. It was effective in its innovative use of weapons. Although most Hezbollah fighters did not seek death, the organization was willing to accept casualties. Hezbollah was perfectly willing to accept a loss ratio of about five Hezbollah fighters to one IDF soldier. Hezbollah's intelligence performance was surprisingly effective. As Ralph Peters observed, "Israel fought as a limping stepchild of Clausewitz. Hezbollah fought as Sun Tzu's fanatical son."[86]

As suggested above, the sort of hybrid threats generated by complex irregular warfare and illustrated by Hezbollah may well constitute the most probable, most demanding, and potentially most costly type of future conflict. Implications of wars against hybrid threats include the likelihood that they will be extremely lethal and protracted, that since they will often take place in contested urban zones, they will be manpower intensive, and that they will be widely distributed by distance, complexity, and mission. In most cases, these hybrid threats will seek to win the war of perceptions, waging a conflict among the people. To prevail against such a threat requires cultural intelligence and exploitation of the human terrain.

The operational environment in such conflicts very likely will be characterized by close encounters between friendly forces and an enemy that seeks to blur the distinctions between the conventional and the unconventional and between combatants and noncombatants, between conflict and stability operations, and between the physical and the psychological. After all, hybrid war is a competition for influence and legitimacy in which perceptions are paramount. As the conflict in Iraq illustrated, in the battle for legitimacy religious identity may trump or negate better governance and economic benefits.

In general, hybrid foes will attempt to exploit the political effects of a conflict, seeking to undermine the legitimacy of US military actions. Thus these enemies will try to leverage "lawfare," the use of the rules of warfare against the United States (while ignoring these rules themselves)—for example, by taking refuge within the civilian population in an attempt to maximize civilian casualties.[87]

Principles of American Warfare

Greatly influenced by a future characterized by irregular warfare waged by hybrid threats, American warfare is defined by four key characteristics. First, it is comprehensive, designed to enable partners, to wage major combat, and to create conditions to transition to civil authorities; defeating an enemy is no longer sufficient for declaring victory. Next, the American way of warfare is multidomain and full-spectrum, capable of operating under the seas and ice to outer space. Next, to unify command of large military formations with competing service agendas, the American way of warfare is joint. Finally, given national priorities, the American way of warfare is internationalized through military alliances and coalitions. The United States rarely fights alone for legitimacy, instead sharing the burden of warfare, filling skill gaps, and exploiting cultural knowledge.

Comprehensive

Maj. Gen. Robert Scales has argued that military personnel will "have to possess the flexibility and skill to transform themselves from close combat specialists to providers of humanitarian assistance and social services. . . . These cannot be mass-produced."[88] As somber evidence of this challenge, Antulio Echevarria notes "while the U.S. military's preference for fighting major wars may have compromised its ability to succeed in small ones, it is also clear that the nation-building tasks it was typically asked to perform tended to prove too complex for the military tool alone."[89] As Harlan Ullman wrote, "National Security can no longer be defined by national defense. We had that luxury during the Cold War. Now the aperture must be greatly expanded. That expansion applies well beyond the Department of Defense, the State Department, and the CIA—the traditional centerpieces for national security. Today, Treasury, Transportation, Homeland Security, Commerce, Health and Human Services, Agriculture, and Interior all have large national security roles."[90]

In the absence of true participation of multiple federal agencies in combat zones, current doctrine attempts to divide military operations across six distinct phases: shape, deter, seize initiative, dominate, stabilize, and enable civil authority.[91] Shape includes various government activities performed to dissuade or deter potential adversaries and to assure or solidify relationships with friends and allies. Deter includes efforts to prevent undesirable adversary action

Table 5.2: Principles of Joint Operations

Principle	Purpose
Objective	Direct every military operation toward a clearly defined, decisive, and achievable goal.
Offensive	Seize, retain, and exploit the initiative.
Mass	Concentrate the effects of combat power at the most advantageous place and time to produce decisive results.
Maneuver	Place the enemy in a position of disadvantage through the flexible application of combat power.
Economy of Force	Expend the minimum essential combat power on secondary efforts in order to allocate the maximum possible combat power on primary efforts.
Unity of Command	Ensure unity of effort under one responsible commander for every objective.
Security	Prevent the enemy from acquiring unexpected advantage.
Surprise	Strike at a time or place or in a manner for which the enemy is unprepared.
Simplicity	Increase the probability that plans and operations will be executed as intended by preparing clear, uncomplicated plans and concise orders.
Restraint	Limit collateral damage and prevent the unnecessary use of force.
Perseverance	Ensure the commitment necessary to attain the national strategic end state.
Legitimacy	Maintain legal and moral authority in the conduct of operations.

Source: Joint Staff, *Joint Publication 3-0: Joint Operations* (Washington, DC: Department of Defense, August 11, 2011), Appendix A.

by demonstrating the capabilities and resolve of the joint force (e.g., military exercises). Seizing the initiative includes operations designed to gain access to theater infrastructure and to expand friendly freedom of action while degrading enemy capabilities with the intent of resolving the crisis at the earliest opportunity. The dominate phase focuses on breaking the enemy's will and depends on overmatching the adversary through force. The stabilize phase occurs where there is no operating civil authority and the military provides or facilitates

Figure 5.1: Phases of Warfare

SHAPE Phase 0	DETER Phase 1	SEIZE INITIATIVE Phase 2	DOMINATE Phase 3	STABILIZE Phase 4	ENABLE CIVIL AUTHORITY Phase 5
PREVENT PREPARE	CRISIS DEFINED	ASSURE FRIENDLY FREEDOM OF ACTION	ESTABLISH DOMINANT FORCE CAPABILITIES	ESTABLISH SECURITY	TRANSFER TO CIVIL AUTHORITY
		ACCESS THEATER INFRASTRUCTURE	ACHIEVE FULL-SPECTRUM SUPERIORITY	RESTORE SERVICES	REDEPLOY

Based on figure III-17 in Department of Defense, *Joint Publication 5-0 Joint Operation Planning* (Washington, DC: Department of Defense, 2011), III-41, www.dtic.mil/doctrine/new_pubs/jp5_0.pdf.

delivery of basic services to a population. The final phase is transitioning to civil authority, which would enable the military to redeploy from the operating area once a civilian government is created.

Phasing operations from zero to five is a useful construct when thinking about combat operations with other states that have a clear beginning, middle, and end to fighting (e.g., Yugoslavia in 1999 and Iraq in 1991), but conflict cannot be easily conducted in phases. Militaries more often find themselves engaged in Krulak's three-block wars, in which combat, reconstruction, and humanitarian assistance occur simultaneously in relatively confined areas. For example, in 2003 after the United States invaded Iraq and there was no clear sovereign authority, the United States (principally through its military) assumed the role of occupying power. For postinvasion Iraq, this meant the military provided Iraqi civilians with electricity, water, sewage treatment, and trash removal in addition to basic security such as policing and border control. Restarting the economy was viewed as essential to bringing normalcy to Iraq by reducing levels of violence. In the ideal, nonmilitary parts of the federal government would provide these services. Yet, at the national level, there is no expeditionary reconstruction capability outside of the military. In spite of calls by the secretary of state and secretary of defense to mobilize the interagency of federal departments, there were very few nonmilitary or nonintelligence civilians in Iraq and Afghanistan.

Multidomain

Preserved from the legacy of preparing to fight the Soviet Union, the American way of warfare is multidomain. It can fight on land, on or below the sea, in the air, and in space, with an emerging capability to fight in cyberspace. Across these different domains, as Barry Posen writes, the United States can command the commons because "it can credibly threaten to deny their use to others; and that others would lose a military contest for the commons if they attempted to deny them to the United States."[92]

Historically the military services tended to divide by domain; the navy fights on the sea, the Marine Corps fights from the sea, the air force fights from the sky, and the army fights on land. Congress does designate core missions for the services to preserve some differentiation, but the DOD further designates missions for its major components. As noted in Directive 5100, the navy and Marine Corps comprise the nation's principal maritime force, the air force is the principal air and space force, and the army is the principal land force. To be sure, the services do have unique capabilities or core competencies often defined by platforms. The navy, for example, has the unique capability to control the seas through its warships and conduct antisubmarine warfare with its submarine fleet. The air force maintains long-range strategic airlift capabilities with C-17 aircraft. The services also define core competencies by capacity. While the Marine Corps is a significant ground force, the army has a greater size and logistical capacity, giving it greater staying power.

In spite of this, there are significant areas of overlap. Both the navy and air force have significant tactical air assets; they differ on basing at sea or on land. When both services begin to fly the F-35 (Joint Strike Fighter), capability differences will further narrow. Both the Marine Corps and army have significant infantry components; they differ on deployment lengths and debarkation points. Both the navy and air force have nuclear weapons; they differ on delivery mechanisms. All three services have engineering capabilities: the navy has its construction battalions (CBs, or SeaBees), the army has its Corps of Engineers, and the air force has its Rapid Engineer Deployable Heavy Operational Repair Squadron Engineers, or RED HORSE squadrons. And in the cyber domain, the navy has its Tenth Fleet, the air force has its Twenty-Fourth Air Force, and the army has its 780th Military Intelligence Brigade. Redundancy occupies a significant place in the US military.

Joint

As the preceding discussion suggests, the services differ primarily in degree rather than in kind. Over the last thirty years, the independent military services have been unified through joint warfighting. As noted in chapter 2, jointness has gradually emerged from the ashes of World War II and was reinforced by changes in law that charged the services with recruiting, training, and equipping the forces that are employed by combatant commanders in a joint way. Since the passage of the Goldwater-Nichols Department of Defense Reform Act of 1986, "jointness"—cooperation and harmony among the armed services—has been the watchword of the US military. In passing the act to respond to the operational deficiencies it perceived to be plaguing the military in the 1980s, Congress expected that jointness would spur cooperation among the services at all stages of the defense process, from research and development and procurement through to operations, thereby ending the baleful effects of interservice rivalry. (President Harry Truman once remarked that "if the Army and the Navy had fought our enemies as hard as they fought each other, [World War II] would have ended much sooner."[93])

In practice jointness means a navy attack aircraft can get fuel from an air force tanker and provide close air support for an army unit. Implicit in this joint example is that navy aircraft have refueling probes and communication systems that are compatible with air force tankers. The navy pilot also has the ability to communicate with a forward air controller on the ground who directs the munitions. And the navy pilot has an appreciation for the appropriate size of a weapon necessary to support a ground unit without causing fratricide or collateral damage that would impact national reconciliation efforts. Indeed, recent successes on the battlefields—from Iraq to Afghanistan—have been attributed to the new culture of "jointness" that enabled the United States to deploy more effective military force across the entire spectrum of conflict. In August 2011, then chairman of the Joint Chiefs of Staff Adm. Mike Mullen argued that in the two decades since the law had passed, "we have built an incredibly joint force in ways that many of us could not have imagined." He then made the plea to "leverage not only what has happened here, but recognize the importance and opportunity in places like cyber, like space, (and) in intelligence. As we get smaller as an institution, that mandates that we work more closely together."[94]

Warfare undoubtedly underscores how, why, and when to integrate service capabilities. But it was various mandated actions and operational experiences that truly institutionalized jointness. In a combat zone, for example, the commander may be from the army, his deputy may be from the navy, and the chief of staff may be from the air force. The command is unified under a single leader who works to unite the best the services have to offer. The idea that jointness is a pejorative is fading as the senior ranks become populated with officers commissioned after the 1986 legislation that mandated it.[95]

Operations have not only reinforced the imperative of unity of command, but also exposed flaws in the services. As apparent in the major conflicts of the last seventy years, the military had the capacity to deploy large numbers of personnel, but it did not have the capability or culture to create social harmony and promote economic development. In Vietnam this was addressed through the Civil Operations and Revolutionary Development Support (CORDS) program. In Iraq and Afghanistan, the Provincial Reconstruction Teams, or PRTs, were created to build infrastructure and gain the trust of indigenous civilians. To ensure that the military has the necessary civilian agencies with it in the future, there has been an attempt to expand the concept of jointness to include agencies and departments across the government, international, intergovernmental, and nongovernmental communities. While the military can make this change in its doctrine, government departments outside of the DOD continue to limit their exposure to combat zones.

Internationalized

As jointness was gradually realized in the DOD, military operations of the 1990s internationalized the American way of warfare. While the United States intended to fight the Soviet Union with its NATO allies in an internationalized way, coalition operations became the norm for legitimacy and burden sharing. For example, when NATO deployed the Stabilization Force (SFOR) to Bosnia-Herzegovina in 1996, thirty-five countries participated. Fifty countries' forces operated in Afghanistan in 2014. Headquarters, both abroad and in the United States, are also incorporating international officers into traditionally US-only staffs. At the center of the coalitions is a US-sponsored framework to enable partners to contribute to international security. This is both cost-effective and consistent with US values.

To improve coalition operations, non-NATO countries have adopted NATO standards and doctrine, which have become the lingua franca of defense interoperability. These standards are practiced during predeployment training and regular multinational exercises. Integrated operations are also visible at sea where Bahrain-based naval coalitions are patrolling the Gulf of Aden and the Indian Ocean to reduce illicit trafficking and piracy. To be sure, burden sharing is a virtue. However, internationalizing operations have costs. These costs include national caveats, incompatible systems, diverse tactics, varying national interests, and disparate resource levels.[96] At times this can lead to stress among partners, but by and large, operational commanders leading coalition forces understand the constraints each country imposes and seek to mitigate those.

To ensure that the United States has partners whose militaries are capable of working with it on a variety of missions, the US military has increasingly devoted more of its time and effort to what is labeled "security force assistance" (SFA), a set of activities to develop the capacity and capabilities of foreign security forces and their supporting institutions. We often associate SFA with weak states, but these activities also occur with dozens of treaty allies and are intended to promote international cooperation. With shared challenges of terrorism and nuclear proliferation, and shared goals of development and protecting human security, there are unprecedented levels of international cooperation to share information, target terrorists, and provide governments the tools they need to confront national threats before they become regional ones.

Pragmatically, the United States likes to see its partners fulfill regional and global security roles. However, underinvestment in logistics, intelligence, and weapons limits partners' abilities to meet their foreign policy goals. This regularly causes concern on both sides of the Atlantic. For example, NATO deputy secretary general Alexander Vershbow said, "This transatlantic capability gap is simply not sustainable in the long term. . . . We should be aiming for the day when no single Ally needs to provide more than 50% of certain critical NATO capabilities."[97] To guarantee alliance operations are not simply American ones, NATO's "smart defense" initiative attempts to generate the defense capabilities the alliance needs. As defense budgets decline further, this problem will be exacerbated unless developed countries begin to match their strategic objectives with the military means required.

To be sure, developed countries do place significant demands on the United States, but we cannot overlook how partners support a shared basis for international security. This comes in the form of allies deploying forces (Germany is the core country in Kosovo), allies providing host-nation support (Japan provides billions annually to support US forces), and allies bringing their own unique capabilities to coalition operations (Italy trains Afghan police). This is recognized by President Barack Obama, as he intends to continue the American tradition of enabling partners and reinforcing allies throughout the globe. As he noted in his second inaugural address, "America will remain the anchor of strong alliances in every corner of the globe. And we will renew those institutions that extend our capacity to manage crisis abroad. For no one has a greater stake in a peaceful world than its most powerful nation."[98]

Conclusion

Tensions regarding what the military should be prepared to do remain unresolved. On the one hand, one group clearly believes the United States wasted vast resources and failed to achieve core objectives in Vietnam, Iraq, and Afghanistan. Consequently, members of this group contend that the military should focus its efforts on "real" warfighting. The novelist Mark Helprin captured this mood and eloquently wrote that we need to acknowledge that victory is not "leaving divided, violence-plagued, tinder-box nations hostile to American interests, friendly to its enemies, and largely unchanged despite our mission of transformation."[99] For Helprin and others, the United States needs to exercise restraint when it comes to military intervention and focus on major war preparation and deterrence.

On the other hand, another group says that even if we wanted to, we cannot run away from the past because the future will be dominated by the United States leading coalitions to combat subnational and transnational forces. Frank Hoffman, for example, writes that we cannot overlook "America's global leadership role and the destabilizing effects of the withdrawal of U.S. forces and the concomitant decline in American access and influence it would produce."[100]

Hoffman and others like him point out that conventional warfighting is actually the exception in US history and that counterterrorism, counterinsurgency, and security force assistance are therefore core military missions. They argue, therefore, that the American military should do its best to learn the lessons from Iraq and Afghanistan. This group draws strength from the last decade and notes that we could have done better by listening to voices such as Krulak's that attempted to drive strategic thinking and planning toward the types of conflicts the United States was likely to wage.

Thus multidimensional war in the future is likely to be characterized by distributed, weakly connected battlefields, unavoidable urban battles with unavoidable collateral damage exploited by an adversary's strategic communication, and highly vulnerable rear areas. On such battlefields, friends and enemies are comingled, and there is a constant battle for the loyalty of the population. All of this is exacerbated by the proliferation of militarily useful technology, including nuclear weapons and delivery systems. While we can identify a way of American warfare, Colin Gray is astute: "Two caveats in particular need to be stamped in red ink on every manuscript that presents a generally favorable view of the concept of a national way of war. First, it is necessary to beware of caricature; second, it is mandatory to be alert to evolution and change."[101]

To be sure, depictions of the future security environment are important if the American way of warfare rather than rationale for war continues to dominate national security. Thus retired Marine Corps general James Mattis hit the nail on the head several years ago when, paraphrasing Sir Michael Howard, he remarked, "We are not likely to get the future right. We just need to make sure we don't get it too wrong."[102] One way to ensure that we don't get the future "too wrong" is not to confuse the *nature* of war—which is immutable—with the *character* of war—which is infinitely variable. In thinking about future war, planners cannot afford to make this mistake but are limited by their roles as advisers to those engaged in statecraft and should heed Lt. Gen. Michael Short's advice:

> When the decision is made to use force, then we need to go in with overwhelming force, quite frankly, extraordinary violence that the speed of it, the lethality of it . . . the weight of it has to make an incredible impression on the adversary, to such a degree that he is stunned and shocked and his people are immediately asking, "Why in the world are we doing this? If this is just the first night, then what in the world is the rest of it going to be like? How long can we endure it, and more importantly, why are we having to endure it? Let's ask our leaders why this is happening."[103]

Short is clearly impressed with the military's ability to annihilate an adversary and seems grounded in American history, but Russell Weigley later took issue with a narrow interpretation and with the primacy of annihilation in American military thinking: "The taste for overwhelming force tended to prevent or delay military intervention in situations where the national interest or considerations of a superpower's moral responsibilities would otherwise have called for intervention, but geography or political pressures militated against overwhelming force. I should have made it clearer that the historic American way of war should not cause us to believe if we cannot apply absolutely, unquestionably decisive force, the alternative must be to apply no force at all."[104]

Because of tension between the military preference for annihilation and the political preference for action, the institutional military appears to precariously navigate the civil-military divide. With dissatisfying outcomes in conflict zones, the military appears to be running away from a hybrid future by closing the book on recent wars and shifting to the Asia-Pacific region. While many want to run away from the last twenty years as astrategic, we must consider that the wars were only different in degree from previous conflicts in the

Balkans or the Middle East. As the United States attempts to shift its strategic focus to Asia, we must think deeply and discuss honestly the changing American way of warfare that is defined by being comprehensive, multidomain, joint, and internationalized. Warfare needs to be placed back in the context of war as the pursuit of political ends and national objectives, rather than being another (albeit important) tool of power. To paraphrase Leon Trotsky, the US military may not be interested in hybrid warfare, but hybrid warfare is interested in the US military.

Notes

1. Carl von Clausewitz, *On War*, ed. and trans. Michael Howard and Peter Paret (Princeton, NJ: Princeton University Press, 1976), passim; Alan Beyerchen, "Clausewitz, Nonlinearity, and the Unpredictability of War," *International Security* 17, no. 3 (Winter 1992–93); Barry D. Watts, *Clausewitzian Friction and Future War*, McNair Paper 52 (Washington, DC: National Defense University Press, 1996); Mackubin Thomas Owens, "Reflections on Future War," *Naval War College Review* 61, no. 3 (Summer 2008).

2. Michael Howard, *War in European History* (Cambridge: Cambridge University Press, 2001), ix–x.

3. Russell F. Weigley, *The American Way of War: A History of United States Military Strategy and Policy* (New York: Macmillan, 1973), xxii.

4. Antulio J. Echevarria II, *Toward an American Way of War* (Carlisle, PA: US Army War College, Strategic Studies Institute, March 2004), 4.

5. Brian Linn, "'The American Way of War' Revisited," *Journal of Military History* 66, no. 2 (April 2002), 506.

6. Colin S. Gray, "The American Way of War: Critique and Implications," in *Rethinking the Principles of War*, ed. Anthony D. McIvor (Annapolis, MD: Naval Institute Press, 2005), 15.

7. Antulio J. Echevarria II, *Toward an American Way of War* (Carlisle, PA: US Army War College, Strategic Studies Institute, March 2004), 2, www.strategic studiesinstitute.army.mil/pdffiles/pub374.pdf.

8. Grant T. Hammond, "The U.S. Air Force and the American Way of War," in McIvor, *Rethinking the Principles* (see note 6), 115.

9. Echevarria, *Toward an American Way of War*, 7.

10. Harlan Ullman, "On War: Enduring Principles or Profound Changes," in McIvor, *Rethinking the Principles* (see note 6), 88.

11. Echevarria, *Toward an American Way of War*, 16.

12. Samuel P. Huntington, *American Military Strategy*, Policy Paper 28 (Berkeley: Institute of International Studies, University of California, Berkeley, 1986), 13.

13. Brian Linn, *The Echo of Battle: The Army's Way of War* (Cambridge, MA: Harvard University Press, 2007).

14. Robert H. Scales, "The Second Learning Revolution," in McIvor, *Rethinking the Principles* (see note 6), 47.

15. Arthur Cebrowski, "Foreword," in McIvor, *Rethinking the Principles* (see note 6), x–xi.

16. Echevarria, *Toward an American Way of War*, 1. For critical sources on victory and strategy, see John I. Alger, *The Quest for Victory: The History of the Principles of War* (Westport, CT: Greenwood, 1982); J. Boone Bartholomees, "Theory of Victory," *Parameters* 38, no. 2 (Summer 2008): 25– 36; Stephen Biddle, *Military Power: Explaining Victory and Defeat in Modern Battle* (Princeton, NJ: Princeton University Press, 2004); Richard Hobbs, *The Myth of Victory: What Is Victory in War?* (Boulder, CO: Westview, 1979); Dominic D. P. Johnson and Dominic Tierney, "Essence of Victory: Winning and Losing International Crises," *Security Studies* 13, no. 2 (Winter 2003–4): 350–81; Robert Mandel, *The Meaning of Military Victory* (Boulder, CO: Lynne Rienner, 2006); William C. Martel, *Victory in War: Foundations of Modern Strategy* (New York: Cambridge University Press, 2011); William C. Martel, "Grand Strategy of 'Restrainment,'" *Orbis* 54, no. 3 (Summer 2010): 356–73; Raymond O'Connor, "Victory in Modern War," *Journal of Peace Research* 6, no. 4 (Special Issue on Peace Research in History, 1969), 367–84.

17. Gray, "The American Way of War."

18. Ralph Peters, "Speed the Kill: Updating the American Way of War," in McIvor, *Rethinking the Principles* (see note 6), 95.

19. Ibid., 106.

20. Frederick W. Kagan, *Finding the Target: The Transformation of American Military Policy* (New York: Encounter Books, 2006), 66.

21. Thomas G. Mahnken, *Technology and the Way of War since World War II* (New York: Columbia University Press, 2010), 2.

22. John A. Lynn, *Battle: A History of Combat and Culture* (Boulder, CO: Westview, 2003), 321.

23. H. H. Gaffney, "The American Way of War through 2020" (Alexandria, VA: Center for Strategic Studies, CNA Corp., 2006), 3.

24. Michael P. Noon, "Next-War-itis, This-War-itis, and the American Military," Foreign Policy Research Institute E-Notes (January 2009).

25. Sam C. Sarkesian, *Beyond the Battlefield: The New Military Professionalism* (New York: Pergamon, 1981).

26. George C. Herring, "American Strategy in Vietnam: The Postwar Debate," *Military Affairs*, April 1982, 88.

27. Andrew J. Bacevich, "The Petraeus Doctrine," *Atlantic*, October 2008.

28. Ibid.

29. "An Interview with George W. Casey, Jr." *Joint Force Quarterly*, no. 52 (1st Quarter 2009): 19.

30. Colin Gray, "Future Warfare or the Triumph of History," *RUSI Journal* 150, no. 5 (October 2005): 16–19.

31. Two major theater wars (2MTWs) was a notional force planning construct used to determine the appropriate size of the US military.

32. John Hillen, "Superpowers Don't Do Windows," *Orbis* 41, no. 2 (Spring 1997): 242.

33. Charles J. Dunlap Jr., "Forget the Lessons of Iraq," *Armed Forces Journal*, January 2009.

34. Department of the Army, *U.S. Army Strategy* (Washington, DC: Department of Defense, 2008), 7, http://pksoi.army.mil/training_education/documents/Army_Strategy_20081.pdf.

35. Quoted in "Executive Summary," *Joint Force Quarterly*, no. 52 (1st Quarter 2009): 13.

36. *Field Manual 100-5, Operations* (1986), quoted in Gian Gentile, "Let's Build an Army to Win All Wars," *Joint Force Quarterly*, no. 52 (1st Quarter 2009): 27.

37. Gentile, ibid.

38. Gian P. Gentile, "Think Again: Counterinsurgency," *Foreignpolicy.com*, January 2009, www.foreignpolicy.com/articles/2009/01/12/think_again_counterinsurgency.

39. Mackubin Thomas Owens, "Reflections on Future War," *Naval War College Review* 61, no. 3 (Summer 2008).

40. Echevarria, *Toward an American Way of War*, vii.

41. Department of Defense, *Transformation Planning Guidance* (Washington, DC: Department of Defense, 2003), 3.

42. For example, see Michael Vickers and Robert Martinage, *The Revolution in War* (Washington, DC: Center for Strategic and Budgetary Assessments, 2005).

43. Max Boot, "The New American Way of War," *Foreign Affairs* 82, no. 4 (July/August, 2003): 42.

44. Ariel E. Levite and Elizabeth Sherwood-Randall, "The Case for Discriminate Force," *Survival* 44, no. 4 (Winter 2002–3), 81–98.

45. Quoted in *Battle Plan under Fire*, PBS Nova, www.pbs.org/wgbh/nova/wartech/transform.html.

46. William Owens, "System-of-Systems: U.S.'s Emerging Dominant Battlefield Awareness Promises to Dissipate 'Fog of War,'" *Armed Forces Journal International*, January 1996.

47. Arthur K. Cebrowski, "New Rules, New Era," *Defense News*, October 21–27, 2002, 28.

48. The new rules of information-age warfare included information superiority, shared awareness, self-synchronization, dispersed forces, and demassed forces. At the same time, operations should emphasize deep sensor reach and speed. Defense Department, *Military Transformation: A Strategic Approach* (Washington, DC: Office of Force Transformation, 2003), 32.

49. Charles Dunlap, "America's Asymmetric Advantage," *Armed Forces Journal*, September 2006.

50. Ronald R. Fogelman, "Information Technology's Role in 21st Century Air Power," *Aviation Week & Space Technology*, February 17, 1997, 17.

51. Michael C. Short, television interview, *Frontline: War in Europe: NATO's 1999 War with Serbia over Kosovo*, 2000, Public Broadcasting Service, www.pbs.org/wgbh/pages/frontline/shows/kosovo/interviews/short.html.

52. Mackubin Thomas Owens, "Technology, the RMA, and Future War," *Strategic Review*, Spring 1998.

53. National Research Council, *Avoiding Surprise in an Era of Global Technological Advances* (Washington, DC: National Academy of Sciences, 2005).

54. Stephen Biddle challenged the view that the Afghanistan war was fought in a revolutionary way. See "Afghanistan and the Future of Warfare," *Foreign Affairs* 82, no. 2 (March/April 2003): 31–39.

55. Boot, "New American Way of War," 44.

56. Ralph Peters, "A New Age of Warfare," *New York Post*, April 10, 2003.

57. Antulio J. Echevarria II, "What Is Wrong with the American Way of War?," *Prism* 3, no. 4 (February 2012), http://cco.dodlive.mil/files/2014/02/prism108-115 _echevarria.pdf.

58. Quoted in *Battle Plan under Fire*, PBS Nova, www.pbs.org/wgbh/nova/wartech/nature.html.

59. Robert Scales, "Transformation," *Armed Forces Journal*, March 2005, 24.

60. H. R. McMaster, "Learning from Contemporary Conflicts to Prepare for Future War," in *Defense Strategy and Forces: Setting Future Directions*, ed. Richmond M. Lloyd (Newport, RI: Naval War College Press, 2007), 72.

61. Thomas Ricks, *The Gamble: General David Petraeus and the American Military Adventure in Iraq, 2006–2008* (New York: Penguin, 2009), 160–61.

62. Philip Bobbitt, *The Shield of Achilles: War, Peace, and the Course of History* (New York: Knopf, 2002), xxi.

63. John Nagl, "Let's Win the Wars We're In," *Joint Force Quarterly* 52 (1st Quarter 2009): 25.

64. Thomas Hammes, "Fourth-Generation Warfare: Our Enemies Play to Their Strengths," *Armed Forces Journal*, November 2004, 40–44.

65. Tim Benbow, "Talking 'bout Our Generation? Assessing the Concept of 'Fourth-Generation Warfare,'" *Comparative Strategy* 27, no. 2 (2008): 148–63.

66. *Field Manual 3-07: Stability Operations* (Washington, DC: Department of the Army, 2008).

67. Scales, "Transformation," 25.

68. Nagl, "Let's Win," 21.

69. Robert M. Gates, *Duty: Memoirs of a Secretary at War* (New York: Knopf, 2014), 118.

70. Nagl, "Let's Win," 22.

71. David Galula, *Counterinsurgency Warfare: Theory and Practice* (Westport, CT: Praeger, 2006), 72.

72. Ibid., 4–5.

73. Doug King, "Hybrid War," briefing to the Defense Science Board, May 24, 2007.

74. Frank G. Hoffman, *Conflict in the 21st Century: The Rise of Hybrid Wars* (Arlington, VA: Potomac Institute for Policy Studies, 2007), 28.

75. "An Interview with Charles Krulak," *Newshour with Jim Lehrer,* June 25, 1999, www.pbs.org/newshour/bb/military/jan-june99/krulak_6-25.html.

76. "Lessons of Combat: 25th Anniversary of U.S. Withdrawal from Vietnam," *PBS Newshour*, April 12, 2000, www.pbs.org/newshour/bb/asia-jan-june 00-vietnam_4-12/.

77. Dominic Tierney, *How We Fight: Crusades, Quagmires, and the American Way of War* (New York: Little, Brown, 2010).

78. Cited in John Robb, *Brave New War: The Next Stage of Terrorism and the End of Globalization* (Hoboken: John Wiley, 2007), 14.

79. Ibid., 14–15.

80. Ibid., 102.

81. Ibid., 103.

82. Michael Evans, "From Kadesh to Kandahar: Military Theory and the Future of War," *Naval War College Review* 56, no. 3 (Summer 2003): 132–50.

83. Robert Gates, "Remarks as Delivered, Maxwell-Gunter Air Force Base, Montgomery, AL," April 15, 2009, www.defense.gov/transcripts/transcript.aspx ?transcriptid=4214.

84. Michael G. Mullen, *Capstone Concept for Joint Operations Version 3.0* (Washington, DC: Department of Defense, 2009), 14.

85. Quoted in Thom Shanker, "Military Sees Broader Role for Special Operations Forces, in Peace and War," *New York Times*, April 2, 2013.

86. Ralph Peters, "Lessons from Lebanon: The New Model Terrorist Army," *Armed Forces Journal*, October 2006.

87. William H. Taft IV, "The Law of Armed Conflict after 9/11: Some Salient Features," *Yale Journal of International Law* 28 (2003).

88. Scales, "Second Learning Revolution," 45.

89. Echevarria, *Toward an American Way of War*, 6.

90. Ullman, "On War," 93.

91. Based on figure IV-9 in Department of Defense, *Joint Publication 5-0: Joint Operation Planning* (Washington, DC: Department of Defense, 2011), www.dtic.mil/doctrine/new_pubs/jp5_0.pdf, III-41.

92. Barry Posen, "Command of the Commons: The Military Foundation of U.S. Hegemony," *International Security* 28, no. 1 (Summer 2003): 5–46.

93. Quoted in Charles Stevenson, *SECDEF: The Nearly Impossible Job of Secretary of Defense* (Washington, DC: Potomac Books, 2006), 7.

94. Quoted in Jim Garamone, "Mullen Stresses Lessons of Jointness," Armed Forces Press Service, August 2, 2011, www.af.mil/news/story.asp?id= 123266402.

95. But the argument that the Goldwater-Nichols legislation has habituated the US military to the conditions of "jointness" must be weighed against a more likely explanation for the tradition of cooperation. Simply, high defense budgets assured each of the services that their favored programs would be funded. That era is coming to an end—and with it, contrary to Mullen's predictions, the expectation that "jointness" can continue in conditions of budgetary austerity.

Jointness works best when all of the services get most of what they want. From the Reagan defense buildup of the 1980s up to today, the defense budget, though less than 4 percent of gross domestic product and less than 20 percent of the federal budget, was sufficient to allow the services to build the capabilities required to implement their respective "strategic concepts." Doing so mitigated interservice rivalry.

But defense planning and budgeting are, in essence, about managing risk. Given the security environment that prevailed after the fall of the Soviet Union, the US military was not required to balance risk in a way that benefited one service at the expense of another. The United States was rich enough—and, even after 9/11, safe enough—that the country did not have to choose less land power in order to acquire more sea or air power. The services could also eagerly meet all joint requirements because doing so did not come at the expense of any perceived "core" missions of the services.

This, of course, is changing. Undoubtedly jointness will remain the official position of the military in the future, and the US military will not soon lose the ability to conduct effective multiservice operations. But reduced defense budgets are likely to pit the roles, missions, and associated programs of the services against each other. In an era of fiscal austerity, real trade-offs will be made and declining defense budgets may restoke the interservice budget and doctrine battles of the late 1940s. If this occurs, the historical record demonstrates that declining defense budgets can lead to a degree of interservice competition that threatens the very security of the United States.

96. Joint Staff, *Enduring Lessons from the Past Decade of Operations* (Suffolk, VA: Department of Defense, 2012).

97. Alexander Vershbow, "Closing the Gap: Keeping NATO Strong in an Era of Austerity," speech, February 11, 2013, NATO website, www.nato.int/cps/en/natolive/opinions_98350.htm.

98. Barack Obama, "Second Inaugural Address," January 21, 2009, www.whitehouse.gov/the-press-office/president-barack-obamas-inaugural-address

99. Mark Helprin, "A Primer for American Military Intervention," *Wall Street Journal*, July 4, 2012.

100. Frank G. Hoffman, "Striking a Balance: Posturing the Future Force for COIN and Conventional Warfare," *Armed Forces Journal*, July 2009, www.armedforcesjournal.com/2009/07/4099782/.

101. Gray, "The American Way of War," 26.

102. Cited in Mackubin Thomas Owens, "America's 'Long War(s),'" FPRI (Foreign Policy Research Institute) e-note, January 2008, www.fpri.org/articles/2008/01/americas-long-wars.

103. Short, television interview, *Frontline*.

104. Russell Weigley, "'The American Way of War' Revisited," *Journal of Military History* 66, no. 2 (April 2002): 532.

6

The American Way of Peace

Security is a critical foundation of prosperity. Trade cannot flourish in waters that are contested by forces; societies cannot thrive under the threat of terrorism; and commerce cannot be sustained in areas devastated by natural disasters.

—Secretary of Defense Chuck Hagel, 2013

The American way of peace flows directly from the American way of warfare. Given the evolution of the American way of warfare that puts greater emphasis on allied collaboration, the American way of peace places its emphasis on the reconstruction and transformation of former foes into new friends who can take their place within a US-led global order. The American way of peace is the complete opposite of what might be termed the traditional way of peace, when postconflict negotiations focused on neutralizing an enemy's potential for starting a new war. Often this was guided by the precept *vae victis* (woe to the vanquished). The losing nation would be stripped of territory, obliged to pay reparations (sometimes of a crushing nature), accept significant disabilities in terms of trade, and be required to disarm in some fashion. Sometimes this approach would be tempered, as occurred with France following the final victory of the allied powers over Napoleon in 1815, but the traditional "way of peace" was largely rooted in a concept whereby the vanquished needed to be penalized, such as Germany and Austria-Hungary were in 1918.[1] The traditional way of posthostilities stressed the subordination of the losers to the victors and sought to perpetuate subordination as long as possible. It often nurtured a desire on the part of the losing side for revenge to reverse the effects of defeat, while the winners were forced to either maintain their military advantage or risk losing the peace. The Unites States does not practice this.

Since the Second World War, the United States has sought to change the postconflict negotiation paradigm from retribution against past enemies to reconstruction and reconciliation with future friends. Part of the US strategy for securing the peace has been to construct collective security organizations and to promote closer economic integration through free trade, based on the assumption that US interests are best served through a global order that promotes the spread of open societies lightly defended and tied to the United States through shared economic and security interests. (This approach was successful in Western Europe and East Asia but has produced mixed results in the Middle East and Central Asia.) Yet, resurrecting former foes into friends that integrate into an Americanized international order is the dominant paradigm for the American way of peace.

The American way of peace is facilitated through rules-based international institutions such as the United Nations (UN), the International Monetary Fund (IMF), the World Bank, the North Atlantic Treaty Organization (NATO), the General Agreement on Tariffs and Trade (GATT), and the World Trade Organization (WTO), reflecting American faith in the value of international cooperation. This has not been done outside of national interests; rather, the United States uses international institutions to find ways for it to either maintain a preponderance of influence by controlling the largest bloc of voting shares in an international financial organization such as the IMF or building in some form of veto power in a political organization such as the UN. This tension—between the stated desire for a rules-based order and preserving the right of the United States to bend or break those rules—continues to be a major fault line within US foreign policy to this day. With fiscal challenges weighing on the United States and the backdrop of unsatisfying postwar outcomes in the 2000s, the next twenty years will test US ambivalence for the institutions it largely funds and an American way of peace that seeks to move past international tradition that emphasizes *vae victus*.

Lessons from American Presidents

What might be termed an "American way of peace" flows from the advice and perspectives offered by early US presidents. The first precept is to reject the notion that any country is a permanent foe of the United States. George Washington, in his "Farewell Address," counseled, "Harmony, liberal intercourse with all nations, are recommended by policy, humanity, and interest," warning against "inveterate antipathies against particular nations."[2] In theory all nations can and should become friends and partners of the United States. This is the basis of a long-standing American attitude that no conflict is perpetual and that it is possible, and even desirable, for former enemies to become future friends.[3] This principle explains how the Britain that burned the White House in 1814 could become the Britain that is the most important bilateral partner of the United States today.

The second is the necessity for postwar reconstruction of the defeated foe. Abraham Lincoln, in his Second Inaugural Address, plucked the strings of American idealism in proclaiming that after the destructive Civil War, the way forward should be one of reconciliation: "With malice toward none, with charity for all, with firmness in the right as God gives us to see the right, let us strive on to finish the work we are in, to bind up the nation's wounds, to care for him who shall have borne the battle and for his widow and his orphan, to do all which may achieve and cherish a just and lasting peace among ourselves and with all nations."[4]

Lincoln's vision was expanded by Woodrow Wilson, who, in justifying American involvement in the First World War in his 1918 State of the Union Address, insisted that after military victory was achieved "the world be made fit and safe to live in; and particularly that it be made safe for every peace-loving nation which, like our own, wishes to live its own life, determine its own institutions, be assured of justice and fair dealing by the other peoples of the world as against force and selfish aggression. All the peoples of the world are in effect partners in this interest, and for our own part we see very clearly that unless justice be done to others it will not be done to us."[5] Since the mid-twentieth century, the Wilsonian imperative has been embodied in the expectation that after a conflict concluded, the "United States will leave behind [in the defeated country] a free-market, liberal state committed to the rule of law, a strong civil society and peaceful intentions."[6] This approach is the complete opposite of *vae victis* and enabled America's World War II adversaries Japan and Germany to become essential security, economic, and diplomatic partners of the United States.

As Harry Truman put it, "if any nation would keep security for itself, it must be ready and willing to share security with all. That is the price that each nation will have to pay for world peace. Unless we are all willing to pay that price, no organization for world peace can accomplish its purpose."[7] Additionally, the breakdown of the world economy during the interwar period had "convinced leaders that a new set of cooperative monetary and trade arrangements was a prerequisite for world peace and prosperity."[8] Indeed, as Truman continued, "a just and lasting peace cannot be attained by diplomatic agreement alone, or by military cooperation alone. Experience has shown how deeply the seeds of war are planted by economic rivalry and by social injustice." Consequently, the new world order that rose after 1945 was made to prevent World War III and traced its roots in the lessons from World Wars I and II.

Lessons from War

The contemporary American way of peace also builds on the lessons learned from the failures to secure the peace after the First World War.[9] In spite of President Wilson's vision to remake the postwar international system, there were no effective institutions and mechanisms to arbitrate international disputes that could lead to war. Americans' penchant for neutrality was made clear following the war, as expressed by constitutional lawyer Zechariah Chafee who said, "We will not be represented at Geneva [at the League of Nations]. We will not be represented at The Hague [at the World Court]. We will not take an effective part in any economic conference."[10]

Without a new paradigm, the Versailles settlement was still strongly defined by the traditional way of peace—aimed at the subjugation of Germany rather than its reintegration—and despite Wilson's idealism it did not succeed in creating a global order that prevented trade conflicts and strategic rivalries among the nations from destabilizing the international system.[11] Significantly, the United States and other countries left the task of creating the economic prosperity so foundational to maintaining a peaceful international environment largely to the private sector in the immediate years following the war—but private capital remained largely unwilling to finance the necessary reconstruction, certainly in the absence of any governmental guarantees.[12]

Having learned these lessons, US statesmen during the Second World War realized that the United States would have to take the lead in creating a new international architecture to secure the peace—and would have to be prepared to make significant contributions in terms of resources but also sacrificing some of America's freedom of action.[13] This became a political challenge. After all, the Senate had been unwilling to sanction American membership in the League of Nations in 1920 out of fear that the obligations of the organization would constrain American options or compel American involvement in world affairs. In summoning the conferences at Bretton Woods (New Hampshire) and Dumbarton Oaks (Washington, DC) to lay out the design for postwar organizations (the UN, the IMF, and the World Bank)—and later spearheading the development of regional organizations from what was to become the European Union (EU) to the Organization of American States—US policymakers were guided by a vision of guaranteeing America's own national security by a "wiring of trade and treaty" that would enmesh other nations of the world in a cooperative system that would decrease the attractiveness of war and conflict as tools of statecraft.[14]

Active efforts to reshape and restructure the international environment, rather than simply "come home" after the close of the fighting, were not guided by some sense of misguided altruism but based on the assumption that US interests are best served through an American-led global order that coincided with the construction and maintenance of a more liberal world system.[15] The American way of peace would not only "encourage an upward cycle of global peace and prosperity," but would also serve concrete US interests by decreasing threats and alleviating the costs of security.[16] Extending olive branches to former enemies was nurtured with trade and diplomatic preferences to prevent future conflict.

Table 6.1: US Mutual Defense Treaty Allies

Year Established	Parties
1949	NATO: Albania (2009), Belgium (1949), Bulgaria (2004), Canada (1949), Croatia (2009), Czech Republic (1999), Denmark (1949), Estonia (2004), France (1949), Germany (1955), Greece (1952), Hungary (1999), Iceland (1949), Italy (1949), Latvia (2004), Lithuania (2004), Luxembourg (1949), Netherlands (1949), Norway (1949), Poland (1999), Portugal (1949), Romania (2004), Slovakia (2004), Slovenia (2004), Spain (1982), Turkey (1952), United Kingdom (1949), and United States (1949)
1951	Philippines and United States
1952	ANZUS: Australia, New Zealand, and United States Note: The US mutual defense pact with New Zealand is suspended but remains in effect between Australia and New Zealand.
1953	Republic of Korea and United States
1954	Japan and United States
1954	Thailand and United States

To realize a lasting peace, since the close of World War II the United States has offered other countries around the world what John Ikenberry has labeled a "grand bargain" whereby Washington gives existing partners and former foes unprecedented access to its markets, makes available substantial assistance for development and reconstruction, and as necessary extends security guarantees. In return, participating countries are expected to offer diplomatic, military, economic, and logistical support to US initiatives. A subsidiary bargain was that in return for accepting US leadership of the community of nations, other countries would get a voice in the system and assurances that the United States would allow itself to be bound by the rules.[17] If its prerogatives of leadership were recognized, US policymakers were prepared to move away from the time-established logic of the Melian Dialogues (the weak suffer what they must, the strong do what they like) in favor of reaching decisions through what Secretary of State Edward R. Stettinius Jr. described as "the hard and the exacting day-to-day work of consultation, negotiation, and adjustment which are the essence of successful cooperation among free peoples."[18]

Linking Peace and War

The American way of peace flows directly from the American way of warfare. Americans no longer understand "victory" simply to be the military defeat of an adversary and the destruction of an enemy's conventional military forces, followed by return of US forces to the United States. Instead US leaders have extended the definition of warfare to encompass what is achieved in the post-conflict period. This builds on an observation made by Gen. Dwight D. Eisenhower, in speaking to his staff after the surrender of Germany in 1945. He noted that judgments as to American success or failure after World War II "can only be judged fifty years from now. If the Germans at that time have a stable, prosperous democracy, then we shall have succeeded."[19]

Gen. Tommy Franks, the American commander who led the 2003 invasion of Iraq, echoed Eisenhower almost sixty years later in response to a question as to what constitutes victory:

> We also find that in almost every case we became involved in wars in order to gain security, either for ourselves or for friends; that at the end of the conflict, as a result of treaty, or pact, or alliance, this security was guaranteed. Security for friends—meaning both allied countries as well as for pro-American forces within a given country—has also inevitably become a part of the objective of victory. That is how we establish the metrics of defining victory. There are always secondary objectives. The opening and securing of lines of communication are sometimes components in defining what constitutes victory. Sometimes there are economic benefits. Sometimes victory is said to have been achieved when a particular country has been introduced (or reintroduced) into the community of nations, as happened with Germany and Japan after World War II. This may entail the establishment of the rule of law and some form of representative government.[20]

Indeed, although by traditional standards the United States won an overwhelming victory in Iraq in 2003—destroying the regime in a matter of weeks and capturing Saddam Hussein by the end of the year—the assessment as to whether or not America had "won the war" ultimately rested upon the postwar outcome: whether or not the post-Saddam government was perceived as democratic and friendly to US interests, willing to be integrated into larger US-led political and economic institutions, and prepared to support US security objectives for the Middle East.[21]

The American ways of warfare and peace have merged into one continuous spectrum. The willingness to use military power and security guarantees to create and maintain an open, liberal, rules-based economic order—which in turn generates prosperity, which decreases the prospects of conflict—is at the heart of what Robert Gilpin termed the "American system," a series of "economic, political and security arrangements" between the United States and countries in Europe, East Asia, and the Middle East.[22]

The American Way of Peace in Practice, 1944–71

The first practical steps toward implementing a new postwar American way of peace came in the midst of the Second World War. The Roosevelt administration was cognizant of the fact that Wilson's idealistic plans had failed in part due to lack of congressional buy-in. In the fall of 1943, resolutions sponsored by J. William Fulbright in the House of Representatives and Thomas Connally in the Senate endorsed US participation in a new international collective security organization. The Connally resolution broke with a traditional understanding, that the United States would only resort to war if faced with a direct and imminent threat to its own territory or interests, by accepting the need for the United States to participate in order "to prevent aggression and to preserve the peace of the world." During the debates Sen. Claude Pepper, while defending Congress's constitutional right to declare war, advanced the proposal that it might be necessary for US forces to be deployed as a "police force" to stop aggression—even without prior congressional approval—in order to nip a larger war in the bud.[23]

These resolutions cleared the way for the Roosevelt administration to begin negotiations with the other major Allied powers (Britain, the Soviet Union, and China) on the future international collective security organization. At the Dumbarton Oaks conference in the summer and fall of 1944, the structure that would become the UN was largely put into place. The conference in San Francisco in spring 1945 finalized the draft of the UN Charter. The United States made significant concessions, from the point of view of American isolationists: It accepted that the Security Council could determine what constituted threats to international peace and security and that it could compel member states—including the United States—to take actions to support its directives (per Articles 24 and 25) anywhere in the world. This went beyond the initial concept of the United States as the "policeman" largely responsible for security only in the Western Hemisphere and made it easier to accept the idea that the United States should offer security guarantees to countries around the world, not just in its immediate geographic neighborhood. The passage of the United Nations Participation Act (Public Law 79-264) by Congress in December 1945 confirmed that the president did not need to seek prior authorization from Congress to take measures enacted by the Security Council under Articles 41 and 42 of the charter (for instance, imposing economic sanctions but also "such action by air, sea, or land forces as may be necessary to maintain or restore international peace and security").

Table 6.2: Top Contributors to the UN Operating Budget

Country	Contribution as Percentage of UN Operating Budget
United States	22
Japan	10.8
Germany	7.14
France	5.59
United Kingdom	5.17
China	5.14
Italy	4.44
Canada	2.98
Brazil	2.93
Spain	2.97
Russia	2.43
Australia	2.07

Source: United Nations Secretariat, "Assessment of Member States' Contributions to the United Nations Regular Budget for the Year 2013 and of New Member States' Advances to the Working Capital Fund for the Biennium 2010–2011 and Contributions to the United Nations Regular Budget for 2011 and 2012," December 24, 2012, http://daccess-dds -ny.un.org/doc/UNDOC/GEN/N12/664/15/PDF/N1266415.pdf?OpenElement.

In keeping with the principle identified by Ikenberry that the US way of peace requires giving other countries—even small nations—input into the system, the United States accepted modifications to the draft charter developed at Dumbarton Oaks and ratified at the San Francisco Conference, most notably to allow the General Assembly to play a "subsidiary role in the maintenance of international peace" and to be able to discuss and recommend nonbinding measures.[24] This decision gave small countries such as Afghanistan, Costa Rica, and Uruguay equal status with the great powers in the General Assembly. Finally, the United States became the single largest financial contributor to the work of the new organization and remains so to the present day.[25]

Given the link between security and economic development, the United States pursued an interest in the economic health of other states (to remove causes for war and strengthen efforts to keep the peace), and US and British experts laid the basis for the postwar economic system.[26] This effort grew out of Secretary of State Cordell Hull's observation that "if we could get a freer flow of trade . . . in the sense of fewer discriminations and obstructions . . . so that one country would not be deadly jealous of another . . . the living standards of all countries might rise, thereby eliminating the economic dissatisfaction that breeds war."[27]

The United States invited representatives of all forty-four Allied countries to an economic conference at Bretton Woods in July 1944. This meeting was designed to set up the rules and institutions necessary for facilitating international trade and investment—particularly to guarantee acceptable means of payment—as well as to ensure sufficient liquidity in the global economic system. Cognizant of the reality that the interwar system had failed because of a lack of a lender of last resort, trade barriers, and a dearth of acceptable currencies for payment, the United States accepted the responsibility to keep the dollar fully convertible into gold and for other currencies to be pegged against the dollar (with provisions to allow for their appreciation or depreciation in order to facilitate trade and economic growth).

The United States would make the largest single contribution to the creation of the IMF, which would allow countries to borrow to meet their debt obligations (and so avoid a major problem prior to World War II of countries defaulting on their loans and so paralyzing international capital markets). The United States would also be the single largest contributor to the proposed International Bank for Reconstruction and Development, which would be in a position to support reconstruction and development efforts, avoiding the mistakes of the interwar period of leaving this task up to a risk-averse private sector. While efforts to create an international trade organization did not succeed at Bretton Woods (and the charter developed at the 1947 UN conference in Havana was never ratified), subsequent meetings of countries to find ways to reduce and eliminate tariffs created the basis for GATT.[28] The United States thus committed itself to the lion's share of the work (and the cost) of "constructing two global arteries, one for trade and the other for the international circulation of money."[29] In doing so, Washington was willing to accept a number of short-term economic disadvantages to get the system up and running, including some restrictions of the full convertibility of other currencies for dollars and the maintenance of some barriers against American exports.[30]

Americanized Multilateralism

The international conferences that created the postwar global architecture reflected an American approach that projected the sense that US decisions were "consultative, cooperative and multilateral in design."[31] However, these institutions also locked in American predominance by design.[32] In the UN, the veto power granted to the United States (and four other major powers) meant that action could not be taken in defiance of American preferences. This also proved an important selling point to skeptical American lawmakers, underscoring that the United States would never be forced into any international action against its will. With this recourse, the United States could cede UN leadership to people from other countries and illustrate the importance of democratic standards in the institution through the General Assembly.

In contrast to the UN, voting rights in the IMF and the World Bank were structured like a corporation where countries' voting rights were based on the number of shares each country "bought" through contributions to the fund. In this case, as the largest contributor, the United States could set the agenda for both institutions and, if necessary, block or veto undesirable action. At the same time, leadership of the IMF would be granted to a European, while an American has perpetually served as World Bank president.

Through these arrangements, US policymakers were confident that they had found a way to embed US priorities within a cooperative multilateral framework, by stressing the compatibility of US interests with the successful functioning of these institutions.[33] Other countries were willing to accept the bending of principles of state equality and binding authority in order to ensure that domestic US politics supported the new institutions and prevented a repeat of what happened after World War I when the United States failed to join the League of Nations.[34] This gave the Roosevelt and Truman administrations the flexibility needed to get legislative approval for the United States to join the UN, the IMF, the World Bank, and GATT.[35] An important component in this domestic support for the American way of peace came from the business community, which mobilized support for US international engagement as something good for the expansion of the American economy. US business leaders were well aware that the health of the US economy rested on maintaining the growth caused by the war—and that part of that process meant keeping "sufficient demand in America and abroad to keep that level after the war."[36]

American policy toward the defeated Axis powers was the second major building block in the emerging American way of peace. Initially, in concert with their British and Soviet allies, American officials (primarily Secretary of the Treasury Henry Morgenthau) were prepared to apply the traditional way of peace, especially vis-à-vis Germany: a punitive approach designed to destroy the industrial base of the defeated powers and exact revenge for the war through crippling reparations.[37]

Over time, however, the US approach shifted. Ensuring a stable postwar world required more than the military defeat of the Axis powers—it needed their successful reintegration into the community of nations, especially the global economy, and in particular the willingness of the United States to assume the burden of funding their international deficits.[38] US officials recast the occupations as necessary assistance for these countries "to win their way back to an honorable place among the free and peace-loving nations of the world."[39]

Believing that the draconian peace settlements of previous eras (including the Versailles Treaty) had merely laid the foundation for new wars, the US approach concentrated on "taming" a former enemy's military capabilities but at the same time providing generous incentives to rejoin the community of nations and to support US initiatives. The State Department's political adviser to the US military occupation in Germany, Robert Murphy, argued in December 1948 against a "Carthaginian" approach to peace with Germany (defined by imposing crushing reparations or placing prohibitions on industrial development), pointing out these measures were not successful "as a means of obtaining security." He further noted that it was "inconsistent with our basic policy of reconstructing a peaceful and self-sustaining Germany."[40] (The US predilection for turning former enemies into friends was satirized by Leonard Wibberley in his 1955 novel *The Mouse That Roared*—about a small European country in financial distress that decides its best course of action is to declare war on the United States, lose, and then receive large amounts of developmental aid to reconstruct its economy—which played on the American desire to rebuild former enemies into newfound friends.)

Initially the Rooseveltian vision of the American way of peace was meant to be global in scope, but the onset of the Cold War meant that a significant portion of the Eurasian landmass now lay outside the emerging American system. While the USSR and its satellites remained in the UN, they eschewed entry into the IMF, the World Bank, and GATT. In turn, the emergence of a Soviet bloc led the United States to create a new set of more limited institutions for Western Europe, Latin America, and East Asia, beginning with NATO in 1949. These newer organizations followed the patterns set in the creation of the postwar international institutions: multilateral in structure, with a consultative role for all members big and small but with clear mechanisms for ensuring US dominance.

The Soviet threat "provided the political glue" that helped to forge a US-led political and economic order by forcing the United States and its allies to "subordinate their short-term economic and other differences to the long-term political priority of containing Soviet power."[41] It allowed the United States to create regional "coalitions of the willing" to block Soviet expansionism (and to bring together states that otherwise might not have joined together in common security and economic efforts with each other and with the United States.[42]

The US strategy was to "maintain a sphere of influence . . . an expanded zone of responsibility—with the consent of those who live within it" in order to "nurture the long-term vitality and interdependence of an American-led, liberal international order outside the Communist bloc."[43] To do this, Americans had to undertake several related initiatives: finding ways to revive the economies of the noncommunist states, guaranteeing their military security against the threat posed by the USSR, and, last but not least, linking Americans psychologically with allies overseas to "prevent a retreat into isolationism like that which had followed World War I."[44] The last challenge required convincing Americans that the geographic isolation provided by the Pacific and Atlantic Oceans was no longer sufficient to provide security for the United States and that a United States standing alone would be overwhelmed if the Soviet Union could harness the resources of the Old World. American leadership of what began to be termed "the Free World" was necessary to ensure the domestic peace and prosperity of the United States. US attitudes about the desirability of having the Treasury fund development and reconstruction aid also needed to be changed from seeing this as charity to the "more urgent purpose of alleviating social and economic conditions which might breed communism."[45]

Mobilizing the Nonstate

To get these messages across, the Truman administration relied upon what has been termed "state-private" networks (bringing together government officials and nongovernment organizations) to make the case for programs such as the Marshall Plan and the North Atlantic alliance.[46] Such domestic support was critical because, by some estimates, the Marshall Plan cost approximately $13 billion and effectively transferred the equivalent of 1.5 percent of US gross national product to the recipients.[47]

The American approach was to offer "alliance on easy terms, placing few demands on its partners and preferring to see them 'as a pool of potential volunteers rather than conscripts to its cause.'"[48] The United States did not conquer or dominate its allies, which made its hegemonic position within the international system easier for other states to accept.[49] Likewise, organizations such as NATO solved the European security dilemma best captured by its first secretary-general, Hastings Ismay, who famously summed up the importance of the organization designed "to keep the Americans in, the Russians out, and the Germans down."[50]

All of the countries of the Free World did not receive identical offers from the United States, and there were some critical differences between how the American system was built in Western Europe versus in East Asia and in other parts of the world. Nevertheless, there were some common features, which included

- an offer of a bilateral security pact (such as the US-Japan Security Treaty or the mutual defense treaty between the United States and the Republic of Korea) or membership in an American-led multilateral defense treaty (such as NATO, SEATO, or CENTO), which would commit the United States to come to the defense of the other state;
- an offer of development and reconstruction aid (via the Marshall Plan or another program in different regions of the world);

- an offer of access to the American market for their exports; and
- the ability to peg the country's currency to the dollar and to have access to loans in order to ease balance-of-payments problems.

This is why the American system has sometimes been described as an "empire by invitation"—since countries were free to reject American offers of help and assistance.[51]

The Cold War provided countries an alternative worse than the American-dominated international order.[52] While the United States was willing to devote major expenditures to rehabilitating the former Axis powers, the Soviet Union did the opposite by stripping their occupation zones of industrial equipment, experts, and other assets in line with the traditional *vae victis* approach. In contrast to programs such as the Marshall Plan, which funneled US reconstruction assistance to Western Europe, the Soviet Union constructed an economic system for their satellites based on the principle of subordinating their economies to Soviet needs.[53]

To reassure weaker states, the United States in the immediate postwar period engaged in a policy of "strategic restraint—to reassure weaker states that it would not abandon or dominate them." In practice this meant that "the leading state does not need to use its power assets to enforce order and compliance."[54] (This approach enabled France, for example, to withdraw from NATO's military committee in 1966 yet retain its place in NATO's political institution.) In contrast, the Soviet Union under Joseph Stalin pursued an opposite approach, imposing strict political controls on its Eastern European satellites (which backfired in the case of Josip Broz Tito in Yugoslavia), but wavered in its support of Mao Zedong in China—sending precisely the signals of domination and abandonment.[55]

In contrast, the US security presence sought to reassure partners without creating the impression of outright domination. If Soviet forces were perceived as occupiers wherever they were stationed—instruments to enforce economic and political subservience—the deployment of the US military overseas was not only seen as a guarantee of protection but as an economic windfall for the host countries. The United States spent lavishly to project its Cold War military power, and the impact of military transfers to Europe to set up and maintain a deterrent force amounted to nearly 3 percent of the total gross domestic product (GDP) of Western Europe.[56] In Japan, US military expenditures averaged $550 million per annum from 1950 to 1960.[57]

As the Cold War progressed, other countries in the American system were expected to make some contribution to common expenses.[58] However, it was understood that the United States would take on the major share of the expenses, both in per capita and in absolute terms, for the functioning of postwar institutions, beginning with the UN but also organizations such as NATO. Each

US ally paid some costs—but Washington was willing to overpay for several reasons. The first was that even if others acted as free riders to some extent, it was still cheaper overall for the United States than trying to bear the burden of maintaining the system alone. Nor did the United States want to run the risks of losing its strategic advantage if it, in retaliation, decided to cut back on its own contributions. US overpayments also helped to ratify US predominance in these institutions.[59] Finally, in some cases the United States did not want some of its partners to develop advanced militaries. Instead, the United States guaranteed Japan's and Germany's defense in order to reassure neighbors that neither country would reemerge as a threat.[60]

However, the United States also did not act as an international benefactor, dispensing benefits without seeking advantages. While offering easy terms for alliance—a guarantee to potential partners that they would not be drained like Soviet satellites—the United States also needed to avoid the Soviet mistake of tying up so much of its productive capacity in defense-related expenditures. In July 1953, the director of policy planning at the State Department, Paul Nitze, noted: "The actual and potential capabilities of the US and of allied and friendly states are very large. The problem appears to be more the effective organization, direction and leadership of these capabilities and the distribution of emphasis in developing new capabilities than it is one of an overall insufficiency of actual and potential capabilities. We can within the next several years gain preponderant power."[61] Nitze followed up that observation by advising:

> The United States should continue to pursue a policy of limited mobilization designed to develop and maintain a favorable power position without resort to an armament effort that would disrupt the economies of the free nations and thus undermine the vitality and integrity of free society. Such a power position should be sufficient to (1) maximize the chance that general war will be indefinitely postponed, (2) provide an effective counter to local aggression in key peripheral areas, and (3) provide the basis for winning a general war should it occur.[62]

Washington used the leverage that aid and security guarantees gave it as incentives to get other partners to do things for the United States. Marshall Plan aid, for instance, was made conditional on governments undertaking a whole series of reforms—from altering legal systems to changing the rules for businesses—and, critically, on commitments to move away from the protectionism that had led to the "beggar-my-neighbor" policies of the 1919–39 era in favor of the free flow of goods and capital across borders.[63] In contrast to Soviet imposition of central planning and other Soviet techniques on its satellites, "postwar Americanization . . . involved not only a transfer of US production techniques and management methods . . . but also a partial transformation of economic structures, institutions and sociocultural practices."[64] A critical quid pro quo that Washington extracted from European recipients of aid, for instance, was the pledge to treat the subsidiaries of American multinational firms as the equivalent of domestic firms, which opened the door for US firms to sell their products on better terms than during the interwar period.[65] Japan was not asked to make major economic concessions to American business interests but instead gave the United States complete access to air and naval bases from which the United States could secure its interests in the entire Asia-Pacific region (and that would not simply be used solely for the defense of the Japanese islands).[66] All US partners were also asked to take steps that were not in their economic self-interest, such as restricting their trade in advanced industrial goods or critical raw materials to the Soviet Union or the People's Republic of China, but that served overall US security interests.[67]

The United States also used its influence to try to encourage its partners to end their quarrels with each other—with significant success in terms of Franco-German reconciliation but even, in the cases of historic foes such as Greece and Turkey and Japan and Korea, using the carrots it could provide to ameliorate potential conflicts.[68] Security guarantees provided by the United States provided the safety for countries to take risks in trying either to resolve or at least lower tensions. The threat of Soviet land invasion facilitated Franco-German reconciliation, but the maritime space of Asia prevented the US-Japanese relationship from developing into a multilateral organization like NATO.

The US-led alliance systems also generated imperatives toward institutionalizing the Free World, to create "a wide array of economic and political agreements that have helped generate unprecedented levels of integration and cooperation among the countries of Western Europe, North America and Northeast Asia."[69] Annual NATO summits, trade rounds under the auspices of GATT, the conclaves of "the Groups" (the Group of Seven [G-7], etc.) all provided regular contacts not only between the heads of state but the relevant bureaucracies, helping to build the sense of an international community.

Regional Integration

The United States also led the push for regional integration, in part based on the theory that larger, more efficient markets would help generate the prosperity needed to hold the Soviet Union at bay and reduce the attractiveness of communism as a competing ideology, but also so that over time US partners would be in a better position to contribute more to maintain and preserve the American system. Prosperity would, following Nitze's formulation, increase the resources available to the United States to contain the Soviet Union.[70] Western European states, under NATO's umbrella, began to forge closer economic associations that would culminate in the Treaty of Rome in 1957, laying the foundations for what would become the EU, as well as other regional and subregional associations.[71]

In order to support the process of European economic integration, the United States was prepared to accept some degree of pan-European protectionism (notably in agriculture) if it promoted intra-European trade. But again there was a long-term logic at play: focusing on export-led growth would allow European states to improve their overall balance of payments with the United States.[72]

This process was less successful in Asia, but the United States sponsored Japan's entry into the "Western club" of advanced industrial democracies through the G-7. While there was no Asian equivalent of the European Common Market, the United States did use its influence to push for a more open trading system in Asia.[73]

Finally, states that were part of the American system were expected to support US predominance in international organizations, particularly in Washington's ability to set global and regional agendas. By having a bloc of supporters, this would also help to cloak the exercise of US power, for "when people around the world believe that US primacy advances broader global interests, Washington finds it easier to rally international support for its policies, leaving its opposition isolated and ineffective."[74] As a result, "the American system of alliances across the Atlantic and the Pacific provided the political framework within which American political and economic influence expanded around the globe until the expansionism was brought to an end at least temporarily in the jungles of Vietnam."[75]

But the American system had also brought clear benefits to its members. The US focus on promoting export-led growth in other countries—and backstopping the Bretton Woods institutions, which provided the necessary safety nets for the international economic system—helped to facilitate a sixfold expansion in world trade from 1948 to 1973.[76] Continual reductions in tariffs alone helped spur very high rates of world trade growth during the 1950s and 1960s—around 8 percent a year on average.[77] Even after the shocks of the 1970s and the aftermath of the collapse of the Soviet Union, the system endured. Today it is difficult to argue with the results of the American way of peace. The Peterson Institute has estimated that the efforts to promote a stable and open economic order by promoting international trade added $1 trillion annually to US GDP.[78] Other studies calculate that the United States enjoyed a 12 percent increase in its national income due to its openness to international trade.[79] At the same time, however, America's partners also benefited. The United States was a "wealth-generating and voluntary" hegemonic power whose partners benefited as much from these arrangements as the United States and had real incentives both to align with the United States and to voluntarily reform their own political and economic institutions along liberal lines to qualify for membership.[80]

Building Blocks of the American Way of Peace

Despite smaller conflicts that erupted on the periphery, the world from 1945 onward did not experience another Great Depression or another world war, and the industrial countries of the world achieved an unprecedented level of integration.[81] Moreover, the institutions created in the aftermath of the Second World War "had the flexibility to evolve with economic circumstances and take on new roles in the maintenance of international cooperation."[82] The postwar American experience benefited from a stable international security environment but was also nurtured by the American way of peace, which relied on public-private partnerships, economics of security, and the provision of international public goods.

Many discussions of postwar American efforts have focused primarily on the role of the US government, and it is very true that the initial heavy lifting, especially in terms of aid, was done by the Treasury and that the "grants of the late 1940s represented political decisions on the part of Washington"[83] But the American private sector followed because, unlike what had happened after World War I when many private investors lost as a result of economic collapse in Europe, there were now government guarantees in place—both economic and military—that offered a greater sense of security for new investments.[84] A concerted effort was made to replicate domestic guarantees at the international level through initiatives such as the Overseas Private Investment Corporation (OPIC), created in 1969 to offer political risk insurance to American companies for their investment efforts around the world (initially in some eighty countries; OPIC now operates in nearly one hundred fifty). Tools such as OPIC were meant to reaffirm "United States policy to encourage productive private United States investment in developing countries" in order to "harness private sector funds and energies to realize public policy goals." [85] As Sen. Jacob Javits noted, OPIC was a way to "apply business methods and business accounting procedures to the business operations of project development, investment, insurance, guarantees and direct lending—that is, to private activities which are sensitively and directly geared into the development of the less developed areas which we propose to help in the foreign aid program."[86]

The US government could never have succeeded in rebuilding the economies of Western Europe and East Asia or in spurring development in other parts of the world on its own resources. It could, however, create conditions for this to occur. One of the more lasting impacts was the US influence in getting partner countries to modify their legal and business frameworks to be more accommodating to American concerns. In turn, this helped to facilitate foreign direct investment on the part of American firms, which often served to transfer technology and advanced industrial methods to US partner countries, enabling them to more rapidly develop their own domestic economies.[87] As countries received US aid, they often turned to American firms for goods and services. In the immediate postwar years, "private business enterprises such as capital equipment suppliers, consultancies and final goods suppliers also played an important and growing role" in rebuilding economies shattered by the Second World War.[88] US businesses found a number of ways to profit from the American way of peace, from selling licenses for using US patents and processes, to providing needed goods and inputs, to branching into new markets by partnering with local suppliers and distributors.[89] A further benefit to US firms was that in a number of places, the transfer of technology and know-how lowered the costs of inputs (from raw materials to parts) imported by American businesses, thus cutting their costs.[90]

The American way of peace rests on the assumptions that shared prosperity diminishes the likelihood of conflict within the group and reinforces shared security ties. The postwar experience conclusively demonstrated that free trade drew America closer to its military allies, who then became its chief trading partners.[91] It reinforced the proposition that states that rely on each other for security are also likely to benefit from economic trade.[92] As Dan Drezner has concluded, "the greater economic growth and dynamism produced by the free exchange of goods and services, and capital across borders rewards all the actors in the system."[93] Of particular importance over the last seventy years in helping to cement US security ties with other countries has been the rise of middle classes who have directly benefited from trade between their nations and the United States—and who helped to ensure a continuation of pro-American policies.[94] The starkest example is evident in US-German trade and US-Japanese trade. Once existential enemies of the United States, both Germany and Japan are important security and economic partners. As relations are restored between the United States and Vietnam, it is conceivable that significant trade and security cooperation will progress over the coming decades, which will signal a clear restoration of normalcy in spite of the horrific losses and still extant bitterness on both sides that resulted from the Vietnam War.

Declaring war against the United States (and losing) is not always a magical recipe for economic development. This is particularly true if US government assistance has not created conditions where private capital is prepared to follow. This is most apparent in countries where civil war followed US intervention: The environment was simply too dangerous for companies to operate, and so it proved impossible to replicate the postwar Japanese and German economic miracles.

Additionally, attempts to create lasting, enduring security relationships have failed when there has been little development of trade and business relations to cement ties. One of the main examples of this in recent years has been the failure of grandiose proposals for US-Russian cooperation. For years congressional legislation prevented normal trading relations between the two countries, and as of 2013 bilateral trade lagged at under $40 billion. (In contrast, the value of

Russian-Chinese trade is more than double, at $83.5 billion, and both countries, in strengthening their strategic partnership, have pledged to increase that figure to $200 billion by the end of the decade.[95]) At the same time, even if a country has a strong balance of trade with Washington—but the benefits are kept in the hands of an oligarchic few—it may result in strengthening rather than diminishing anti-American feeling, as demonstrated in parts of the Middle East.[96] Finding ways to draw rising middle classes around the world into recognizing their stake in productive relations with the United States helps to advance the American security agenda by creating subnational constituents for the current international system.

John Ikenberry has noted that the American way of peace was grounded in a bargain whereby the United States "provides some array of public goods in exchange for cooperation of other states."[97] The US system was characterized by extended deterrence and regional trade linkages and was organized around a dense array of rules, institutions, and partnerships spread across global and regional security, economic, and political realms.[98] These have helped to provide international (or global) public goods, making progress to "achieve crucial goals such as financial stability, human security or the reduction of environmental pollution" and other such issues that cross borders and impact entire regions or the world as a whole.[99] US leadership has created an international system that permitted the maintenance of "open seas, open trade and open societies lightly defended."[100] This permitted the rise of globalization and the emergence of a more interdependent world economy. Other uses of US power have been to guarantee the free flow of energy, particularly from the Persian Gulf, to consumers around the world and to work with other states to hold back the proliferation of weapons of mass destruction.[101] Even states that might otherwise oppose the United States have grudgingly accepted the benefits that the American way of peace has generated, particularly in recent decades. For example, the current system benefits rivals such as India and China, which both rely on unrestricted commerce from the Persian Gulf.

American Way of Peace 2.0

The American way of peace began to falter in the late 1960s as the costs of maintaining the system began to tax a US economy struggling to pay the bills for the Vietnam War and the Great Society programs. Moreover, because of US efforts to rehabilitate the economies of Western Europe and Northeast Asia after 1945, America's overall share of the global economy had shrunk—and with it, some of the margins for supporting the postwar international system. With the United States now seeing its reserves collapse—and the value of the dollar overpriced relative to gold—President Richard Nixon issued Executive Order 11615 on August 15, 1971, ending the automatic convertibility of dollars into gold. An effort in December 1971 (the so-called Smithsonian Agreement to try and restore convertibility of the dollar to gold within fixed trading parameters) failed.

Ending the gold standard signaled the end of the original Bretton Woods system and led to a new era where currencies would be allowed to "float" on the foreign exchange markets rather than have a fixed, defined value vis-à-vis gold or a single reserve currency. US status would no longer be determined by its hard assets; rather, reputation emerged as the sine qua non of US power. In the midst of the Cold War and a very costly Vietnam War, this was risky. Many predicted that this would be the end of the postwar US-led international economic system. However, the system did not collapse because other countries were now sufficiently invested in it as stakeholders and did not want to risk their own security and prosperity. Keeping the value of the dollar stable in order to facilitate global trade and investment and to have a secure storehouse of value (and accurate way to price goods) was in the interest of all participants in the global economy. Moreover, retaining the US ability to be the main provider of global public goods, starting with security, meant that other states—especially Germany and Japan—had an incentive to backstop the American system. In essence, "the international role of the dollar has been maintained primarily through the informal co-operation of the American, German and Japanese central banks . . . largely out of fear of what would happen to the international economic and political system if the monetary system were to break down."[102]

Nitze's vision of an effective organization of US and allied capabilities in order to achieve preponderant power in the international system came to fruition by the 1980s. Despite impressive Soviet gains on paper, the Free World outclassed the USSR and its bloc and exposed its weaknesses. The stress of attempting to maintain the Soviet system led to its collapse—while the US-led community of states demonstrated its strengths and flexibility. As the USSR itself began to implode, proposals would be advanced to finish the postwar task of peace-building by providing a new Marshall Plan to rebuild the economies of the ex–Soviet bloc states (including Russia itself), to have them join NATO, and to restore the Rooseveltian vision of international order.[103] Similar optimistic appraisals were offered for the Middle East after the success of the Gulf War in 1991 in the hope that new Arab-Israeli talks could produce a lasting peace settlement. There was also a sense that both Latin America and Africa would be positioned to advance as Cold War–era conflicts and civil wars there were settled.

There was also the reality that while the American way of peace had been "most successful in Western Europe and East Asia," Washington had "had more mixed results in other parts of the world," particularly in the Middle East.[104] The challenge of the 1990s—and beyond—would be to expand the zones of peace and prosperity in Western Europe and East Asia to the rest of the world—and in so doing, preserve America's position of leadership and primacy.

One of the things that was most striking was how postwar institutions, starting with NATO, endured after the collapse of the USSR ended the apparent raison d'être of the Americanized international system. Even after the Soviet threat evaporated, countries that were part of US-led alliances did not want them to dissolve, on the grounds that a continued American presence overseas, even if not always welcomed by every nation, was still a sine qua non for providing systemic stability for Europe and East Asia.[105] In particular, no country wanted to see an American withdrawal create vacuums of power that could only be remedied by expensive and destabilizing regional arms races. US security guarantees—backed up by American military capabilities—were seen as indispensable to keeping the peace and to keeping an increasingly globalized world functioning. Since there was no other system or state willing or able to provide the same degree of international public goods, the United States became the default provider.

Moreover, given the astonishing success of those Western European and East Asian states that had been part of the American system during the Cold War, a whole host of new applicants—former Soviet bloc states, newly democratizing Latin American and African countries, and nations across the Greater Middle East—wanted "in." This dovetailed with an immediate post–Cold War focus on expanding the number of market democracies (which would then become part and parcel of the American system) through a strategy of expanding and deepening existing institutions such as NATO.[106] One singular success was the institutionalization of GATT into the WTO via the agreement concluded at Marrakech, Morocco, in April 1994. NATO undertook a limited expansion to bring in Central and Eastern European states and launched a series of programs and dialogues designed to connect more far-flung parts of the world with the Atlantic alliance, starting with the Partnership for Peace.

But it soon became clear that the American system could not operate under the same terms as before. There were concerns that existing regionally based institutions might lose their "coherence in the long run" if they became more global in scope and that "the agenda of continuous expansion" might "culminate in fatigue from over-stretching"—a concern most often voiced when ambitious plans to expand the EU and NATO to encompass a wider neighborhood (Eurasia and parts of the Middle East and North Africa) were discussed.[107] The WTO, launched with such fanfare in 1995, did succeed in institutionalizing existing rules governing international trade, but the latest round of multilateral talks designed to further lower trade barriers and increase flows of global trade—the Doha Round, launched in 2001—has stalled for over a decade without results. Plans for a globe-spanning version of NATO or a League of Democracies—which would tie together such countries as Britain, Germany, Poland, and

France with Japan, India, Australia, South Korea, Colombia, and Chile into a single security and economic community—have never left the drawing board.

The main reason was that the United States no longer possessed the resource margins it did in 1945 when it was responsible for more than half the world's GDP and could afford to "overpay" to maintain institutions such as the UN and NATO. (Michael Mandelbaum has noted a shift in US policy language as a result: The United States no longer commits to create or build institutions but instead falls back on more indeterminate language—to "foster" and "encourage" and "promote.")[108] The United States attempted to compensate for this by convening coalitions whereby other partners would contribute a larger share of the costs, recognizing that it alone could not carry out new peace missions. Increasingly the United States looks to others to take on more of the burdens. The headline of April 1, 2011, "Defense Secretary Robert Gates: Other Nations Should Take Lead on Libya," is but one example of Washington policymakers searching for other states to take the lead.[109] It reflects a growing attitude that America's allies and partners can now "assume responsibility for their own security including its costs."[110] Usually this is accompanied by the hope that others—the UN as a whole, the EU, or other international organizations—will take over the tasks of building and sustaining regional and global security architectures, with the United States playing only a supporting role, satirized as "leading from behind." Richard Haass, president of the Council on Foreign Relations, advises US policymakers to "resist wars of choice" and to "cut back" on trying to transform other societies. Moreover, he encourages greater efforts to "*integrate* other countries [emphasis added] into concerted efforts to strengthen weak states, rein in hostile ones, and build the international mechanisms needed to manage globalization's most pressing challenges."[111]

As Dov Zakheim, former comptroller for the Department of Defense, observes that "the United States can certainly make a major contribution toward helping a state get back on its feet if it acts in concert with other states, and if it lets others take the lead in the nation-building effort."[112] In Afghanistan the United States contributed the bulk of the military forces, but while it was the largest single donor for Afghan reconstruction, US contributions only accounted for some 40 percent of the pledged total—and more important, if other nations who have promised aid do not deliver the full amounts, Washington is in no position to make up the difference.[113] There are both valid fiscal and strategic reasons, but the uneasy relationship with the government in Kabul and high levels of corruption stunt any major assistance effort.

Thus the United States is in no position to bankroll new Marshall Plans or Bretton Woods or Dumbarton Oaks–style arrangements.[114] In keeping with President Bill Clinton's mantra that the "era of big government is over," the American way of peace shifted gears from a focus on massive multilateral programs in favor of a more piecemeal and bilateral approach.[115] The challenge has been to find more cost-effective ways to deliver the main components of the American way of peace. In particular, the United States now has an interest in nurturing self-reliant partners who would be able to take responsibility for their own security and for sustaining some portion of the American way of peace—without taking up US resources.[116]

Trade and Assistance

Two ways in which the United States has sought to pursue this approach have been to use bilateral free-trade agreements using the lure of complete access to the American market and to proffer security assistance.[117] Both tools have been used to get other countries to modify domestic institutions and realign foreign policies to meet US strategic objectives. This was done even if the end result did not quite meet what Western European states and Japan received from the United States during the 1950s—especially a security commitment.[118] Such efforts, however, have had some success in creating a more informal pool of partners for Washington.[119] Indeed, what was striking about the coalition that the United States assembled for operations in Afghanistan and Iraq was the extent to which America relied not upon its formal alliances and institutions for support, but on bilateral appeals backed up by promises of US aid or assistance.[120] These looser security and economic arrangements, it is hoped, can still provide "mechanisms and venues to build political relations, conduct business, and regulate conflict."[121]

The United States in the last two decades has embraced an approach that sees trade policy as the pursuit of diplomacy by other means.[122] When he was US trade representative, Robert Zoellick was quite clear in signaling that the United States would prioritize the pursuit of preferential trade agreements, including concluding free-trade agreements, with those countries that supported US foreign and security policies.[123] Indeed, pieces of legislation such as the Africa Growth and Opportunity Act, passed in 2000, contain provisions that countries are eligible to take advantage of US largesse as long as they do "not engage in activities that undermine US national security or foreign policy interests." Recent trade agreements have also included provisions that address US concerns about labor rights, environmental issues, and protection of intellectual property, which are designed to bring legislation in other countries into closer conformity with US standards.

The first iteration of the American way of peace consciously cultivated "semi-sovereign" states (certainly in the cases of postwar Japan and Germany), with others prepared to turn over a good part of managing the global security agenda to Washington.[124] Further, as previously noted, this includes a willingness on the part of Washington to "overpay" to retain preeminence, but the world of the early twenty-first century presents different challenges. For one, with a few exceptions (for instance, small ex-Soviet republics and some Asian countries with unresolved border issues), most countries in the world today do not face a single overarching security threat from a single major power. Instead their security is threatened by a host of problems, ranging from transnational terrorism to dislocations caused by climate change. In turn, the United States faces no one peer competitor, but US national security can be negatively impacted by a multitude of small threats that, taken together, would overwhelm its capacity to respond—especially the threats emanating not from strong states but from weak ones that cannot control what happens on their territories.[125] As a result, there has been a broadening of what constitutes national security "to include a wider range of threats, ranging from economic and environmental issues to human rights and migration."[126] With an expansive view of security, there is a focus on building up state capacity around the world to deal with problems before they metastasize into major threats to the United States or to the global system. This focus is based in part on the realization that America does not have the wherewithal to fix every last problem, but it is also grounded in the sober realization that one cannot safely ignore any problem area in the world without running the risk that this will be the genesis of the next catastrophic attack on America or American interests.[127] This is why US officials now routinely note that "the increased interconnectedness associated with global economic advances, while bringing prosperity to more countries and regions, has also meant that the security of the United States can be affected by events in more places, more countries, and more regions. This has led to an increased demand to expand our partnerships and deepen our security relationships."[128] At the same time, the United States has to find ways to be more frugal with its disbursement of resources—and so shifting from alliance commitments to security cooperation is seen as a way to preserve a US coordinating role (and an initial or core investment) but with others prepared to take on more of the day-to-day burdens.[129]

As with the proffer of a trade pact, a US security assistance package may be quite attractive to other countries, as it may include an entire menu of options, including training and combined exercises, operational meetings, contacts and exchanges, security assistance, medical and engineering team engagements, cooperative development, acquisition and technical interchanges, and scientific and technology collaboration. It may also carry with it the opportunity to purchase (or to receive) advanced US military technology.[130] In return it offers a way to get other countries to amend or alter both foreign and domestic policies—and for those nations to focus on US security priorities (such as combating the proliferation of weapons of mass destruction and engaging in regional peacekeeping or antipiracy patrols in areas where the United States is unable or unwilling to operate) or to offer tangible support to American needs (such as providing basing rights).[131] The United States has dozens of formal allies—countries that are bound to Washington by concrete security guarantees—but has expanded its list of partners via security cooperation to encompass almost every country around the world. US-provided military training and defense equipment help governments control their airspace, monitor their maritime zones, and reduce the impact of subnational and transnational threats. While a gang like MS-13 can be addressed by the Los Angeles Police Department as a criminal matter, the government of El Salvador treats the same organization as a national security threat requiring external assistance from the US military. While the Federal Aviation Administration can monitor US airspace and the Air National Guard can interdict suspicious flights, Colombia cannot do the same without US equipment and expertise.

Through building partnership capacity, US partners gain obvious benefits through security assistance. These include access to the US defense base, opportunities to attend US professional military education institutions, and the ability to serve in US-led military commands. The United States does assume some risk by maintaining a nonexclusive list of partners. Yet the benefits are not one-sided. Partners provide access to forward bases as logistical hubs, the basis for future military coalitions, and even billions in host-nation support. The latter may increase in importance as the defense budget declines and forces draw down from Europe, the Middle East, and Asia.

Building up partner capacity also makes sense as domestic political support for robust American engagement in the world falters. Ever since the end of the Cold War, there has been a decline in public support for the United States paying the majority of the cost in providing international public goods, a trend accelerated during the wars in Iraq and Afghanistan. Polling data released in summer 2013 revealed that more than half of the American public "feels little responsibility and inclination to deal with international problems that are not seen as direct threats to the national interest," and some 83 percent want the government to focus on domestic issues rather than foreign policy.[132]

The United States shows no signs of retreating altogether from a global leadership role but seeks partnerships as a key component of its strategy. In the era of declining defense budgets, enabling partners through security force assistance is a sure way to retain influence and limit US deployments. With shared challenges of terrorism and nuclear proliferation, and shared goals of development and protecting human security, there are unprecedented levels of international cooperation to share information, target terrorists, and provide governments the tools they need to confront national threats before they become regional ones. This was on display in Afghanistan where fifty countries operated under the International Security Assistance Force flag and in the Indian Ocean where twenty-nine countries operated as Combined Maritime Forces. At the center of the coalitions is a US-sponsored framework to enable partners to contribute to international security. This is both cost-effective and consistent with US values. Moreover, this approach is not necessarily expensive and can reduce the burden on American taxpayers. By training and equipping other militaries, the goal is to reduce US military presence internationally and allow others to provide for their own security. This has positive benefits both for the US defense budget (e.g., an Afghan soldier is paid hundreds of dollars per month compared to an American soldier who is paid thousands) and, if European and Asian navies can patrol strategic waterways, for international security.

If the US focus in the intermediate aftermath of World War II was on Western Europe (and to some extent East Asia), the American way of peace version 2.0 has concentrated on identifying and cultivating partners in other geographic regions of the world. During the first decade of the 2000s, for instance, the United States concentrated on concluding free-trade agreements with countries in parts of the world where it wanted to also be able to better project power (Australia, New Zealand, Singapore, Chile, Oman, Bahrain, and Peru) as well as with countries where it wished to deepen its engagement (Colombia, South Korea, and Panama). There was a particular effort to try to move forward with new agreements with "friendly Middle Eastern countries in order to solidify bilateral relationships and extend U.S. economic, security and political influence in the region."[133]

Conclusion: The Future of the American System

The piecemeal approach of the American way of peace 2.0 has been criticized by some who feel that the approach of the last few years has produced an impressive list of US partners on paper but who in practice are unable to provide serious capabilities nor are in any position to help sustain the global system. They hope that if the US economy recovers by the end of the decade, America could again undertake the heavy lifting needed to renovate existing alliances and create new ones. In particular, there is a good deal of optimism that the United States could restore its position as the center of a global system by creating two new multilateral partnerships—the trans-Pacific Partnership and the Transatlantic Trade and Investment Partnership—in which the United States would act as the dynamo and hub.[134]

Others, however, question the value of the postwar American way of peace for the future security and prosperity of the United States. Some argue that the American system, in recent years, has acted as a drag on America's ability to take vigorous steps in its own defense by giving other countries too much influence on Washington's decision making. A related argument is that the United States has been financing international public goods that primarily benefit other states and no longer directly impact US interests. A troubling trend for Washington to consider is that American expenditures in support of NATO have increased since the end of the Cold War and the disappearance of the Soviet threat. Washington now foots the bill for nearly 75 percent of the alliance's costs—up from 63 percent in 2001.[135] Considering allies' limited efforts to share burdens, former secretary of defense Robert Gates wrote, "NATO is not a 'paper member-ship' or a 'social club' or a 'talk shop.' It is a *military* alliance—one with very serious real world obligations."[136] At the same time, however, American overpay-ment for NATO does not lead European countries to compensate the United States in political or commercial affairs.[137] Russia's 2014 provocations should compel European governments to spend more on defense, but Europeans will likely find accommodation given the important role Russian capital plays in Western Europe.

One of the principal manifestations of this debate is whether the United States should continue to provide the security for the free flow of energy around the world as America moves closer toward being able to supply its needs from domestic and hemispheric sources. Other countries—especially the rising China and India—ought to be able to invest in the capabilities needed to continue to sustain and manage the global commons. However, this also raises the risk of declining US influence as other countries acquire greater power in the inter-national order.

To compensate, NATO secretary-general Anders Fogh Rasmussen was one of the proponents of a "smart defense" concept that would shift the empha-sis away from "spending more" in favor of "spending better"—drawing on the American way of peace 2.0 to pursue "multinational approaches, making the transatlantic compact more strategically oriented, and working with emerging powers to manage the effects of the globalization of security."[138] No other coun-try wishes to take on the burdens of global management—yet almost all are loath to let the American system break down. This suggests, as Ikenberry con-cluded, that the "United States itself, while remaining at the center of the order, also continues to experience gains and losses" but that the benefits that have accrued to most states serve "to mitigate the interest that particular states might have in replacing it."[139] For the foreseeable future, propping up the American system—and the US ability to continue to manage it—will remain the domi-nant feature of global politics.

Notes

1. See, for instance, the discussion in Henry Kissinger, *A World Restored: The Politics of Conservatism in a Revolutionary Age* (New York: Universal Library, 1964), esp. 138–39, 144–47.

2. George Washington, "Farewell Address" (1796), Avalon Project, http://avalon.law.yale.edu/18th_century/washing.asp.

3. Charles A. Kupchan, *How Enemies Become Friends: The Sources of Stable Peace* (Princeton, NJ: Princeton University Press, 2010), 2.

4. Abraham Lincoln, "Second Inaugural Address," March 5, 1865, Avalon Project, http://avalon.law.yale.edu/19th_century/lincoln2.asp.

5. Woodrow Wilson, "State of the Union," March 5, 1917, Avalon Project, http://avalon.law.yale.edu/20th_century/wilson2.asp.

6. James Jay Carafano and Dana R. Dillon, "Winning the Peace: Principles for Post-Conflict Operations," *Backgrounder* (Heritage Foundation), no. 1859 (June 13, 2005): 3.

7. Harry S. Truman, "Address in San Francisco at the Closing Session of the United Nations Conference," June 26, 1945, archived online by Gerhard Peters and John T. Woolley, American Presidency Project, www.presidency.ucsb.edu/ws/?pid=12188.

8. Kathryn M. E. Dominguez, "The Role of International Organizations in the Bretton Woods System," in *A Retrospective on the Bretton Woods System: Lessons for International Monetary Reform*, ed. Michael D. Bordo and Barry Eichengreen (Chicago: University of Chicago Press, 1993), 357.

9. Charles S. Maier, "The Two Postwar Eras and the Conditions for Stability in Twentieth-Century Europe," *American Historical Review* 86, no. 2 (April 1981): 341.

10. Comments of Zechariah Chafee, as quoted by Clarence Berdahl, "The Leadership of the United States in the Postwar World," *American Political Science Review* 38, no. 2 (April 1944): 237.

11. G. John Ikenberry, "Power and Liberal Order: America's Postwar World Order in Transition," *International Relations of the Asia Pacific* 5 (2005): 134.

12. Maier, "Two Postwar Eras," 341.

13. Berdahl, "Leadership of the United States," 240, 245.

14. Per the phrasing of Michael Vlahos, as quoted in Nikolas K. Gvosdev, "Picking on Both Sides of the Aisle," *National Interest*, August 10, 2010, http://nationalinterest.org/commentary/picking-sides-aisle-3883.

15. Ikenberry, "Power and Liberal Order," 134.

16. Colin Dueck, "Hegemony on the Cheap: Liberal Internationalism from Wilson to Bush," *World Policy Journal* 20, no. 4 (Winter 2003–4): 6.

17. Ikenberry, "Power and Liberal Order," 140–41. On the idea of the United States as "self-binding" to follow rules and norms, see Lisa Martin, *Multilateral Organizations after the US-Iraq War of 2003*, report of the Weatherhead Center for International Affairs (Harvard University), August 2004.

18. Edward R. Stettinius Jr., "A Charter Convention, Not a Peace Conference," speech delivered to the Council on Foreign Relations, April 6, 1945, in *Vital Speeches of the Day* 11, no. 13 (April 1945), 389.

19. Joseph E. Persico, *Roosevelt's Centurions: FDR and the Commanders He Led to Victory in World War II* (New York: Random House, 2013), 533.

20. Tommy Franks et al., "The Meaning of Victory: A Conversation with General Franks," *National Interest*, November/December 2006, 86, http://nationalinterest.org/article/is-this-victory-1287.

21. See, for instance, the discussion by Paul Saunders and Nikolas K. Gvosdev, "Defining Victory," *National Interest* 81 (Fall 2005): 5–7.

22. For a more detailed exposition, see Robert Gilpin, "The Rise of American Hegemony," in *Two Hegemonies: Britain 1846–1914 and the United States*

1941–2001, ed. Patrick Karl O'Brien and Armand Clesse (Aldershot, UK: Ashgate, 2002), 165–82.

23. 89 Cong. Rec. at 9101.

24. N. D. White, *The United Nations and the Maintenance of International Peace and Security* (Manchester: Manchester University Press, 1990), 3.

25. Brett D. Schaefer, "U.S. Funding of the United Nations Reaches All-Time High," Heritage Foundation WebMemo #2981 on Foreign Aid and Development, August 13, 2010, www.heritage.org/research/reports/2010/08/us-funding-of-the-united-nations-reaches-all-time-high.

26. Derek S. Reveron and Kathleen Mahoney-Norris, *Global Security in a Borderless World* (New York: Westview, 2011).

27. Cordell Hull, *The Memoirs of Cordell Hull: Volume 1* (New York: Macmillan, 1948), 81.

28. Jeffrey A. Frankel, "Globalization of the Economy" (working paper 7858, National Bureau of Economic Research, Cambridge MA, August 2000), 5–6.

29. Michael Mandelbaum, "The Inadequacy of American Power," *Foreign Affairs* 81, no. 5 (September/October 2002), 68.

30. Maier, "Two Postwar Eras," 344.

31. Jan S. Prybyla, *The American Way of Peace: An Interpretation* (Columbia: University of Missouri Press, 2005), 17.

32. John Lewis Gaddis, *Surprise, Security, and the American Experience* (Cambridge, MA: Harvard University Press, 2004), 53.

33. Prybyla, *American Way of Peace*, 17; Gaddis, *Surprise*, 59.

34. For some of the background, see, for instance, Stephen Schlesinger, "Can the United Nations Reform?," *World Policy Journal* 14, no. 3 (Fall 1997): 47–52.

35. See, for instance, the comments of John S. Odell, in G. John Ikenberry, "The Political Origins of Bretton Woods," in Bordo and Eichengreen, *A Retrospective* (see note 8), 186.

36. Comments of Eric Johnston, president of the US Chamber of Commerce, in 1944, in W. H. White, *Report on the Russians* (New York: Harcourt, Brace, 1945), 23. See also Odell's comments in Ikenberry, "Political Origins of Bretton Woods," 186.

37. See, for instance, Michael Beschloss: *The Conquerors: Roosevelt, Truman and the Destruction of Hitler's Germany, 1941–1945* (New York: Simon & Schuster, 2002), esp. 1–188.

38. Maier, "Two Postwar Eras," 350–51.

39. Comments of Secretary of State James Byrnes in 1946, quoted in Beschloss, *Conquerors*, 277. Gen. Douglas MacArthur had expressed similar sentiments about redirecting Japanese efforts to develop "vertically" as part of a vision of an "emancipated Pacific basin" when he accepted the Japanese surrender aboard the USS *Missouri* on September 2, 1945.

40. Letter of December 13, 1948, to Undersecretary of State Robert Lovett, in *Foreign Relations of the United States: Volume II, 1948* (Washington, DC: Government Printing Office, 1948), 1339, 1340, http://digital.library.wisc.edu/1711.dl/FRUS.FRUS1948v02..

41. Gilpin, "Rise of American Hegemony," 167.

42. Prybyla, *American Way of Peace*, 39.

43. Gaddis, *Surprise*, 61; Dueck, "Hegemony," 4.

44. Gilpin, "Rise of American Hegemony," 168.

45. John Lewis Gaddis, *The United States and the Origins of the Cold War, 1941–1947* (New York: Columbia University Press, 1972), 317.

46. See, for instance, Steven Casey, "Selling NSC-68: The Truman Administration, Public Opinion, and the Politics of Mobilization, 1950-51," *Diplomatic History* 29, no. 4 (2005): 655–90.

47. Gilpin, "Rise of American Hegemony," 168.

48. Nikolas Gvosdev (also quoting Conrad Black), "Vesting Shareholders," *National Interest*, September 17, 2003, http://nationalinterest.org/article/vesting-shareholders-2430.

49. Stephen M. Walt, "Taming American Power," *Foreign Affairs* 84, no. 5 (September/October 2005): 110.

50. Quoted in Joseph Nye, *The Paradox of American Power* (London: Oxford University Press, 2002), 33.

51. See, for instance, Geir Lundestad, "Empire by Invitation? The United States and Western Europe, 1945–1952," *Journal of Peace Research* 23, no. 3 (1986): 263.

52. Gaddis, *Surprise*, 63.

53. For a firsthand account of Soviet methods, see Vladimir Dedijer, *Tito* (New York: Simon & Schuster, 1952), 268, 277–82. See also Dieter Heinzig, *The Soviet Union and Communist China, 1945–1950: The Arduous Road to the Alliance* (Armonk, NY: M. E. Sharpe, 2004), 69; Victor S. Mamatey, *Soviet Russian Imperialism* (New York: Van Nostrand Reinhold, 1964), 96–97; Karl Hardach, *The Political Economy of Germany in the Twentieth Century* (Berkeley: University of California Press, 1980), 111–14.

54. G. John Ikenberry, "Institutions, Strategic Restraint and the Persistence of American Postwar Order," *International Security* 23, no. 3 (Winter 1998–99): 45.

55. Mamatey, *Soviet Russian Imperialism*, 80–97.

56. See J. Bradford DeLong, "Post-WWII Western European Exceptionalism: The Economic Dimension," paper for the University of California / National Bureau of Economic Research, drafted September 1997 and revised December 1997, www.j-bradford-delong.net/Econ_Articles/ucla/ucla_marshall2.html.

57. Aaron Forsberg, *America and the Japanese Miracle: The Cold War Context of Japan's Postwar Economic Revival, 1950–1960* (Chapel Hill and London: University of North Carolina Press, 2000), 84–85.

58. DeLong, "Post-WWII."

59. Mancur Olson Jr. and Richard Zeekhauser, "An Economic Theory of Alliances," *Review of Economics and Statistics* 48, no. 3 (August 1966): 273, 276, 279.

60. Mandelbaum, "Inadequacy of American Power," 63.

61. "Memorandum by the Director of the Policy Planning Staff (Nitze) to the Deputy Under Secretary of State (Matthews)," Washington, July 14,

1952, G/PM files, lot 68 D 358, "'NSC 135,'" at Department of State, Office of the Historian, http://history.state.gov/historicaldocuments/frus1952-54v02 p1/d13.

62. Statement of Policy Drafted by the Director of the Policy Planning Staff (Nitze), "Reappraisal of United States Objectives and Strategy for National Security," Washington, July 30, 1952, PPS files, lot 64 D 563, "NSC 68 & 114," in *Foreign Relations of the United States, 1952–1954, Volume II, Part 1*, National Security Affairs, Document 14, https://history.state.gov/historicaldocuments/frus 1952-54v02p1/d14.

63. DeLong, "Post-WWII."

64. Jonathan Zeitlin, "Introduction: Americanization and Its Limits," in *Americanization and Its Limits: Reworking United States Technology and Management in Postwar Europe and Japan*, ed. Jonathan Zeitlin and Gary Herrigel (Oxford: Oxford University Press, 2000), 8.

65. Gilpin, "Rise of American Hegemony," 168; Zeitlin, "Introduction," 25.

66. Gilpin, "Rise of American Hegemony," 170.

67. Such requests were handled through the Coordinating Committee for Multilateral Export Controls. For more on US influence over the process, see United States Congress, Office of Technology Assessment, *Technology and East-West Trade* (Washington: Government Printing Office, 1979), 158–70.

68. For instance, on the Greek-Turkish dynamic and the NATO role in managing tension, see Fotios Moustakis, *The Greek-Turkish Relationship and NATO* (London: Frank Cass, 2003), esp. 51.

69. Ikenberry, "Power and Liberal Order," 138.

70. John R. Oneal, "The Theory of Collective Action and Burden Sharing in NATO," *International Organization* 44, no. 3 (Summer 1990): 401; Gilpin, "Rise of American Hegemony," 169.

71. Oneal, "Theory of Collective Action," 390.

72. DeLong, "Post-WWII."

73. See Charles C. Kolb, review of Aaron Forsberg's *America and the Japanese Miracle: The Cold War Context of Japan's Postwar Economic Revival, 1950–1960*, H-Net, November 2000, www.h-net.org/reviews/showrev.php?id=4716; Gilpin, "Rise of American Hegemony," 170.

74. Walt, "Taming American Power," 116.

75. Gilpin, "Rise of American Hegemony," 171.

76. Prybyla, *American Way of Peace*, 20, 26.

77. World Trade Organization, "The GATT Years: From Havana to Marrakesh," at www.wto.org/english/thewto_e/whatis_e/tif_e/fact4_e.htm.

78. Scott Bradford, Paul Grieco, and Gary C. Hufbauer, "The Payoff to America from Global Integration," in *The United States and the World Economy: Foreign Economic Policy for the Next Decade*, ed. C. Fred Bergsten (Washington, DC: Peterson Institute for International Economics, 2005).

79. Frankel, "Globalization of the Economy," 27.

80. See, for instance, William Odom and Robert Dujarric, *America's Inadvertent Empire* (New Haven, CT: Yale University Press, 2004).

81. Comment of Alberto Alesina, in Dominguez, "Role of International Organizations," 401.

82. Dominguez, "Role of International Organizations," 391.

83. Maier, "Two Postwar Eras," 341.

84. DeLong, "Post-WWII."

85. Steven Franklin and Gerald T. West, "The Overseas Private Investment Corporation Amendments Act of 1978: A Reaffirmation of the Developmental Role of Investment Insurance," *Texas International Law Journal* 14, no. 1 (1979), 2.

86. Remarks on the floor of the Senate, December 12, 1969, as recorded in the *Congressional Record*, vol. 115, part 29, 91st Cong., 1st Sess. (December 12, 1969 to December 18, 1969), 38697.

87. For a discussion of this process in the abstract, see Edwin Mansfield, *Intellectual Property Protection, Foreign Direct Investment, and Technology Transfer*, International Finance Corporation Discussion Paper no. 19 (Washington, DC: World Bank, 1994), 1. See also Edwin Mansfield and Anthony Romeo, "Technology Transfer to Overseas Subsidiaries by U.S.-Based Firms," *Quarterly Journal of Economics*, 95, no. 4 (December 1980): 743.

88. Zeitlin, "Introduction," 25.

89. Ibid., 25–26.

90. Mansfield and Romeo, "Technology Transfer," 744.

91. Mandelbaum, "Inadequacy of American Power," 70.

92. James Morrow, "Alliances and Asymmetry: An Alternative to the Capability Aggregation Model of Alliances," *American Journal of Political Science* 35, no. 4 (November 1991): 904–33.

93. Daniel W. Drezner, "Military Primacy Doesn't Pay (Nearly as Much as You Think)," *International Security* 38, no. 1 (Summer 2013): 68.

94. The Federal Republic of Germany and the Republic of Korea both provide excellent examples of countries where, despite significant electoral shifts between right- and left-leaning governments, close business and security ties with the United States have remained unchanged.

95. Nikolas K. Gvosdev and Christopher Marsh, *Russian Foreign Policy: Interests, Vectors and Sectors* (Thousand Oaks, CA: CQ Press, 2013), 139.

96. Ray Takeyh and Nikolas K. Gvosdev, "Democratic Impulses versus Imperial Interests: America's New Mid-East Conundrum," *Orbis* 47, no. 5 (Summer 2003): 422.

97. G. John Ikenberry, *Liberal Leviathan: The Origins, Crisis, and Transformation of the American World Order* (Princeton, NJ: Princeton University Press, 2011), 72

98. Ikenberry, "Power and Liberal Order," 134.

99. Inge Kaul, Isabelle Grunberg, and Marc A. Stern, "Introduction," in *Global Public Goods: International Cooperation in the 21st Century*, ed. Inge Kaul, Isabelle Grunberg, and Marc A. Stern (New York: Oxford University Press, 1999), xii.

100. Observations of Charles Krauthammer, quoted in Nikolas K. Gvosdev, "Battle for the High Seas," *National Interest*, October 12, 2012, http://national interest.org/commentary/battle-the-high-seas-7559.

101. Mandelbaum, "Inadequacy of American Power," 65.

102. Gilpin, "Rise of American Hegemony," 178.

103. See, for instance, Coral Bell, "Why Russia Should Join NATO: From Containment to Concert," *National Interest* 22 (Winter 1990–91): 37–47.

104. Carafano and Dillon, "Winning the Peace," 3.

105. Mandelbaum, "Inadequacy of American Power," 63–64.

106. Dueck, "Hegemony," 6.

107. Alok Rashmi Mukhopadhyay, "NATO at 60: A Reality Check," Institute for Defence Analyses and Studies, April 2, 2009, www.idsa.in/specialfeature/NATOat60arealitycheck_armukhopadhyay_020409.

108. Michael Mandelbaum, "Inadequacy of American Power," 73.

109. Cf. Donna Cassatta and Lolita C. Baldor, "Defense Secretary Robert Gates: Other Nations Should Take Lead On Libya," Associated Press, April 1, 2011, as archived by the Huffington Post, www.huffingtonpost.com/2011/04/01/defense-secretary-robert-gates-opposed-arming-rebels_n_843428.html.

110. The argument as presented by Michael Mandelbaum, *The Ideas That Conquered the World: Peace, Democracy and Free Markets in the 21st Century* (New York: PublicAffairs, 2002), 153.

111. Richard Haass, *Foreign Policy Begins at Home: The Case for Putting America's House in Order* (New York: Basic Books, 2013), 162.

112. Dov Zakheim, "Confessions of a Vulcan," *Foreign Policy*, May 13, 2011, www.foreignpolicy.com/articles/2011/05/13/confessions_of_a_vulcan/.

113. See, for instance, Lydia Poole, *Afghanistan: Tracking Major Resource Flows, 2002–2010*, briefing paper, January 2011, Global Humanitarian Assistance, http://www.globalhumanitarianassistance.org/wp-content/uploads/2011/02/gha-Afghanistan-2011-major-resource-flows.pdf.

114. "US Can't Afford 'Marshall Plan' for Arab Spring Transitions, Says Clinton," *Democracy Digest*, August 17, 2001, www.demdigest.net/blog/2011/08/us-cant-afford-marshall-plan-for-arab-spring-transitions-says-clinton/#sthash.BnNloe44.dpuf.

115. David Auerswald and Caroline Shaver, *It's Not Just the Economy, Stupid: Linking Free Trade and the War on Terror*, Georgetown University Institute for the Study of Diplomacy case 293 (2007), 14; Uri Dadush, "The Accidental Trade Policy," *Politica Exterior*, May 9, 2013.

116. Derek Reveron, "Defense Reduction through Security Force Assistance," *New Atlanticist*, February 8, 2013, www.acus.org/new_atlanticist/defense-reduction-through-security-force-assistance.

117. William Cooper, *Free Trade Agreements*, report RL31346 (Washington, DC: Congressional Research Service, 2005), 3. For instance, for the United States, the main driver for the creation of a North American Free Trade Agreement (NAFTA) was not primarily economic; the United States already possessed the

benefits of a continent-wide market within its own borders. Given the relative size of the US economy, Canada and Mexico would benefit more. Indeed, as one American negotiator told his Canadian and Mexican interlocutors, one was not dealing in reciprocity when, in exchange for "access to our $7 trillion market," the other two countries were offering "access to your $250 billion and $500 billion markets." Maxwell A. Cameron and Brian W. Tomlin, *The Making of NAFTA: How the Deal Was Done* (Ithaca, NY: Cornell University Press, 2000), 15.

118. The Republic of Georgia learned this to its detriment in 2008 when it clashed with Russia over the separatist territories of Ossetia and Abkhazia and discovered that being a "strategic partner" of the United States did not carry with it an ironclad guarantee of US protection. Nevertheless, President Mikheil Saakashvili justified continued Georgian involvement in the wars in Afghanistan and Iraq as a way to receive US security and economic aid and that Georgia would be more protected as a result. See Doug Bandow, "Poking the Bear," *National Interest*, January 15, 2010, http://nationalinterest.org/article/poking-the-bear-3354?page=show.

119. For example, even though the draft agreement never explicitly dealt with security matters, NAFTA was "nevertheless replete with implications for regional security cooperation. In one sense, it could serve as a catalyst for closer coordination on a broad array of common concerns, particularly with regard to transnational security matters." Michael Dziedzic, "NAFTA and North American Security," *National Defense University Strategic Forum* 18 (January 1995), 2.

120. Sometimes sarcastically referred to as being members of "coalitions of the billing," a number of the countries that have joined US efforts have done so because of targeted economic or security aid. For a critical overview, see Laura McClure, "Coalition of the Billing—or Unwilling," *Salon*, March 12, 2003, www.salon.com/2003/03/12/foreign_aid/.

121. Ikenberry, "Institutions, Strategic Restraint," 69. The quote refers to the overall thrust of the American system

122. Dadush, "Accidental Trade Policy."

123. Auerswald and Shaver, *It's Not Just the Economy*, 3.

124. Ikenberry, "Institutions, Strategic Restraint," 69.

125. Stephen D. Krasner and Carlos Pascual, "Addressing State Failure," *Foreign Affairs* 84, no. 4 (July/August 2005): 153–63.

126. Keith Krause and Michael C. Williams, "Broadening the Agenda of Security Studies: Politics and Methods," *Mershon International Studies Review* 40, no. 2 (October 1996): 230.

127. Krasner and Pascual, "Addressing State Failure," 153.

128. Andrew J. Shapiro, "A New Era for U.S. Security Assistance," *Washington Quarterly* 35, no. 4 (Fall 2012): 23. At the time of writing, Shapiro was the assistant secretary of state for political-military affairs.

129. Reveron, "Defense Reduction."

130. Jennifer D. P. Moroney, Joe Hogler, Lianne Kennedy-Boudali, and Stephanie Pezard, *Integrating the Full Range of Security Cooperation Programs into Air Force Planning: An Analytic Primer* (Santa Monica, CA: RAND Corp., 2011), 2, also 105, 106.

131. Shapiro, "New Era," 28; see Moroney et al., *Integrating the Full Range*, 2, 3.

132. See section 7, "Values about Foreign Policy and Terrorism," of the Pew Research Center for the People and the Press research report *Partisan Polarization Surges in Bush, Obama Years: Trends in American Values: 1987-2012*, issued June 4, 2012, www.people-press.org/2012/06/04/section-7-values-about-foreign-policy-and-terrorism/. The conclusions are reinforced in later research; see Bruce Stokes, "Americans' Foreign Policy Priorities for 2014," *FactTank*, Pew Research Center, December 31, 2013, www.pewresearch.org/fact-tank/2013/12/31/americans-foreign-policy-priorities-for-2014/.

133. Auerswald and Shaver, *It's Not Just the Economy*, 14–15.

134. Dadush, "Accidental Trade Policy."

135. Steven Erlanger, "Shrinking Europe Military Spending Stirs Concern," *New York Times*, April 23, 2013, A3.

136. Robert M. Gates, *Duty: Memoirs of a Secretary at War* (New York: Knopf, 2014), 157.

137. Malcolm Chalmers, "The Atlantic Burden-Sharing Debate: Widening or Fragmenting?," *International Affairs* 77, no. 3 (2001): 573.

138. Anders Fogh Rasmussen, "NATO after Libya: The Atlantic Alliance in Austere Times," *Foreign Affairs* 90, no. 4 (July/August 2011): 4.

139. Ikenberry, "Institutions, Strategic Restraint," 78.

7

Financing the American Way

We shall need prosperous markets in the world to insure our own prosperity, and we shall need the goods the world can sell us.

—President Franklin D. Roosevelt, 1945

In his seminal work *The Rise and Fall of the Great Powers*, Paul Kennedy identified the economic drain caused by "imperial overstretch" as the main reason a great power declines over time. Unable to pay the costs of its preferred international order, the leading nation is forced to give way to its challengers. As Kennedy noted in his introduction, "the triumph of any one Great Power . . . or the collapse of another, has usually been the consequence of lengthy fighting by its armed forces; but it has also been the consequences of the more or less efficient utilization of the state's productive economic resources in wartime, and, further in the background, of the way in which that state's economy had been rising or falling, relative to the other leading nations."[1]

Kennedy's 1987 book initiated a robust debate over whether the United States was in decline—and whether it could sustain its ways of war and peace in the future. Some were predicting that rising powers—first Germany and Japan, later India and China—would supplant a United States that would find itself exhausted from trying to maintain its international arrangements and commitments.[2] Writing fifteen years later, however, the *Economist* editorialized that the prospect for American decline "still looks far-fetched," and while "the burdens of America's world role are large and expanding," they were "not overwhelming." It added that the "resources produced by America's economy are vast" and could continue to sustain the American system.[3]

Nevertheless, Kennedy's thesis about overstretch is an important reminder that America's superpower status does not solely rest on military instruments alone. The country's macroeconomic performance is also critical "if the nation is to maintain a position of leadership in national security affairs worldwide"—

a point that gained renewed currency after the economic crisis of 2008–9.[4] To explain the important role the economy plays in national security, this chapter reviews the relationship between domestic programs and national security, the domestic benefits of foreign policy, and the dollar as global reserve currency. But first it is important to understand what leads to imperial overstretch.

The Road to Exhaustion

Traditionally most great powers have either extracted the surplus needed to sustain their international position from the domestic economy (e.g., Russia) or have drained their colonies or partners (e.g., Spain). Others attempted to maintain a particular regional or global balance of power that forced potential rivals to devote their time and attention to coping with each other, giving the principal power freedom to maneuver (e.g., Britain). Sooner or later, however, all of these aspiring hegemons reached a point of exhaustion where they were unable to sustain their position (for instance, France at the end of the Napoleonic period), or else the international system changed, making a strategy of balancing unfeasible (as occurred to imperial Germany after 1890).

America's Cold War rival—the Soviet Union—ultimately failed as a superpower because it could not finance the burdens of its status.[5] Despite massive investments in the defense sector and a number of technological "firsts" (including putting the world's first satellite into orbit), the USSR was never able to convert these accomplishments into the dynamos that could have unleashed the capacities of the civilian economy and led to sustained economic growth. Soviet aid was zero-sum; funds sent to support Soviet allies or clients came at the expense of domestic spending. Soviet partners were reluctant contributors to maintaining the cohesiveness of the Soviet bloc. Finally, the USSR could force its satellites to accept payments in nonconvertible rubles, but for its international transactions it had to rely on a finite amount of hard currency to finance its trade.

In all of these cases, the end results were identical every time: When treasuries ran dry, the tenure of a particular great power ended. In fact, this historic fact set the table for the United States to emerge as the leading power after World War II because most of its potential rivals were badly damaged by the war. With significant surpluses at its disposal, the United States funded the construction of its preferred postwar global architecture.[6] At the height of its economic dominance, this preferred order fulfilled President Franklin D. Roosevelt's vision of a prosperous global market.

The favorable alignment of exhausted rivals and US economic revival could not last forever. In the 1970s, the Bretton Woods accords collapsed, US currency was delinked from the gold standard, and inflation undermined domestic economic activity. Since then, the US share of global economic output has been

Table 7.1: World GDP in Comparison (by Percentage)

	1870	1913	1929	1950	1960	1970	1980	1990	2000	2008
China	17.10	8.83	7.05	4.59	5.24	4.63	5.20	7.83	11.77	17.48
Germany	6.50	8.68	6.74	4.97	6.62	6.12	5.52	4.66	4.24	3.36
India	12.15	7.47	6.23	4.16	3.88	3.41	3.18	4.05	5.18	6.70
Japan	2.29	2.62	3.29	3.02	4.45	7.36	7.83	8.55	7.16	5.70
United Kingdom	9.03	8.22	6.46	6.52	5.37	4.35	3.64	3.48	3.30	2.84
United States	8.87	18.93	21.68	27.29	24.27	22.39	21.12	21.39	21.89	18.61

Source: Wolfgang Keller, Ben Li, and Carol H. Shiue, "Shanghai's Trade, China's Growth: Continuity, Recovery, and Change since the Opium War," working paper 17754, National Bureau of Economic Research, January 2012, 51, at www.nber.org/papers/w17754, © Wolfgang Keller, Ben Li, and Carol H. Shiue.

in steady decline as countries such as Germany, Japan, South Korea, and China became global economic players (see table 7.1). These events led some to assume that the American system was likewise at the end of its lifespan—either because the United States could no longer afford to maintain it or because major changes in the international system would unleash new challengers that would make it too costly for the United States to retain its traditional role as a leading power.

Predictions of US decline did not hold true. In contrast to the Soviet Union, the United States was able to use its military and foreign aid spending as a stimulus to, rather than a drain upon, the larger civilian economy. It was able to get its partners to assume some of the burdens of maintaining the US-led international system. Finally, the dollar's emergence as the world's de facto reserve currency, in essence taking some of the role previously played by gold, meant that it served as the vehicle for facilitating most international transactions—thus giving many countries a vested interest in keeping the value of the dollar stable and predictable.[7]

Consequently the United States has enjoyed enormous financial and fiscal advantages not shared by its rivals or predecessors. The US dollar is the currency of international trade, a status reaffirmed by the decision of major energy producers to price their products in dollars. This provides a major stimulus for the expansion of US business overseas and helps to fuel American corporate dominance. This reality also created a worldwide demand for the dollar as a trading instrument and storehouse of value with stakeholders located beyond its borders. However, global interest in the fate of the dollar has allowed the US government to run deficits, secure in the knowledge that there is a built-in demand for dollars as well as an incentive not to let the dollar lose significant value. Thus at various points during the Cold War—and continuing into the twenty-first century—the United States has been able to tap into a broader resource flow emanating from allies and partners (and sometimes even potential rivals) to pay for its national security enterprise.

The National Security Budget as Domestic Spending

Historically many countries have found that high levels of defense spending brought few benefits to the domestic economy and often choked off development. Some rising imperial powers sought to limit expenditures by deliberate strategic choices (e.g., Portugal's decision to concentrate on maintaining a chain of outposts rather than to control large swaths of territory and Britain's choice to forgo a powerful land force in order to concentrate on naval power). Indeed, empirical evidence has amply demonstrated that "defence expenditures may retard economic growth by crowding out investment, health and education spending and infrastructural improvement."[8] Thus it was generally accepted that any country had a binary choice to make between "guns" and "butter."

In creating its national security establishment after World War II and desiring to safeguard its wartime industrial expansion, the United States sought to mitigate the effects of the guns/butter dichotomy. While this is generally a false choice, US military spending found a good balance among funding for personnel, acquisitions, operations, and research. By retaining a leading role for the US government in promoting and financing research and development (R&D), the government fostered a multisector partnership that would involve the business community and private organizations that would focus on development, production, and utilization.[9] A second factor was to facilitate spillover effects so the company that developed new products, goods, or services for the civilian sector could apply a technology or process originally designed for military needs. Government-funded "innovations . . . would be exploitable for national security, economic growth, and sustained societal benefit."[10] The third was to tie national security spending to other economic policies in order to stimulate growth and development that in turn would positively impact nonmilitary sectors of the economy.[11]

To harness the broader effects of government-funded research, the United States created entire networks of state-run laboratories and research institutions in order to identify and produce defense-related technologies. The most celebrated may be the Defense Advanced Research Projects Agency (DARPA), whose mandate to prevent "technological surprise" from threatening the US defense posture and to support scientific breakthroughs accelerate development to the point where practical technology can be derived.[12] DARPA functions as an incubator of ideas, a supporter of research, and a place where applications can be developed, creating a network to link suppliers of components with researchers and start-up companies in order to develop advanced technology.[13] DARPA's role, for instance, in pioneering the technologies that led to such breakthroughs as the graphic user interface for personal computers, the hardware and protocols that led to the internet, the components that allowed for the development of mobile phones, and the Global Positioning System of satellites that has revolutionized navigation is legendary.[14] In the early twenty-first century, new breakthroughs in nanotechnology and medical sciences driven by battlefield necessity are opening up new areas of productive collaboration between the defense establishment and the American scientific and industrial communities.[15] Recognizing this, the 2014 Quadrennial Defense Review pledges a recommitment of support to maintaining the industrial base and technological edge of the United States.[16]

However, in contrast to the Soviet model, where similar breakthroughs in military technology rarely found their way into the civilian economy, the US Department of Defense (DOD) took conscious steps to ensure that technology originally developed for defense needs would be integrated into the private sector to, in turn, develop the national industrial base. Through such avenues as cooperative research and development agreements between government labs and outside private companies and provisions for private companies to conclude patent license agreements, the DOD's intellectual property can be made available for commercial exploitation by the private sector (as, for instance, medical research by the US Army's Walter Reed Army Institute of Research was licensed to major pharmaceutical companies to develop new drugs and treatments).[17] While the fees paid represent only a fraction of the R&D costs, the indirect payoff comes from the rapid growth that can be engendered when military technology is reengineered to meet civilian demands.

The United States often provides R&D funds to universities and to private firms to develop new technologies. In this role, the DOD in a number of areas acts as an "angel investor." By providing early-stage seed funding for start-ups or by reducing the risk assumed by major corporations, the government assumes some of the burden for financing R&D of new products.[18] Indeed, 60 percent of the funding for IBM's first generation of computers came from the Pentagon, which needed the computing power to run complicated defense systems; however, IBM was then free to retool the designs and market computers for commercial use.[19] In analyzing the impact of the DOD's research activities on the civilian economy, a task force commissioned by the European Commission concluded that "defence-related research plays a major role in innovation in the U.S.; it benefits the whole of industry, including the civilian sector."[20]

In addition to its support for research, the defense budget, because of its economies of scale, allows for the military to buy products, technologies, and services in quantities large enough to make production cost-effective. The "stimulus, support and head start a large defense budget offers" remains a critical factor in how American firms have obtained advantages in bringing new items to the market.[21] When combined with "buy American" provisions in law, which require the DOD to rely on American-produced or American-sourced goods, companies are guaranteed a ready market, giving them time to bring costs down to make mass production more cost-effective.[22] In some cases, the DOD will also encourage a particular component that can be used in military hardware to be developed for a larger civilian market (e.g., brake-by-wire technology for the automobile industry) in order to achieve component cost reductions by the high volume of production for civilian use.[23] For products where there is no civilian application, US policy is to insure companies against loss, not only by having the government fund much of the R&D budget, but also to guarantee that the DOD will pay based on costs rather than on achieving the lowest possible price, with provisions built into contracting rules to permit firms to enjoy a profit on their defense contracts.[24] Defense procurement can also serve as a de facto subsidy for different industries such as aerospace and shipbuilding. Indeed, there have been estimates that DOD support has been worth some $560 million annually to the US commercial aircraft industry.[25]

Critics correctly note that using the military budget as a primary tool of domestic economic stimulus is both wasteful and inefficient.[26] These criticisms forget, however, that the main point of national security spending was never to spur economic growth but rather to prevent damaging dislocations in the domestic economy of the type that ultimately crippled the Soviet Union. It also ignores the reality that the government was never going to engage in any sort of massive spending on this scale on any comparable civilian projects. Nevertheless, as many economists have noted, "defence spending generates a number of positive externalities, such as human capital formation, technological spin-offs and security spillovers. Hence, military expenditure may enhance economic growth through Keynesian type aggregate demand effects. If countries are experiencing under-employment, defence expenditures may have a stimulative effect, with higher aggregate demand, production and employment. Investment in human capital is another area where there may be a substantial positive externality of defence spending on the rest of the economy."[27] In other words, military spending helps to prime the pump and, in theory, can be partially "recouped" because a larger, more dynamic economy will produce the tax revenues needed to sustain the country's national security apparatus.

Economists have long recognized that government spending, particularly defense spending, can jump-start the economy and put people to work. Indeed, one of the concerns of business leaders as World War II came to a close was that massive defense cuts might stall the economy, since civilian demand would not be sufficient to absorb all the capacity. At various points since then, international crises that have led to spikes in US defense spending have helped to maintain growth in the US economy by channeling orders into key industries.[28]

In turn, this leads to spillover effects: The decision to build installations and extend defense contracts in different regions of the country triggers growth in other sectors of the economy—in businesses that provide component parts and services, in the housing sector, and in the general service sector.[29] For instance, increased US military spending, particularly the purchase of high-technology products, was critical in New England's economic recovery starting in the late 1970s. Because of the size and scale of the orders, large-scale defense contracts provided a good number of well-paying jobs and created demand for components and parts, leading to spillover effects in other parts of the economy and contributing to the economic rebound.[30] There is a clear multiplier effect: The increase in jobs from direct employment by the DOD and direct and indirect government spending helps to boost wages; it leads to increases in disposable income, which stimulates consumption. This multiplier effect of government spending "also works through a chain of lower equipment investment, structures investment and residential building."[31] Therefore, sustaining levels of national security spending generates support from across the economy, because significant reductions in demand by the US government will lead to job losses. In turn, this will depress demand, cause slowdowns in other sectors of the economy, and reduce tax revenues.

Most estimates of the multiplier generated by US defense spending place it, on average, around 0.6; that is, for every dollar spent by the DOD, American GDP grew by an additional 60 cents. This multiplier rises when the domestic economy is weaker, with some estimates calculating that the multiplier increases by 0.05 for every percentage point when the unemployment rate is higher than 5.6 percent. At the height of the economic crisis in 2008, when unemployment approached 10 percent, the defense spending multiplier almost reached a factor of one—where each dollar spent on defense was translated into an almost an equivalent dollar in GDP growth.[32] This multiplier is also more cost-effective when the costs of borrowing to pay for defense spending are low, and as we shall shortly discuss, US dollar primacy has created conditions for the United States to finance its deficits on good terms.

Profiting from Aid

US overseas economic and military aid, at first glance, does not seem to fit into any scheme of supporting the domestic economy or helping to generate additional resources. But there is a national security logic to US foreign assistance. First and foremost it is designed to address issues before they can metastasize into more costly problems that might require much more expensive US intervention.[33] The hope is that a small amount of upfront aid might mitigate the need for a more costly operation down the road; similarly, postreconstruction aid is often pitched as the cheapest way to secure the peace.[34]

Table 7.2: Top US Trading Partners (as of July 2013 in Billions of Dollars)

Rank	Country	Exports	Imports	Total Trade	Percentage of Total Trade
—	Total, All Countries	908.6	1,307.0	2,215.6	100.0
—	Total, Top Fifteen Countries	618.5	977.3	1,595.8	72.0
1	Canada	174.0	192.4	366.4	16.5
2	China	63.8	241.6	305.4	13.8
3	Mexico	130.3	162.1	292.4	13.2
4	Japan	37.4	80.7	118.1	5.3
5	Germany	27.3	64.4	91.8	4.1
6	South Korea	23.8	37.1	60.9	2.7
7	United Kingdom	28.0	30.7	58.7	2.6
8	France	18.0	25.7	43.7	2.0
9	Brazil	25.4	15.8	41.2	1.9
10	Saudi Arabia	11.1	28.5	39.6	1.8

Source: US Census Bureau, at www.census.gov/foreign-trade/statistics/highlights/toppartners.html.

The second is that US aid is designed to help other economies recover and so helps to facilitate business ties with the United States. Pro–foreign aid members of Congress have argued that "investment in foreign aid is an investment in global relationships and our shared financial future. As developing nations become more prosperous, they will become less dependent on assistance, and Americans will benefit from our established relationships with these emerging markets."[35] Research has demonstrated that there is a positive link between the amount of foreign aid a country receives and a corresponding increase in the goods and services it purchases as a result from the donor country.[36] As table 7.2 illustrates, five of the top ten trading partners of the United States received significant reconstruction assistance as part of the American strategy to "win the peace" (and as detailed in the previous chapter).

Foreign aid can meet important national security aims but also helps to deal with surpluses or other issues that left unaddressed could create problems for the domestic economy. Americans have supported robust US engagement in the world largely because the responsibilities associated with superpower status could be utilized to drive domestic prosperity. In 1976, Chairman of the Senate Finance Committee Russell Long warned Secretary of State Henry Kissinger, "If we trade away American jobs and farmers' incomes for some vague concept of a 'new international order,' the American people will demand from their elected representatives a new order of their own, which puts their jobs, their security and their income above the priorities of those who dealt them a bad deal."[37]

For instance, US food aid programs have not only delivered aid to the starving (and have, in some cases, helped to improve America's standing in the eyes of the local populations) but also served as a form of direct aid to American farmers by having the government buy up surplus food for distribution to famine victims overseas.[38] Because an additional proviso in foreign aid programs is to mandate that US shipping companies be contracted to deliver the assistance, these aid programs are now estimated to directly sustain some 33,000 jobs and are an important source of support for the US agricultural sector.[39] Other provisions as found in the Foreign Assistance Act of 1961 (Title 22, Section 2381) placed "buy American" requirements on some categories of US foreign assistance—so that US aid, for instance, could only be used to purchase US-produced pharmaceuticals or motor vehicles.

Indeed, until 2012, much of US foreign assistance was conveyed as "tied aid": Some of the funds provided by the US government to other countries—whether to help with development, pursue security cooperation goals, or focus on particular projects—had to be used to purchase US goods and services.[40] The largest recipients of US assistance still receive the bulk of their funds as tied aid, with mandates to spend those dollars buying products from the United States. In Egypt, for instance, much of the military aid given is funneled back to US providers for aircraft, other types of equipment, and technical support.[41] A similar set of provisions governs US aid to Israel, to the chagrin of some who argue that this limits Israel's ability to purchase the best military and security equipment. A controversial 2011 report by the Jerusalem Institute for Market Studies suggests that while Israel might still purchase much of its military equipment in the United States, the requirement that 75 percent of US assistance be used to purchase American-made products constrains Israel's ability to purchase either better-quality or less-expensive equipment from domestic sources or from other suppliers.[42]

While there has been significant criticism of this approach on the grounds that it reduces the effectiveness of US assistance, a corresponding argument is that the "buy and ship American" provisions help to build support for American foreign aid within the US business community.[43] In terms of the impact of "pure" foreign aid (not counting foreign military sales), it is estimated that up to 1.9 million jobs in the United States are derived from foreign aid programs—which facilitate direct purchase of American goods or create conditions for them to be bought, in turn leading to a larger ripple effect to subcontractors and suppliers.[44]

As with domestic defense spending, foreign assistance is an inefficient way to stimulate the economy, but, once again, outflows from the US Treasury can be partially offset by having aid programs structured in such a way as to generate business for American firms. Ironically, as budgets drop, US policymakers may seek out cheaper options to maintain American influence—for instance, turning to overseas providers—as a way to save money. However, this creates a downward spiral that threatens the tacit understanding that US overseas military and economic assistance should, in part, help to stimulate the domestic economy. The Pentagon's announcement in 2010 that it would seek to purchase Russian-manufactured Mi-17 helicopters for the use of Afghanistan's military—in part because of cost factors—drew a great deal of criticism when American firms, which make analogous equipment, were not permitted to bid on the contract. This led in June 2013 to a unanimous vote in the House of Representatives that US funds could not be expended on a contract with Rosoboronexport, the Russian provider of the helicopters. Rep. Rosa DeLauro summed up the general sentiment: "If we are going to spend US taxpayer dollars to provide helicopters to the Afghan National Security Forces, we should be spending those dollars for the purchase of U.S.-made helicopters."[45] Representative DeLauro was making a general point but also supporting her constituents in Connecticut who worked for the Sikorsky Aircraft Corporation, a helicopter manufacturer.

The Rosoboronexport contract debate is but one example of how in recent years the US public has been less willing to sacrifice jobs and programs at home in order to fund efforts to promote security and prosperity abroad. The economic crisis of 2008–9 heightened concerns that the effort to sustain US global leadership has a negative impact on the country's well-being.[46] As a result, President Barack Obama has been at pains to stress that American engagement overseas is part and parcel of a "jobs strategy."[47]

American skepticism that US military and economic involvement brings concrete benefits to the United States has accelerated in the aftermath of the Iraq and Afghanistan campaigns where, despite massive US investment of funds and personnel, many of the potentially lucrative business deals involving both countries' untapped resources have gone to Chinese firms even as China itself has eschewed any participation in efforts to stabilize either nation. This creates the impression among many Americans that "we do the heavy lifting . . . and they pick the fruit."[48] And this was repeated again after the 2011 Libya campaign where the United States bore the lion's share of the costs, but American firms have not benefited from US military and political support for the opposition in terms of new contracts or access to Libya's massive hydrocarbon deposits.[49] All of this suggests that if there is a growing perception that American overseas engagement does not translate into concrete benefits for Americans, there will be a decline in public support for the United States shouldering a disproportionate share of the burden in providing international public goods.

Finding Donors

Another way the United States has financed its "system" and sought to mitigate the risk of overstretch—and to address concerns about "free riding"—has been to find other countries to act as donors, either by providing monetary resources or services "in kind," to help defray expenses.[50] One of the best examples of this in recent history was the financing of the 1990–91 Gulf War. The initial buildup to the conflict—after Iraq occupied Kuwait in September 1990—and the subsequent operations, which expelled Iraqi forces and restored Kuwaiti sovereignty, are estimated to have cost $61 billion. The United States, however, only paid $7 billion of the costs, or about 12 percent. Other countries—including Saudi Arabia, the Gulf emirates, Japan, South Korea, and Germany—contributed the bulk of the finances to pay for expenditures.[51] Some 24 percent of the troops used in the operation were also supplied by coalition partners, and in the case of British forces, the United Kingdom was "reimbursed" for its costs by other countries such as Germany.[52] In addition, other states, particularly Saudi Arabia, supplied food, fuel, and other resources directly to the US-led coalition, reducing the need for the United States to have to transport supplies.[53] In order to bolster US diplomatic efforts to build up a coalition—and to secure the necessary votes at the United Nations (UN) Security Council to authorize the use of force—Saudi Arabia and the Gulf emirates also dispensed financial assistance to countries to encourage them to help augment US efforts.[54]

Indeed, the Gulf War was a model for how the United States could solicit contributions from other states to support its actions in the international system.[55] Even in missions where the United States has assumed most of the burden, both in terms of combat power and in terms of providing resources (such as the 2011 Libya campaign), it has still benefited from the contributions of allies and partners—in terms of military personnel, equipment, and financial resources—which have augmented US efforts and allowed the United States to "stretch" its contributions.[56] (In addition, during the Libya mission, US allies and partners also ended up buying several hundred million dollars' worth of ammunition and parts from American firms to sustain their efforts.[57]) An unresolved question after the Libya operation, however, is whether the ongoing downsizing of allies' capabilities and increased budgetary pressures will make US allies less able to contribute in meaningful ways to future operations.[58]

There are other ways in which US partners can help defray the expenses the United States incurs in maintaining the current international system. For instance, allies in the past have taken on the role of supplying niche military, intelligence, or development capabilities to augment US efforts. Israel's long experience with asymmetrical warfare and with low-intensity conflict meant that its military establishment had pioneered a number of new systems—sensors, unmanned vehicles, etc.—that proved to be useful in helping the United States to develop better tools for the war on terrorism.[59] The Strategic Defense

Initiative (SDI) launched by the Ronald Reagan administration during the 1980s was a particular example of how the United States spread the costs and contracts for a defense system among its allies: By the late 1980s, SDI had led to sixty-seven contracts in eight different countries (Israel, Germany, Japan, Italy, the United Kingdom, France, Netherlands, and Canada) and in so doing allowed the United States to benefit from "technological developments in those countries."[60] Indeed, the United States has been able to draw upon the R&D and industrial endowments of its allies, particularly in the development of broader capabilities, which during the Cold War gave the West an advantage against numerically superior but technically inferior Soviet bloc militaries.

In much the same way, the United States has also benefited from the assets and capabilities of allies' intelligence services that could carry out missions or gain information that US institutions could not.[61] Other intelligence services, especially with much greater regional capabilities and expertise, have been able to augment US efforts, most notably in the Middle East. The United States has also been able to count on allies to undertake smaller military interventions in parts of the world where the United States has less pressing interests or has had to concentrate on other missions, such as various French and British interventions in West Africa and Australia's leading role in assuming responsibility for the East Timor operation in 1999.[62] Greater European experience with and a preference for deploying in support of peacekeeping and peace-enforcement missions—sometimes at the request of the United States and in other cases to follow after a kinetic US operation—has also helped to free up US resources and lessen American commitments around the world. Examples include the rapid US disengagement from missions in Kosovo and Bosnia, where European forces provided the bulk of forces for stability operations.[63]

In addition to capabilities, allies may offer geographic benefits that help reduce costs.[64] The United States has been able to take advantage of a global network of bases and outposts that allow for a cheaper projection of power than if everything had to be based and shipped from the continental United States. The willingness of dozens of countries to make bases, airfields, ports, and other facilities available for American use—even if they stand to benefit in terms of rent and other considerations—has allowed the United States to augment the striking power of its carrier strike groups to be able to carry out operations anywhere in the world, an advantage that no other power possesses.

Some US commentators complain that American allies are too quick to free ride on overwhelming US capabilities without making equal contributions in kind. This ignores, however, the extent to which the United States has also, in turn, been able to hand off responsibility for missions "other than war" to other partners. European countries may not have the ability to match American conventional military capabilities across the entire spectrum of conflict, but their "civilian power"—particularly in deploying personnel and funding institutions to assist in postconflict reconstruction—is formidable.[65] One might argue that the United States deserves much of the credit for "winning" the Cold War, but the European Union has been the most responsible for securing the fruits of victory in Eastern and Central Europe. Further, by shouldering the bulk of the effort to transform the former Soviet bloc countries into contributing new members of Euro-Atlantic institutions, the United States gained a set of new partners.[66] Other European efforts farther afield—in the Middle East, Africa, and across Eurasia—have had more mixed results, but there can be no question that Europe has played a major role in attempting to expand the number of countries that would be able to become fully integrated members of the US-led international system.

More generally, the United States has been able to turn to the UN to handle a number of peacekeeping operations where Washington had an interest in promoting stability (or at least tamping down conflict) but was unprepared to devote US resources or personnel. Even if the United States must foot the financial bill for such operations, having the UN handle the mission (including the recruitment of forces from donor nations), it is still far more cost-effective than having the US staff the mission itself or running the risk of letting an unaddressed conflict fester.[67] Having other countries supply peacekeepers makes UN missions more cost-effective than US-led operations, and even if the United States pays more of the UN peacekeeping budget, it still only funds a plurality, not a majority, of the costs—and it has proven to be far cheaper than US combat operations.[68]

The United States has also had some success in encouraging partners to take over more of the aid burden for fragile or less developed states or, at Washington's request, to provide assistance to particular countries to meet overall US security goals.[69] Having other countries take on projects for the United States or to harmonize their aid programs with US efforts are additional ways in which scarcer resources can be stretched or be made more effective.[70]

American officials perennially complain that allies and partners can always be doing more to assist US efforts. However, the very fact that the United States has a network of countries prepared to make contributions has been of extraordinary value in alleviating the burdens of superpower status and helping to mitigate the risks of overstretch. The Iraq War was a worrisome divergence from this approach, given the degree to which the United States shouldered the costs of the operation, but the preferred option remains to create coalitions in which participants help to lessen the burden on the Treasury. While acknowledging that the United States may bear the largest burden in terms of purely military expenditures, American allies argue that "their contributions to peacekeeping and overseas aid" ought to be also reckoned in any assessment of burden-sharing.[71] Moreover, one of the most important contributions other countries have made to sustain US power has been their support of the global role of the US dollar.

Primacy of the Dollar

America's position as a global leader has been inextricably connected to the strength and influence of its currency and its emergence after World War II as the de facto currency of the global economy. Adam Posen noted: "When the dollar is believed to have underlying strength, it is to traders' advantages to sign contracts and to price in dollar terms and to trade with countries that also deal in dollars—including the United States—so economic ties between dollar-reliant nations deepen. When the dollar is considered universally liquid and a reliable source of value, regimes that are linked to the United States on foreign policy grounds tend to also peg to the dollar or at least use the dollar as a reference currency."[72] By the mid-1980s, nearly three-quarters of total bank assets in the developed world were denominated in dollars.[73] By 2009, some two-thirds of the reserve assets of both industrialized and developing countries were held in dollars.[74]

For many, America's military preeminence as a superpower is reinforced by the leading role in world affairs of its currency.[75] However, the United States did not impose the dollar on other countries by forcing them to use the currency.[76] This is in contrast to the Soviet Union, which did impose on its satellites the use of transfer rubles in intrabloc trade—rubles that had no value in any other part of the global economy and thus locking in countries into making purchases from the USSR. Instead the dollar was voluntarily accepted because, in the immediate postwar period, it was automatically convertible into gold (at the rate of $35 per ounce) and thus a good storehouse of value. An increased willingness to use the dollar has also tended to track with those countries that have close security ties to the United States and that viewed themselves as America's close trading and investment partners, highlighting a "mutually reinforcing interaction between currency, trade, investment and security relationships."[77] In one particular and very important area, energy producers in the noncommunist world during the Cold War were prepared to set the price of oil in dollars, a particular concession whose maintenance over the years has proven to be very valuable for the United States.[78]

From those initial positions, the dollar has emerged as a de facto global currency. Even after the United States left the gold standard, dollars remained the major form of cash currency around the world, in part because of the size of the US economy and because US political and economic stability made its currency both plentiful and desirable. In 2014, twelve countries or territories continue to "dollarize"—that is, use the US dollar as their own national currency—in spite of divergent views of the international economic system (Ecuador being the best example).[79] Additionally, another eighty-nine countries peg their currency's value to that of the dollar.[80] This makes up approximately one-third of the world's total GDP, and with America accounting for another 22 percent, a little more than half of the global economy's value is defined in relationship to the US dollar.[81] This in turn leads to other trends that reinforce the dollar's primacy: It is the leading currency for transactions in foreign-exchange markets, and beyond commodities such as oil it remains the key invoicing currency in international trade. Around 40 percent of all outstanding debt securities in the world—not just those issued by governments but also by private businesses—are denominated in dollars—even when neither the company nor the potential lenders are based in the United States. In addition, countries often prefer to use the dollar in settling accounts with each other.[82] The dollar, even with the difficulties faced by the US economy in recent years, remains the world's reserve currency, and as former Treasury secretary Timothy Geithner noted, the United States as a result enjoys a "special responsibility" to preserve confidence in the strength of its economic system and in the value of the dollar.[83]

Dollar primacy conveys very real and tangible benefits to the United States, which over the years have helped to mitigate concerns about overstretch. In short, as long as the dollar has remained the main facilitator of the global economy, it has meant that the United States could afford to borrow on much better terms than any other country in order to be able to pay for its national security spending.[84] One of the important—and often unsung—legs of America's "structural power" has been the ability to control the supply and availability of credit denominated in dollars. Only the US government has the power to create dollar assets that are accepted and saleable worldwide.[85] This means that the United States has been able to run deficits, particularly when it comes to financing its national security establishment, without serious concerns that it would not be able to obtain the funds; it has been able to avoid the overstretch trap by "borrowing" rather than having "to finance its military adventures . . . with hard cash on the barrelhead."[86] (Charles de Gaulle's chief economic adviser Jacques Rueff once noted that the United States could run deficits "without tears" and without having to make hard trade-offs about taxes, balancing the books, or changing priorities.) Indeed, as long as the markets are willing to accept it, the United States has the "unconstrained right to print money that others could not (save at unacceptable cost) refuse to accept in payment."[87]

Dollar primacy is also an important tool of US soft power. States (and private businesses around the world) develop a vested interest in the value and stability of the dollar because they rely on it to price their goods, finance their operations, and to serve as a liquid storehouse of value. This means, as a result, that they then develop a vested interest in the success of the US economy and of America's policy preferences, since systemic failure could threaten the dollar's value and thus their own interests.[88]

America's dollar primacy is also served by the logic of institutional lock-in: It is easier to retain the dollar than to navigate the risks and costs of trying to displace the dollar.[89] Other alternatives exist—the euro, the yen, the yuan, or the

Table 7.3: Top Twenty Holders of US Debt (as of December 2013)

1. China (Mainland)
2. Japan
3. Caribbean Banking Centers
4. Belgium
5. Brazil
6. Oil Exporters
7. Taiwan
8. Switzerland
9. United Kingdom
10. Hong Kong
11. Russia
12. Luxembourg
13. Ireland
14. Norway
15. Singapore
16. India
17. Germany
18. Mexico
19. Canada
20. South Korea

Source: US Treasury, "Major Foreign Holders of Treasury Securities," at www.treasury .gov/resource-center/data-chart-center/tic/Documents/mfh.txt.

ruble—but there are major concerns about the economic and political stability of their originating institutions or countries.[90] In some cases, the dollar may be displaced at the margin or within certain trading regions (e.g., the Euro zone), but no other currency is poised to take over its global role, which gives the dollar a certain security of incumbency.

This position of incumbency has been aided by the conscious efforts of other states to prop up the dollar. During the Cold War, Germany, other Western countries, and Japan worked consistently to help maintain the value of the dollar as a way to stabilize the global economy.[91] This was also in part due to the fact that these countries were also political and military allies of the United

States and as such depended on Washington's security umbrella. Helping to facilitate America's ability to retain its military predominance by financing US trade and fiscal deficits was seen as part of the bargain that helped sustain the US system.[92]

Former World Bank president Robert Zoellick has warned that the international primacy of the dollar cannot last forever, particularly when some countries that are not allies of the United States (in the fashion of Germany or Japan) but are potential adversaries (like China) have become stakeholders in the dollar.[93] But even countries that might wish, in an ideal world, to see the dollar dethroned have no interest in its rapid and sudden collapse. They will focus not on eliminating but reducing the role of the dollar and with it some of the advantages that dollar primacy currently conveys.

Indeed, even a rising potential challenger to the United States like China nonetheless retains a strong interest in maintaining a US-dominated international economic system. China is the single largest foreign holder of US debt and a key supporter of the US dollar as a global reserve currency. Beijing is now the largest non-US holder of Treasury securities and one of the leading owners of various US-dollar denominated securities as a whole. It is estimated that some 70 percent of China's currency reserves are held in dollars.[94] Beijing does this to protect its exports because China's yuan remains defined by its relationship to the dollar. Maintaining dollar values is critical for keeping China's exports competitive by preventing any rapid appreciation of the yuan that would make Chinese products less affordable. While China has attempted to shift payments for energy, natural resources, and high-technology purchases away from dollars (notably with Iran), the US currency is still the preferred medium of global exchange between China and its trading partners, in part because other countries do not have confidence that the yuan is a reliable storehouse of value and are not always willing to accept it in payment. Additionally, much of China's international investment is financed from its dollar reserves. Finally, while China is seeking to diversify its currency holdings, the fact that a good deal of its surplus remains invested in dollar-denominated securities means that if Beijing chose to crash the dollar, it would also have to accept a significant write-off of its own investments.

China accepts that its continued purchase of US dollar securities tacitly subsidizes the United States to protect the global commons, since China's export-driven economy relies on the stability to ship goods to global markets. In turn, the United States can run significant budget deficits while financing borrowing through low interest rates, which has, among other things, allowed it to sustain its high levels of defense spending—a state of affairs Beijing is prepared to accept for the present.

For the foreseeable future, therefore, US allies and adversaries alike have shared interests in maintaining the dollar vehicle. The United States will be able to continue its ability to sustain external deficits longer and at higher levels than any other country or group of countries—and in so doing, even with expected budget cuts, maintain the most powerful national security establishment in the world.[95]

Conclusion

Americans found that they could accept superpower status because US global leadership did not extract onerous costs from its citizens and brought tangible benefits. The 2014 Quadrennial Defense Review captured this: "Our economic strength is closely tied to a stable international order, underwritten by the U.S. military's role and that of our allies and partners in ensuring freedom of access and the free flow of commerce globally."[96] American military and financial power undergird an international system, which, as Charles Krauthammer noted, provided for "open seas, open trade and open societies lightly defended," which in turn created tangible benefits for Americans.[97] Indeed, a significant minority of Americans—from active-duty military personnel to defense contractors to researchers and scientists—found that their very livelihood was directly connected to the emergence of the postwar US international system—and many others also indirectly benefited as well. With some degree of burden-sharing—and with US policymakers insulated from having to impose a higher tax burden to finance national security spending (and, in being able to borrow, to do so at low interest rates)—Americans were not required to undergo massive deprivation in order to sustain the US global position. The shift to an all-volunteer military force has also removed the burden of conscription from American society, removing some of the domestic political constraints on deploying the US military overseas—thus lessening the perception that such involvement extracts a cost from the average (nonmilitary) American household.[98]

However, as financing grows tighter—as the dollar loses ground in international markets, remaining a preferred currency but no longer the world's only option; as US defense spending is cut, and its multiplier effect diminishes; as allies contribute less to supporting US-led operations—the United States will of necessity need to become more selective in choosing where and when to intervene in the world. The United States has no implicit "will to great power" status where the population will continue to support the maintenance of a massive national security apparatus with global reach at the cost of their own impoverishment.[99] An economic downturn or slowdown will produce an incidental recalibration of America's reach in the world. In examining polling data, Andrew Kohut concluded, "Feeling burned by Iraq and Afghanistan and burdened by domestic concerns, the public feels little responsibility and inclination to deal with international problems that are not seen as direct threats to the national interest."[100] Leaner times will support a strategic reorientation where the United States concentrates its reduced resources and attention on fewer countries—on those that are themselves positioned to make greater contributions to maintaining global security and prosperity.

Notes

1. Paul Kennedy, *The Rise and Fall of the Great Powers: Economic Change and Military Conflict from 1500 to 2000* (New York: Vintage Books, 1989), xv.

2. These include Andrew Hacker, *The End of the American Era* (New York: Atheneuum, 1970); Charles Kupchan, *The End of the American Era: U.S. Foreign Policy and the Geopolitics of the Twenty-First Century* (New York: Knopf, 2002); Fareed Zakaria, *The Post-American World* (New York: Norton, 2008); Christopher Layne, "The Global Power Shift from West to East," *National Interest*, May/June 2012, 6–16.

3. "Imperial Overstretch? More a Question of Psychology than Economics," *Economist*, June 27, 2002, www.economist.com/node/1188741. See also Robert Kagan, "Not Fade Away: Against the Myth of American Decline," *New Republic*, January 11, 2012, www.newrepublic.com/article/politics/magazine/99521/america-world-power-declinism; Robert J. Leiber, "Staying Power and the American Future: Problems of Primacy, Policy, and Grand Strategy," *Journal of Strategic Studies* 34, no. 4: 509–30.

4. Theodore H. Moran, "International Economics and National Security," *Foreign Affairs* 69, no. 5 (Winter 1990): 89.

5. Joseph Nye, "Gorbachev and the End of the Cold War," *New Straits Times*, April 5, 2006, http://belfercenter.ksg.harvard.edu/publication/1531/gorbachev_and_the_end_of_the_cold_war.html.

6. See, for instance, Armin Schäfer, "Stabilizing Postwar Europe: Aligning Domestic and International Goals," working paper 03/08 (July 2003), Max Planck Institute for the Study of Societies MPIfG, www.mpifg.de/pu/workpap/wp03-8/wp03-8.html.

7. Michael Mandelbaum, "The Inadequacy of American Power," *Foreign Affairs* 81, no. 5 (September/October 2002): 70–71.

8. Julide Yildirim, Nadir Ocal, and Halil Keskin, "Military Expenditures, Economic Growth and Spatial Spillovers: A Global Perspective," *Proceedings: International Conference on Applied Economics 2011*, ed. Nicholas Tsounis, Aspasia Vlachvei, Martino Gaetano, and Theodoros Monovasilis (Kastoria: Technological Institute of Western Macedonia, 2011), 811.

9. Shirley Ann Jackson, "The Nexus: Where Science Meets Society," *Science* 310, no. 5754 (December 9, 2005): 1635, http://www.sciencemag.org/content/310/5754/1634.full.

10. Ibid.

11. Richard Florida and Andrew Jonas, "U.S. Urban Policy: The Postwar State and Capitalist Regulation," *Antipode* 23, no. 4 (1991), 362.

12. Andrew James, *U.S. Defence R & D Spending: An Analysis of the Impacts*, rapporteur's report for the EURAB Working Group (Manchester: PREST, January 2004), 23.

13. Erica R. H. Fuchs, "Rethinking the Role of the State in Technology Development: DARPA and the Case for Embedded Network Governance," Carnegie Mellon University Department of Engineering and Public Policy paper 3 (2010), http://repository.cmu/edu/epp/3.

14. James, *U.S. Defence R & D*, 6.

15. Jackson, "Nexus," 1636.

16. See Department of Defense, *Quadrennial Defense Review: 2014* (Washington, DC: Department of Defense, 2014), esp. 7, 9, www.defense.gov/pubs/2014_Quadrennial_Defense_Review.pdf.

17. James, *U.S. Defence R & D*, 22–23.

18. See, for instance, Eric Schurenberg, "The Inconvenient History of Silicon Valley," *Inc.*, May 30, 2012, www.inc.com/eric-schurenberg/inconvenient-history-of-silicon-valley.html; James, *U.S. Defence R & D*, 40.

19. Susan Strange, "The Persistent Myth of Lost Hegemony," *International Organization* 41, no. 4 (Autumn 1987): 570.

20. *European Defence: Industrial and Market Issues; Towards an EU Defence Equipment Policy*, report issued by the Commission of the European Communities, March 2003, 113.

21. Strange, "Persistent Myth," 570.

22. For instance, in terms of programs designed to increase the stock of biofuels and other hydrocarbon alternatives to the US military, "foreign-produced fuel that is used or sold for use outside the United States" is disqualified. Cf. Shawna M. Bligh and Chris A. Wendelbo, "Federal Government as Angel Investor for Environment and Energy Projects?," *Natural Resources & Environment* 24, no. 1 (Summer 2009), www.session.com/news/FederalGovernmentAngelInvestor.pdf.

23. James, *U.S. Defence R & D*, 23.

24. See, for instance, William P. Rogerson, "Economic Incentives and the Defense Procurement Process," *Journal of Economic Perspectives* 8, no. 4 (Autumn 1994): 67–69, 72.

25. James, *U.S. Defence R & D*, 35.

26. Florida and Jonas, "U.S. Urban Policy," 362.

27. Yildirim, Ocal, and Keskin, "Military Expenditures," 811.

28. Florida and Jonas, "U.S. Urban Policy," 362.

29. Robert Levinson, Sopen Shah, and Paige K. Connor, *Impact of Defense Spending: A State-by-State Analysis*, Bloomberg Government Study, November 17, 2011, 3, http://forbes.house.gov/uploadedfiles/bloomberg.pdf.

30. Richard A. Barff and Prentice L. Knight III, "The Role of Federal Military Spending in the Timing of the New England Employment Turnaround," *Papers in Regional Science* 65, no. 1 (January 1988): 151–66.

31. "Defense Spending Cuts: The Impact on Economic Activity and Jobs," background paper issued by the National Association of Manufacturers (n.d.), 11, www.nam.org/-/media/6C787C12117F49D1BDA2B6526A14DC2E.ashx.

32. For a summary of the different ways of calculating the multiplier, see Robert J. Barro and Veronique de Rugy, *Defense Spending and the Economy* (Arlington, VA: Mercatus Center, 2013). See also Dylan Matthews, "Research Desk: Will Defense

Cuts Harm the Economy?," *Washington Post*, October 26, 2011, www.washington-post.com/blogs/wonkblog/post/research-desk-what-does-defense-spending-do-for-the-economy/2011/10/26/gIQANsiQJM_blog.html.

33. Samuel Worthington, "US Foreign Aid Benefits Recipients—and the Donor," *Guardian*, February 14, 2011, www.theguardian.com/global-development/poverty-matters/2011/feb/14/us-foreign-aid-cuts.

34. Ann Vaughan and Trevor Keck, "Securing the Peace," *Foreign Policy in Focus*, May 15, 2008, http://fpif.org/securing_the_peace/.

35. Adam Smith, Jim McDermott, and Bill Clapp, "U.S. Foreign Aid Is Not a Luxury but a Critical Investment in Global Stability," *Seattle Times*, April 17, 2011, http://seattletimes.com/html/opinion/2014788015_guest18smith.html.

36. Helen V. Milner and Dustin H. Tingely, "The Political Economy of U.S. Foreign Aid: American Legislators and the Domestic Politics of Aid," *Economics and Politics* 22, no. 2 (July 2010): 207–8.

37. US Senate, Committee on Finance, *Oversight Hearings on U.S. Foreign Trade Policy*, 94th Cong., 2nd sess. (Washington, DC: Government Printing Office, 1976), 105.

38. Richard Wike, "Does Humanitarian Aid Improve America's Image?," *Pew Research Global Attitudes Project*, March 6, 2012, www.pewglobal.org/2012/03/06/does-humanitarian-aid-improve-americas-image/.

39. Olga Khazan, "Here Are the U.S. States That Benefit Most from America's Wacky International Food-Aid Program," *Atlantic*, April 5, 2013, www.theatlantic.com/international/archive/2013/04/here-are-the-us-states-that-benefit-most-from-americas-wacky-international-food-aid-program/274709/.

40. Claire Provost, "USAID Now Free to Buy Goods from Companies in Poor Countries," *Guardian*, February 6, 2012, www.theguardian.com/global-development/2012/feb/06/usaid-changes-procurement-policy.

41. "The U.S. Defense Contractors That Benefit from Aid to Egypt," National Public Radio, August 19, 2013, www.npr.org/blogs/parallels/2013/08/19/213471071/the-u-s-defense-contractors-that-benefit-from-aid-to-egypt.

42. Yarden Gazit, "Economic and Strategic Ramifications of American Assistance to Israel," Jerusalem Institute for Market Studies report 1/2011 (2011), 2–3.

43. Marian Leonardo Lawson, *Does Foreign Aid Work? Efforts to Evaluate U.S. Foreign Assistance*, Congressional Research Service report R42827, February 13, 2013, 11.

44. Milner and Tingely, "Political Economy," 204–5.

45. "DeLauro Blasts U.S. Purchase of Russian Helicopters," *Shelton Herald*, June 16, 2013, http://sheltonherald.com/19255/delauro-blasts-u-s-purchase-of-russian-helicopters/.

46. One of the earlier articulations of these concerns is Alfred E. Eckes, "Trading American Interests," *Foreign Affairs* 71, no. 4 (Fall 1992): 135–54.

47. Ed Henry, "In India, Obama Pushes U.S. Jobs," CNN, November 6, 2010, www.cnn.com/2010/WORLD/asiapcf/11/06/india.obama.jobs/index.html.

48. Comment of S. Frederick Starr, quoted in Richard Weitz, "Why China's Free-Riding Is OK," *Diplomat*, August 12, 2011, http://thediplomat.com/2011/08/12/why-china%E2%80%99s-free-riding-ok/?all=true.

49. Jacey Fortin, "Whatever Happened to Libyan Oil? For Western Oil Giants, the Crude Is Sweet but China and Russia May Get the Biggest Taste," *International Business Times*, May 24, 2013, www.ibtimes.com/whatever-happened-libyan-oil-western-oil-giants-crude-sweet-china-russia-may-get-biggest-taste.

50. See, for instance, the exchange between Rep. Brad Sherman and Joseph Yun, acting assistant secretary of state for East Asian and Pacific affairs, during a hearing on US aid to East Asia. Cf. US House of Representatives, International Affairs Committee, Subcommittee on Asia and the Pacific, *Assessing US Foreign Assistance Priorities in East Asia and the Pacific* (May 16, 2013), 113th Cong., 1st sess., www.gpo.gov/fdsys/pkg/CHRG-113hhrg80941/pdf/CHRG-113hhrg80941.pdf, esp. 29–31.

51. See appendix P in *Conduct of the Persian Gulf War*, the final official report by the Department of Defense to Congress (Washington, DC: Department of Defense, 1992).

52. Andrew Bennett, Joseph Lepgold, and Danny Unger, "Burden-Sharing in the Persian Gulf War," *International Organization* 48, no. 1 (Winter 1994): 53.

53. *Conduct of the Persian Gulf War*.

54. For instance, Turkey, which suffered some economic dislocation due to sanctions on Iraq, received more than $2.2 billion in loans and grants from Arab and European states and promises of contracts for Turkish firms for reconstruction activities in Kuwait. Bruce R. Kuniholm, "Turkey and the West," *Foreign Affairs* 70, no. 2 (Spring 1991): 38.

55. Todd Sandler and Keith Hartley, "Economics of Alliances: The Lessons for Collective Action," *Journal of Economic Literature* 39, no. 3 (September 2001): 878.

56. See remarks of the US ambassador to NATO, Ivo Daalder, "What the Libya Operation Teaches Us about NATO," delivered at the University of Maryland School of Public Policy, February 28, 2012, http://nato.usmission.gov/ambassador-speeches/what-the-libya-operation-teaches-us-about-nato.html.

57. Philip Ewing, "Cost of U.S. Libya Ops? About 3 Days in Afghanistan," *DODBuzz*, August 23, 2011, www.dodbuzz.com/2011/08/23/cost-of-u-s-libya-ops-about-3-days-in-afghanistan/.

58. Ellen Hallams and Benjamin Schreer, "Towards a 'Post-American' Alliance? NATO Burden-Sharing after Libya," *International Affairs* 88, no. 2 (2012): 325.

59. Michael Eisenstadt and David Pollock, "Friends with Benefits: Why the U.S.-Israeli Alliance Is Good for America," *Foreign Affairs*, November 7, 2012, www.foreignaffairs.com/articles/138422/michael-eisenstadt-and-david-pollock/friends-with-benefits.

60. See the General Accounting Office report *Strategic Defense Initiative Program: Extent of Foreign Participation*, report NSIAD-90-2 (Washington, DC: Government Printing Office, 1990), 11, 14.

61. Derek S. Reveron, "Old Allies, New Friends: Intelligence-Sharing in the War on Terror," *Orbis* 50, no. 3 (Summer 2006): 453–68.

62. Andrew Moravcsik, "Striking a New Transatlantic Bargain," *Foreign Affairs* 82, no. 4 (July/August 2003): 86–88; James Cotton, "'Peacekeeping' in East Timor: An Australian Policy Departure," *Australian Journal of International Affairs* 53, no. 3 (1999): 237–46.

63. Ibid., 86–88.

64. Sandler and Hartley, "Economics of Alliances," 879.

65. See, for instance, *Europe's Global Role: External Policies of the European Union*, ed. Jan Orbie (Burlington, VT: Ashgate, 2008).

66. Keith Hartley and Todd Sandler, "NATO Burden-Sharing: Past and Future," *Journal of Peace Research* 36, no. 665 (1999): 668, 673.

67. This was the conclusion based on cost estimates about different ways to staff a peacekeeping mission in Haiti. Cf. *Peacekeeping: Cost Comparison of Actual UN and Hypothetical U.S. Operations in Haiti*, a report by the Government Accountability Office to the Subcommittee on Oversight and Investigations, Committee on International Relations, House of Representatives, GAO-06-331 (Washington, DC: Government Printing Office, 2006).

68. "U.S. Pays Soaring Amount for U.N. Peacekeeping, but It's Cheaper than War," *Baltimore Sun*, April 29, 1993, http://articles.baltimoresun.com/1993-04-29/news/1993119149_1_peacekeeping-united-nations-religious-turmoil.

69. Hartley and Sandler, "NATO Burden-Sharing," 673; John P. Tuman, Jonathan R. Strand, and Craig F. Emmert, "The Disbursement Pattern of Japanese Foreign Aid: A Reassessment," *Journal of East Asian Studies* 9, no. 2 (2009): 219–48. The authors argue that US security interests have had a partial influence on Japan's overseas development assistance grants, although making the case that "humanitarianism" played a greater role in determining how Japan spent its aid budget. However, humanitarianism (i.e., sending aid to where it is perceived to fill the most need, rather than to obtain concrete economic or security benefits) fits in with the "human security" direction of US national security strategy in recent years.

70. For instance, within the context of the trilateral US-Japanese-Indian dialogue, Washington is able to discuss with India how its aid and development programs in the region can augment US efforts. India's aid assistance in Afghanistan has also complemented US efforts and has allowed the United States to focus its efforts. In some cases India may be a more effective provider of aid than the United States, such as in assisting farmers in Africa with new technologies. Cf. U.S. House of Representatives, International Affairs Committee, Subcommittee on Asia and the Pacific, *Assessing U.S. Foreign Assistance Priorities in East Asia and the Pacific* (May 16, 2013), 113th Cong., 1st sess., 26, 32, www.gpo.gov/fdsys/pkg/CHRG-113 hhrg80941/pdf/CHRG-113hhrg80941.pdf.

71. Hartley and Sandler, "NATO Burden-Sharing," 674.

72. Adam S. Posen, "National Security Risks from Accumulation of Foreign Debt," in *The Long-Term International Economic Position of the United States*, ed. C. Fred Bergsten, Peterson Institute for International Economics special report 20 (2009), 65.

73. Strange, "Persistent Myth," 569.

74. Linda S. Goldberg, "Is the International Role of the Dollar Changing?" *Federal Reserve Bank of New York Current Issues in Economics and Finance* 16, no. 1 (January 2010): 3.

75. Posen, "National Security Risks," 66.

76. Jonathan Kirshner, "Dollar Primacy and American Power: What's at Stake?" *Review of International Political Economy* 15, no. 3 (2008): 428.

77. Posen, "National Security Risks," 68.

78. Kirshner, "Dollar Primacy," 428.

79. The others are Panama, El Salvador, East Timor, Palau, the Federated States of Micronesia, the Marshall Islands, the British Virgin Islands, the Turks and Caicos Islands, Bonaire, Sint Eustatius, and Saba.

80. Bento Lobo, "Demise of the US Dollar?," *Times Free Press*, August 21, 2011, www.timesfreepress.com/news/2011/aug/21/demise-us-dollar/.

81. Goldberg, "Is the International Role," 2, 3.

82. Ibid., 4, 5, 6.

83. Daniel Whitten, "Zoellick Says U.S. Dollar's Primacy Not a Certainty," *Bloomberg*, September 28, 2009, www.bloomberg.com/apps/news?pid=newsarchive &sid=aj_lWM84rMQ8.

84. Posen, "National Security Risks," 66.

85. Strange, "Persistent Myth," 568.

86. Kirshner, "Dollar Primacy," 431.

87. Strange, "Persistent Myth," 569.

88. Kirshner, "Dollar Primacy," 425, 429.

89. G. John Ikenberry, "Institutions, Strategic Restraint and the Persistence of American Postwar Order," *International Security* 23, no. 3 (Winter 1998/99): 69, 72, 73.

90. Kirshner, "Dollar Primacy," 420.

91. William R. Neikirk, "U.S., Allies Work to Wrap Up Deal to Solidify Dollar," *Chicago Tribune*, February 22, 1987, http://articles.chicagotribune.com/1987-02-22/news/8701150029_1_key-currencies-dollar-japan.

92. Kirshner, "Dollar Primacy," 421.

93. Whitten, "Zoellick Says."

94. A full description of China's holdings and its policies is provided in Wayne M. Morrison and Marc Labonte, *China's Holdings of U.S. Securities: Implications for the U.S. Economy*, Congressional Research Service Report RL 34314 (Washington, DC: Congressional Research Service, 2013).

95. Kirshner, "Dollar Primacy," 421.

96. Department of Defense, *Quadrennial Defense Review: 2014*, xx.

97. Charles Krauthammer, quoted in Nikolas K. Gvosdev, "Foreign Policy, Leverage and Charity," *National Interest*, May 19, 2004, http://nationalinterest.org/article/foreign-policy-leverage-and-charity-2658.

98. Karl W. Eikenberry, "Reassessing the All-Volunteer Force," *Washington Quarterly* 36, no. 1 (Winter 2013): 10.

99. In contrast, for instance, with a country like Russia. Cf. Nikolas K. Gvosdev and Christopher Marsh, *Russian Foreign Policy: Interests, Vectors and Sectors* (Washington, DC: CQ Press, 2013), 6.

100. Andrew Kohut, "American International Engagement on the Rocks," Pew Research Global Attitudes Project, July 11, 2013, www.pewglobal.org/2013/07/11/american-international-engagement-on-the-rocks/.

8

Conclusion:
The Future of US Foreign Policy and Defense Strategy

> Foreign policy consists in bringing into balance, with a comfortable surplus of power in reserve, the nation's commitments and the nation's power.
>
> —Walter Lippmann, 1943

There was nothing either accidental or intentional about the rise of the United States as a global hegemon. Instead, the United States incidentally emerged as a superpower after World War II with no intention to become the world's hegemon, even if that is what it eventually became. Safe from the battlefields of Europe and Asia, the United States concluded the war with an economy that accounted for the plurality of global economic output and led the postwar global economic recovery through international assistance and foreign direct investment. Europe was reborn through the Marshall Plan, while Japan benefited from a commitment to global trade and democracy. Strategically the United States connected countries through international commerce while raising living standards at home and abroad.

With an ardent decolonization agenda and a postwar legitimacy as a bulwark against imperial expansionism, the United States attempted to construct a world characterized by cooperation rather than imperialism. Through the Bretton Woods meetings that created the modern international economic system, the United States attempted to stabilize currency markets, provide governments a lender of last resort, and promote interdependence through trade. Through the Treaty of San Francisco, which created the United Nations (UN) system, the United States attempted to prevent conflict by working with the Soviet Union, United Kingdom, France, and China. President Harry Truman captured this optimism during the UN Charter's signing on June 25, 1945: "The Charter of the United Nations which you have just signed is a solid structure upon which we can build a better world. History will honor you for it. Between the victory in Europe and the final victory, in this most destructive of all wars, you have won a victory against war itself. . . . With this Charter the world can begin to look forward to the time when all worthy human beings may be permitted to live decently as free people."[1]

Yet the optimism for a better future without international rivalry quickly faded. Just months later, British prime minister Winston Churchill sounded the alarm of an "iron curtain" descending upon Europe and challenged the United States to consider the importance of its superpower position and the strategic choices it makes:

> The United States stands at this time at the pinnacle of world power. . . . For with primacy in power is also joined an awe-inspiring accountability to the future. . . . You must feel not only the sense of duty done but also you must feel anxiety lest you fall below the level of achievement. Opportunity is here now, clear and shining for both our countries. To reject it or ignore it or fritter it away will bring upon us all the long reproaches of the after-time. It is necessary that constancy of mind, persistency of purpose, and the grand simplicity of decision shall guide and rule the conduct of the English-speaking peoples in peace as they did in war. We must, and I believe we shall, prove ourselves equal to this severe requirement.[2]

American leaders then saw communist consolidation in Central and Eastern Europe as reinforcing this view, and they kept the United States engaged in international affairs in spite of calls for retrenchment. Significant military demobilization and defense disinvestment did occur in the 1940s, which was evident in the early months of the Korean War when the United States struggled. US performance in Korea and concerns of Soviet expansionism eventually provoked leaders to take up the mantle of international leadership and develop a professional standing military. US secretary of state John Foster Dulles wrote in 1954: "If the enemy could pick his time and his place and his method of warfare—and if our policy was to remain the traditional one of meeting aggression by direct and local opposition—then we had to be ready to fight in the Arctic and the tropics, in Asia, in the Near East and in Europe; by sea, by land, by air; by old weapons and by new weapons."[3]

The US-Soviet rivalry was global, but both sides prepared for major war in Europe. Reinforcing its allies, the United States supported friendly governments and insurgent forces to resist takeovers by parties who would have allied themselves with the Soviets. To do this, the United States had to develop an expeditionary military capable of reinforcing allies anywhere in the world. While the Vietnam War tempered the US disposition for war, the defense reforms undertaken in the 1970s and the 1990s led to a professional force capable of projecting and sustaining combat power anywhere on the planet. While future budgetary uncertainty will affect the capacity of the defense establishment, the United States continues to field military capabilities that are comprehensive, multidomain, joint, and internationalized.

Though not facing existential threats like those of the Cold War, the United States is once again facing an important strategic choice. In contrast to foreign policy during the Cold War, when countering a peer competitor such as the Soviet Union was its organizing principle, future foreign policy will center around reinforcing capable partners who can take on stabilizing roles in their regions to deter the possible rise of challengers intent upon changing the existing global order. In an echo of President Franklin D. Roosevelt's Four Policemen, US strategy over the next twenty years will focus on fewer partners than today but will center on countries that can make definitive contributions to economic prosperity and international security. These partners have a shared sense of a world defined by secure lines of communication, free trade, and collective security. To be sure, future US grand strategy will be global and multilateral, but it will be much more selective than it is today.

Factors Shaping US Grand Strategy

As Michael Roskin has observed, every "generation" of US foreign policymakers reacts to the perceived failure of the previous generation's paradigm. For instance, "the bearers of the 'Pearl Harbor paradigm' (themselves reacting to the deficiencies of the interwar 'isolationism') eventually drove interventionism into the ground in Vietnam, giving rise to a noninterventionist 'Vietnam paradigm.'"[4] As this generation comes to terms with the wars in Iraq and Afghanistan, we expect a similar paradigm to take hold, reinforced by other key factors that will drive the next generation of strategic thinkers. Withholding military intervention of Syria in 2013 was the first sign of this.

First, fiscal austerity is a reality in the United States that will affect the expeditionary capabilities and global American presence. While shrinking budgets affect strategy, a second factor is a sclerotic national security bureaucracy that will struggle to reform as it seeks to protect its weakening resource base. Third, the failure of grand plans to reshape the Middle East and Central Asia has instilled an appreciation for the risks involved in large, transformational international security projects. Finally, technological innovation will transform how the United States views the global market and, in particular, allow for a reevaluation of some of its current dependencies. In so doing, it will transform international trade patterns—and change the conception of US national security.

Table 8.1: US Defense Spending, FY 2001–FY 2015

Fiscal Year	Current Dollars in Billions
2001	316
2002	345
2003	438
2004	468
2005	479
2006	535
2007	601
2008	666
2009	666
2010	691
2011	687
2012	645
2013	614
2014 (est.)	581
2015 (est.)	575

Source: Undersecretary of Defense (Comptroller), DOD Budget Request, slide 2, www
.comptroller.defense.gov/Portals/45/Documents/defbudget/fy2015/fy2015_Budget_
Request.pdf.

Fiscal Constraints

There is a direct connection between national security and the economy: A strong economy generates revenue that can be allocated for defense, while an innovative economy creates new technologies that can be employed by the military. With fiscal austerity on the horizon in 2010, then chairman of the Joint Chiefs of Staff Adm. Mike Mullen declared that the national debt is the single biggest national security threat.[5] He noted that an increasing debt would, over time, come to absorb more and more of US government outlays, thus negatively affecting future military spending, particularly for procurement of new equipment, and the ability to sustain the current size of the force. Thus the US military would be less capable to undertake military operations down the road.

Currently the amount the United States spends on its military is nearly half as much as the rest of the world's military expenditures combined. US military capabilities overshadow all potential competitors: Only the United States,

Table 8.2: Defense Spending by Category (FY 2015 President's Budget Request)

Category	Percentage	Dollars in Billions (Excludes Overseas Contingency Operations)
Military Construction and Family Housing	1.33	6.6
Research, Development, Testing, and Evaluation	12.84	63.5
Procurement	18.28	90.4
Military Personnel	27.35	135.2
Operations and Maintenance	40.19	198.7

Undersecretary of Defense (Comptroller), DOD Budget Request, slide 12, www
.comptroller.defense.gov/Portals/45/Documents/defbudget/fy2015/fy2015_Budget_
Request.pdf.

for example, is able to place over a hundred thousand troops eight thousand miles from home and sustain them indefinitely under combat conditions. This capacity is what makes the United States a superpower. However, this capacity is costly, with military spending reaching $581 billion in 2014.[6] Whether the United States will have the same panoply of tools available to finance its national security operations in the future is subject to debate. But as previously discussed, when allies are supportive, they have provided substantial financial support to reduce the cost to the United States through host-nation support or direct payments.

Over the last decade, the US military budget has grown by several hundred billion dollars. Some of the increase is explained by the cost of the Iraq and Afghan wars, but there were also significant new outlays in scientific research and personnel costs. In fact, the US military spends more on health care than India or Germany spends on its entire defense budget. Likewise the US budget for personnel (salaries and benefits) is larger than China's entire defense budget.[7]

Today the US military is trying to rein in personnel and health care costs. However, Congress is often reluctant to cut personnel benefits or raise health care premiums, and so weapons and end strength may eventually become the focus of the cuts. For the first time in many years, the military budget has become a matter for both public and congressional discussion, with topics formerly deemed "off limits" now open for scrutiny (for instance, whether parts of the formerly sacrosanct nuclear triad ought to be decommissioned), particularly the question as to whether defense spending ought to be cut in order to safe-guard entitlement programs such as Social Security and Medicare. If the goal of reducing discretionary spending by $1.2 trillion over a decade is to be reached, there will have to be major budget cuts that will impact national security and whether the United States can sustain its commitments to maintain an international system of its own creation.

Polling data suggest this will occur as the public values domestic policy more than foreign policy: In 2013, just 6 percent said the president should focus on foreign policy, compared to 40 percent in 2007.[8] This trend stems from frustrations with the protracted conflicts in the 2000s but has its roots in the relatively peaceful 1990s. Then Josef Joffe prophetically asked, "Why pay the bill?"[9] Increasingly, the answer from the US public and Congress is "Let someone else pay."

If the United States—and to a similar extent, Europe—ceases to be willing to pay as much for the maintenance of a global architecture, no other state is likely to step forward to fill that vacuum by creating a rival system. Too many countries, including China, benefit from the existing system—even if they are happy to register complaints about US management and try to steer Washington to fulfill their own preference. Major shocks to the system, such as the 2008–9 US recession, have not generated alternatives to an Americanized international order, and the first signs of economic recovery in the United States have stifled predictions of American decline. The "sticky" nature of the international system has positive benefits for the United States and can prevent any conflict with China since its global integration is attractive.[10] Amb. Sun Guoxiang, consul general in New York of the People's Republic of China, expressed as much: "As long as we [the United States and China] treat each other on an equal footing, accommodate each other's core interests and major concerns, and manage our differences, we can enjoy a sound relationship and mutual development."[11]

Bureaucratic Inertia

At the same time, the ossification of the US foreign policy process has rendered Washington far less creative in coming up with new approaches to deal with a changing world. A vast national security bureaucracy and the weight of congressional regulations and mandates put many limits on the executive branch's freedom of action; windows of opportunity can be long closed before the US government marshals the tools it needs to act. This is why even proposals for interagency reform that have been advanced in the past several years, as flawed as they may be, never seem to leave the drawing board.

The growing dysfunction within Congress and the hyperpartisan atmosphere create an environment ripe for stagnation. As former secretary of defense Robert Gates wrote, "we have rarely been so polarized and so unable to execute even the basic functions of government, much less tackle the most difficult and divisive problems facing the country."[12] Consequently it is highly unlikely that the legislative branch is capable of generating the bipartisan consensus needed to formulate and pass any major national security reforms. As chapter 2 notes, the reforms of 1947 and 1986 were not easy, even with the specter of nuclear war that helped provide the impetus for change.

At the same time, bureaucratic inertia in defense policy is in stark contrast to the post-Vietnam era when a number of changes were made that dramatically changed the US military. First, the Abrams Doctrine shifted key specialties from the active component to the reserve component. This slowed the nation's ability to wage war (it took six months to call up reservists and National Guardsmen and to build the force needed for the 1991 invasion of Iraq), partly in the hopes that this would force political leaders to achieve societal buy-in for any future intervention. Second, conscription was abandoned in favor of the all-volunteer force, which was enshrined in part to provide a constant pool of professional forces but also to avoid conscripting unwilling personnel and, important, to tamp down opposition to military action since only volunteers would be involved. Third, and largely rhetorical, the Weinberger and Powell Doctrines advised strict criteria for military intervention, which was intended to prevent gradual escalations leading to full-scale combat. With the exception of the all-volunteer force, all of these reforms were undone during the 2000s to make the US military more usable. The reserve component and National Guard have transformed from a strategic reserve to an operational reserve. And broad conceptions of security have undermined attempts to reduce military internationalism.

Skepticism of Foreign Policy Goals

A review of US diplomatic history illustrates that the United States tends to offer sweeping foreign policy goals, but the track record to achieving those goals is mixed. As discussed in the chapter on the American way of warfare, battlefield success has been difficult to translate into strategic victory. In Iraq and Afghanistan, it took several years before the national security establishment realized it lacked the capabilities to fundamentally transform societies. Consequently, the United States abandoned its grandiose national objectives and shifted emphasis to security force assistance to let Iraq and Afghanistan fight their own civil wars.

As we reflect on other efforts to transform states or reinforce failing states, the results seem grim. Proponents of nation-building often point to successful cases in Japan, Germany, and South Korea. However, there are few contemporary examples where the intervention by an external actor such as the United States has achieved announced objectives of creating security, a representative government, and a developing economy.[13] Indeed, the United States has no recent case where it can point to a success similar to the rehabilitated postwar Axis powers. Since 2000, Colombia has received massive amounts of US security and economic assistance, yet the government has been unable to bring an end to the country's fifty-year-old civil war. In Bosnia-Herzegovina and Kosovo, economic and political development has progressed little since the military interventions of the 1990s halted overt conflict. US efforts to transform Mali into a constitutional democracy with an effective military force were for naught when rebels were able to seize control of the northern part of the country and the government was overthrown in a military coup in 2012, necessitating US-supported French intervention. Egypt was a major beneficiary of US assistance for decades, yet never started a serious reform process under US tutelage or policy objectives. All of these attempts have reinforced growing skepticism about nation-building and highlighted the limited role that external actors can play.

Frustrated Regional Actors

The financial hardships and bureaucratic inertia of the West have been matched by a growing suspicion of ambitious US-sponsored agendas among the rising and resurgent powers of the South and East—the countries the United States expects to take on more of the burden in maintaining the global system. Despite all the claims that we have entered a postideological period—where the often contentious debates of the twentieth century have been settled in favor of markets, democracy, globalization, and the responsibility to protect—a very clear ideological tension persists in international affairs. The "sovereignty club" has increasingly emerged in recent years and its most consistent members are the BRICS (Brazil, Russia, India, China, and South Africa). These states might not share a common set of political or economic values, but they are in firm agreement about a shared set of principles that ought to govern the international order. These include the beliefs that international institutions exist to regulate interstate behavior, not to promote human rights, that states are obligated to carry out only those contractual obligations they have agreed to, and that no country should judge another's internal policies.[14] Sovereignty claims are reinforced by these countries' desires to become regional hegemons free from US interference: Brazil seeks dominance in South America, Russia wants to dominate its near abroad, India projects its influence as the world's largest UN peacekeeper, China develops capabilities to give it freedom of action in Northeast Asia, and South Africa attempts to help the countries of Africa overcome colonial legacies impeding development.

Coupled with this is a belief, justified or not, that proposed rules—whether on trade, climate, or any other issue—are often shaped by Western countries to favor their own interests and to penalize the rising powers. At their 2013 summit in Durban, South Africa, the leaders of the BRICS reaffirmed their contention that "the prevailing global governance architecture is regulated by institutions which were conceived in circumstances when the international landscape in all its aspects was characterised by very different challenges and opportunities" and pledged that they "are committed to exploring new models and approaches towards more equitable development and inclusive global growth."[15] Consequently, we expect to see these countries challenge the United States when it behaves outside international norms and attempt to constrain its behavior.

Energy Security and Technological Innovation

Energy security has figured prominently in US grand strategy since World War II when President Roosevelt struck his bargain with Saudi king Abdul Aziz that the United States would support the House of Saud in return for steady and reliable access to the kingdom's energy resources. Since then, every president has renewed the commitment of a US military presence in the Middle East.

Now on the cusp of a domestic technological revolution, the United States could break the time-honored links between energy imports and national security. With the extensive development of nonconventional oil and natural gas— the so-called shale revolution—the United States might finally achieve what every president since Richard Nixon has placed on the top of the list of its strategic priorities: energy independence. Indeed, there might even be enough domestic supply for the United States not only to meet its own needs, but also to resume its place as one of the world's major energy exporters.

The International Energy Agency predicts that US energy production will exceed Saudi Arabia's by 2020.[16] If shale oil enables the United States to achieve energy independence, a fundamental shift in US foreign policy could occur that would overturn the Carter Doctrine and the Reagan Corollary, which committed the United States to defend the countries of the Persian Gulf. Likewise there would be little strategic logic for the United States to repeat its past efforts to bring Eurasian energy to international markets. For the past twenty years, US policy has promoted new transport routes that would get Caspian and Central Asian energy to Western markets by bypassing both Russia and Iran; the United States has also encouraged European consumers to decrease their dependence on Russian energy supplies, a request given greater urgency by the 2014 crisis over Ukraine. But if the United States could itself export energy to Europe as well as support the emergence of new sources of Central European shale gas, then the economic rationale for US efforts to intervene in the post-Soviet space diminishes. Instead the United States could rethink its security commitments from those defined by dependency to those defined by national interests.

Other technological breakthroughs could curtail American dependence on overseas energy sources, including safer and more environmentally sustainable ways to access domestic sources of raw materials and new manufacturing techniques. These in turn would decrease American dependence on a globalized "just-in-time" system of trade—where it is of vital importance that resources and components produced in different parts of the world make their way quickly and efficiently to final assembly points and then to market. The United States will not withdraw from the international economy, but it may become more cost-effective in the coming years to truly "buy American"—diminishing the country's interest in patrolling and securing the global commons. And if the United States shifts its orientation away from Europe and Asia toward consolidating a hemisphere-wide market for goods and services, then the United States might redirect its security posture away from Europe and Asia in favor of a Western Hemispheric–centered approach. With no significant military challengers in the hemisphere, this approach could facilitate defense cuts.

Lower resource costs could also revitalize other sectors of the domestic economy and challenge notions of American decline. Already there is a small but noticeable trend by which jobs formerly outsourced to lower-cost venues overseas over the past two decades are being repatriated. And if more manufacturing positions return to the US homeland, leading to a situation where more of the products being consumed in the United States are being made on American soil, there is little logic to the argument the United States must take upon itself the lion's share of the burden of securing the infrastructure of globalization because of American dependence on imported goods and raw materials, especially energy. While outbreaks of piracy in the waters off the continent of Africa, for example, might offend Americans' respect for freedom of the seas, under such conditions it would no longer threaten American economic interests or have an appreciable impact on American trade—making it harder to justify American interventions overseas on the basis of threats to core American interests.

Redefining National Interests

Eugene Gholz, Daryl G. Press, and Harvey M. Sapolsky suggest that "the United States intervenes often in the conflicts of others, but without a consistent rationale, without a clear sense of how to advance U.S. interests, and sometimes with unintended and expensive consequences."[17] This perception, with a combination of mandatory defense cuts and a more economically self-reliant country, will lead to shifts in the existing US global security posture and redefinition of the national interest.[18] National interests can be universal and enduring, such as ensuring the security of the state and its people. But national interests can also be the product of national policymakers, such as advancing democratic institutions and protecting the environment. Rediscovering the intensity of national interests is important to set priorities. Hans Morgenthau differentiated between vital national interests and secondary interests, which are more difficult to define.[19] Barack Obama offered his own priorities and maintained that his administration would apply a careful calculus to determine when a situation might require the use of force: "I have made it clear that I will never hesitate to use our military swiftly, decisively and unilaterally when necessary to defend our people, our homeland, our allies, and our core interests."[20] In the same address, President Obama clarified what he thought was a secondary interest: "There will be times though when our safety is not directly threatened, but our interests and values are. Sometimes the course of history poses challenges that threaten our common humanity and common security, responding to natural disasters, for example; or preventing genocide and keeping the peace; ensuring regional security, and maintaining the flow of commerce. In such cases we should not be afraid to act but the burden of action should not be America's alone. As we have in Libya, our task is instead to mobilize the international community for collective action."[21]

To be sure, presidential policy is one source to discern vital interests from secondary ones, yet the multitude of political actors and nongovernmental forces consider three fundamental questions.[22] One is "What are we willing to *die* for?"[23] That is, where is the United States willing to put service members' lives at risk through ground deployment? The other questions are "What are we willing to kill for?" and "What are we willing to pay for?" One relatively simple approach to this rather complex and somewhat ambiguous concept is to stratify national interests and connect to the types of intervention available:

- Vital Interests: What are we willing to die for? Example: Invade Afghanistan with ground forces to destroy al-Qaeda training camps.
- Important Interests: What are we willing to kill for? Example: Participate in a NATO air campaign to conduct regime change in Libya.
- Peripheral Interests: What are we willing to fund? Example: Train and equip African Union peacekeepers for stability operations in Mali.

Given the ability of the United States to achieve air supremacy as well as to launch standoff naval weapons, it can kill with limited risk to its pilots and sailors, giving it a coercive advantage during diplomatic crises. In the 1990s, for example, missile attacks against Iraq and the air war for Kosovo exemplified that the United States was willing to kill to achieve objectives but not willing to die by deploying ground forces. Advances in remotely piloted vehicles over the last decade enhance Americans' ability to conduct casualty-free warfare, as evidenced by regular drone strikes in Pakistan, Yemen, and Afghanistan.

In addition to using military force, the United States also pursues its national interests through friendly surrogates. In cases like these, the United States is willing to fund others to provide humanitarian assistance, conduct peacekeeping operations, or contribute to international military coalitions. The clearest example is through the Global Peacekeeping Operations Initiative (GPOI), which was designed to train and equip foreign peacekeepers for global deployment.[24] A program like GPOI seeks to limit the impact of regional crises while providing the international community a ready response to humanitarian emergencies. Along these lines, the United States was willing to fund African militaries to operate in Mali, but it was not willing to deploy American ground forces or establish a no-fly zone. This approach is likely to increase in an era of burden-sharing where "building partner capacity is an essential military mission and an important component of the U.S. Government's approach to preventing and responding to crisis, conflict, and instability."[25]

Considering the way military forces are used may lead future administrations to consider reviving a form of the Nixon Doctrine. Certainly the original doctrine, promulgated some forty-three years ago, was meant to address a worldwide Soviet threat, yet while conditions have changed, Nixon's attempts to reformulate a grand strategy during a time of economic uncertainty makes it relevant today. At the time, Nixon declared that "the United States will participate in the defense and development of allies and friends, but . . . America cannot—and will not—conceive all the plans, design all the programs, execute all the decisions and undertake all the defense of the free nations of the world. We will help where it makes a real difference and is considered in our interest."[26]

Under this approach, the United States would focus on meeting its treaty commitments but would also require its partners, if the threat emanated from their region of the world, to assume primary responsibility for action, including shouldering the costs. Hints of this have been seen in the Obama administration's unfortunately labeled dictum of "leading from behind." In theory, the 2011 Libya operation was supposed to be an example of other partners taking the lead in a regional security operation, with the United States only supposed to provide support. In reality, the United States still ended up bearing a significant majority of the costs of that action. Moving forward, however, the United States will have to make it clear that it is not prepared to deploy a fiscal or military safety net to make up for partners' shortfalls the next time its foreign policy exceeds its military capacity. The era when American policymakers were willing to see vital interests at stake in every corner of the globe is coming to an end.

Searching for Grand Strategy

In general, a good strategy should answer three basic questions: (1) What do we wish to achieve—that is, what are the desired ends? (2) How do we get there; what are the ways? (3) And what resources are available, or what means will be used? Simply, strategy is about how leadership can use the power available to the state to exercise control over people, places, things, and events to achieve objectives in accordance with national interests and policies. The Cold War imposed a certain discipline and focus on American strategy. After the Soviet collapse, however, the irrelevance of the Cold War containment strategy spurred a cottage industry as different contenders for a post–Cold War grand strategy emerged in the US foreign policy community.[27] In the absence of a guiding post–Cold War strategic narrative, scholars attempted to articulate distinct strategies that would

Table 8.3: Grand Strategy Alternatives

Primacy or National Liberalism	Liberal Internationalism or Cooperative Security
How does the United States preserve its hegemony? Core tenet: hegemonic stability End: preponderance of military power Way: prevent emergence of rivals Geographic focus: global	How does the United States export security? Core tenet: democratic peace End: strategic interdependence Way: promote democracy Geographic focus: global
Strategic Restraint or Neoisolationism	**Offshore Balancing or Selective Engagement**
How does the United States guarantee security? Core tenet: deterrence End: strategic independence Way: conserve power Geographic focus: Western Hemisphere	When does the United States use its power? Core tenet: balance of power End: regional stability Way: confront non-conforming states Geographic focus: Europe, Asia, Middle East

govern US international behavior, set geographic priorities, and consider how the United States contributes to international security (see table 8.3).

For the last two decades, scholars, public intellectuals, and politicians have argued about what America's role in the world ought to be. There are some who make the case for a grand strategy of restraint so Americans can "be free, enjoy peace, and concentrate more on the problems closer to home."[28] Citing the relative safety of the world, the costs associated with maintaining unipolarity, and the risks associated with military interventions, these individuals argue that American national security is best achieved through withdrawal from international institutions and restraint against temptations to remake the world in America's interests.[29] The idea became more popular in response to the frustration with the Iraq and Afghan wars.

Another form of disengagement has been promoted as offshore balancing by scholars such as Christopher Layne; the strategy calls for a reduction in US international presence and a withdrawal from alliance commitments in Asia and Europe. Layne writes that it is important to move away from a strategy that preserves hegemony and that "the United States would be more secure in a multipolar system than it would be by attempting to perpetuate its current preeminence."[30] In the aftermath of the Iraq War, offshore balancing gained prominent supporters, including Stephen Walt who writes that the strategy would "eschew nation-building and large onshore ground and air deployments. . . . It would acknowledge that Americans are not very good at running other countries . . . [and] it would take advantage of America's favorable geopolitical position."[31] Simply, the safety of peaceful neighbors and bordering oceans, the lack of a great-power rival, and the costs associated with large-scale stability operations should temper military interventions and reset America's defense posture.

The appeal of disengagement strategies increases during times of foreign policy frustration and fiscal austerity, when American global leadership is recast in terms of burdens on the country. But complete disengagement is not endorsed by most Americans. Polling data suggest that some 70 percent of Americans want the United States to remain the global leader—but to share the burdens and responsibilities with other powers.[32] Given the benefits of existing alliances, Robert Art sees a United States more active in the world but limited to the key regions of Europe, the Middle East, and Northeast Asia. He argues that the United States needs "to continue with an activist, internationalist, global leadership policy rather than retreating into isolationism or offshore balancing."[33] The problem is not leading, but rather problems result when the United States operates alone or operates apart from the institutions it sustains. Consequently some scholars advocate a liberal internationalist strategy where grand strategy "should pursue five goals: increasing equality of opportunity, assuming responsibility, smartly managing interdependence, leading coalitions and recasting global bargains, and building the democratic community."[34]

Bridging the importance of leading in a multilateral way, another set of scholars sees the United States globally engaged to prevent "the emergence of a new rival . . . [because] U.S. power is good not only for the United States itself but also the rest of the world."[35] For them "primacy is not strategy but a fact of international life: even if America 'came home' and slashed military spending, it would retain the world's greatest latent power potential."[36] They draw their historical connection from a 1947 Department of State Policy Planning Staff memo: "To seek less than preponderant power would be to opt for defeat. Preponderant power must be the object of U.S. policy."[37]

Primacists argue that despite the costs of such a strategy, the United States obtains critical benefits. Among these are enhanced security, tranquility among great-power rivals, peaceful conditions conducive for trade, and maximum influence for the United States.[38] To maintain its preponderant power, the United States leads through formal international institutions such as the UN and World Trade Organization (WTO) and military coalitions such as the International Security Assistance Force in Afghanistan and the Combined Maritime Coalition in the Indian Ocean.

As academics and public intellectuals argued these issues, different ideas found their way into US government documents.[39] The 1986 Goldwater-

Nichols Act included provisions requiring the president to publish, on a regular basis, a national security strategy. It was hoped that this document would describe "the worldwide interests, goals, and objectives[;] . . . the foreign policy, worldwide commitments, and national defense capabilities of the United States necessary to deter aggression[;] . . . the proposed short-term and long-term uses of the political, economic, military, and other elements of national power of the United States to protect or promote the interests[; and] . . . the adequacy of the capabilities of the United States to carry out the national security strategy."[40]

US presidents have regularly released national security strategies since the law went into effect. While each president responded to particular security challenges during his tenure (the ending of the Cold War for Ronald Reagan and George H. W. Bush and the rise of nationalist conflicts and global terrorism for Bill Clinton and George W. Bush), their respective strategies have also enunciated policies related to trade, America's leadership in global affairs, and the promotion of international organizations to unify action. Each also maintains a recurring theme to improve national security through global engagement.

These documents attempted to answer the question of where the United States should be prepared to invest its resources and put the lives of its service members at risk—and under what conditions. Given that the United States does not have any immediate security threats—the American cause to war is tempered by the reality of peaceful neighbors—US strategies had to make the case, on wider security as well as on ideological grounds, why trends elsewhere in the world (communism, radical nationalism, terrorism, and religious extremism) required US involvement.

US national security strategies have, in turn, sought to redefine what constitutes national security in light of attempts in the 1990s and 2000s to defuse situations before they become crises and to provide the rationale for support for governments that confront shared security challenges such as terrorism and transnational organized crime.[41] Since the 1990s, the limits (and frustration) with US grand strategy tend to be explained by this expansive view of security. Additionally, engaging with almost every country in the world dilutes resources and generates distractions from core interests. While burden-sharing through coalition operations is a norm, the United States increasingly identifies more challenges than it and its partners can manage. Colin Dueck captured the impact of this and notes the American approach to strategy is flawed: "Sweeping and ambitious goals are announced, but then pursued by disproportionately limited means, thus creating an outright invitation to failure."[42] Likewise, attempting to articulate clearly defined doctrine tends to lead to false expectations that are "problematic at best and counterproductive at worst."[43]

Global Interest

Since the early days of the Republic, the United States has always been tied to global interests. While it did its best to refrain from the European wars of the nineteenth century, the United States had an active global agenda. With Europe, the country concluded major agreements with France and Russia to expand its territory in North America. In Asia, the United States established a treaty with Thailand in 1833, opened trade with Japan in 1854, and began administering the Philippines in 1898. Subsequent to the peace treaty ending the Spanish-American War, President William McKinley captured the incidental nature of US great-power status: "We cannot be unmindful that without any desire or design on our part the war has brought us new duties and responsibilities which we must meet and discharge as becomes a great nation on whose growth and career from the beginning the Ruler of Nations has plainly written the high command and pledge of civilization."[44]

In the Western Hemisphere, the United States also created barriers to competitive states. President James Monroe declared in 1823 "that the American continents . . . are henceforth not to be considered as subjects for future colonization by any European powers."[45] The timing enabled newly independent states of Latin America to be free of new claims made by Spain and Portugal but later paved the way for US primacy in the region through the Roosevelt Corollary to the Monroe Doctrine. President Theodore Roosevelt asserted that countries in the hemisphere must behave according to "acceptable international standards of behavior. Chronic wrongdoing, or an impotence which results in a general loosening of the ties of civilized society, may in America, as elsewhere, require intervention by some civilized nation."[46] Far from isolationist, the United States was quite active in Latin America during the early twentieth century through small wars.

When it came to the world wars of the twentieth century, the United States maintained its distance for several years. It did not enter World War I until 1917 (nearly three years after it commenced) and World War II until 1941 (two years after Germany invaded Poland and four years after Japan invaded China). In both cases, the United States came to realize that militarism and fascism in Europe and Asia posed an existential threat to America itself. With the advent of nuclear weapons and the challenge of Soviet subversion around the world, US leaders saw they could not sit on the sidelines for years as the country did in the world wars. Instead, the United States affirmed its global standing not by assuming control of European colonies, but by promoting decolonization, international cooperation, and trade.

Defense and Trade

The United States seeks trade relations with almost every country in the world, and its special trade relationships are geographically dispersed. Through the

159 members of the WTO and the fourteen free-trade agreements with twenty countries, there are very few limits on trade relationships. America is willing to trade with virtually any nation on earth.

When it comes to defense, however, the same cannot be said—not all countries are seen as equally vital to America's own national security. In general, the United States sees Eurasia as a key geographic area. While the Soviet threat vanished in 1991, US commitments to European defense did not. The NATO alliance expanded three times since 1991, increasing its membership from sixteen when the Soviet Union fell to twenty-eight today. Russian provocations in Ukraine in 2014 will stimulate additional commitment to Europe. Likewise, US defense commitments in Asia remain enduring; all non-NATO treaty allies are in Asia, and uncertainty about China's intentions is keeping the United States focused on Asia and developing new relations with India, Vietnam, and Myanmar.

While there are no formal defense treaties with countries in the Middle East (though many are implied, including with Israel and Saudi Arabia), presidents have consistently defined the Middle East as a vital area due to the concentration of oil and natural gas there. President Jimmy Carter in 1980 said, "An attempt by any outside force to gain control of the Persian Gulf region . . . will be repelled by the use of any means necessary, including military force."[47] What became known as the Carter Doctrine led to the stationing of US military forces throughout the region, reversing Iraq's occupation of Kuwait in 1991, and balancing regional powers that may threaten stability.

Largely left out of US trade and security assistance are the fifty-four countries of Africa. US assistance there is primarily focused on improving public health. What little security assistance there is in Africa primarily addresses efforts to combat terrorism and professionalize the countries' small militaries. With no major military power, no risk of nuclear proliferation, and limited threats to natural resource exports, there will be limits on US involvement in Africa. As fiscal austerity sets in and societies develop the capacity for their own development, Africa will remain a peripheral interest.

The same can be said for Latin America. While the region accounts for a significant amount of US trade, the nearly universal acceptance of democracy (including illiberal democracy) keeps the region free of interstate conflict. Transnational organized crime engaged in illicit trafficking does generate civil instability, but the uneasy history of US intervention in the region and increasing capacity of Latin American countries temper any notion of engaging directly to confront their internal challenges. The United States is more likely to follow its Plan Colombia example, which limited US involvement to training, equipping, and advising Colombian forces, rather than participate in military action there.

Finally, when it comes to the so-called global commons (the high seas, the atmosphere, outer space, and cyberspace), the United States is willing to take the lead but no longer assume the full burden of maintaining open and free access. The United States used its "convening power," its network of global bases, and its naval units to form the core of the coalition assembled in 2009 to deal with the threat that piracy emanating from Somalia posed to vital shipping lanes in the Indian Ocean and the Red Sea. However, the initial task force developed, in accordance with the emerging twenty-first-century American way of war, into a joint and international operation, Combined Joint Task Force 150 (CTF-150), which by 2010 encompassed naval, other military, and intelligence assets from twenty-five nations. Working in parallel with CTF-150 was a European Union (EU) naval operation (EU-NAVFOR-Atalanta), as well as task forces sent by China, India, South Korea, and Russia. In 2014, this coalition expanded to twenty-nine countries.

A Grand Strategy for Our Time

For the last seventy years, the United States has largely defined its grand strategy in opposition to threats while pursuing its national interests of security and prosperity. From 1945 to 1991, countering the Soviet Union through global presence and containment dominated US foreign policy. While important international institutions were built, such as NATO, it was not until Soviet collapse that cooperation developed for security purposes could be channeled into new economic institutions such as the EU. While there were significant internal conflicts around the world during the 1990s (particularly in sub-Saharan Africa and southeastern Europe), economic integration, global trade, and economic development were the defining features of the international environment. This led many countries to declare a "peace dividend," which resulted in significant disinvestment in defense infrastructure. By the 2000s, European countries could not match their foreign policy objectives with the military forces required to carry them out in sub-Saharan Africa and Central Asia.

The al-Qaeda terrorist attacks in the United States, Europe, and Africa prompted a return to a threat-focused grand strategy in 2001. The decentralized nature of international terrorist groups reinforced the importance of a global cooperative strategy that found partners in capitals around the world, including Beijing and Moscow. With few exceptions, governments condemned terrorism, and efforts to control it began at the nation-state level. While many states cooperated with the United States, public outrage occasionally challenged the counterterrorism-centric strategy. Key allies, such as Italy and Canada, objected to the use of extraordinary rendition programs. Other countries, such as Pakistan and Argentina, objected to detention centers and missile strikes by remotely piloted vehicles. The counterterrorism-centric approach led to missteps, such as the invasion of Iraq in 2003, and the expansion of the US and NATO missions in Afghanistan in 2009. While military operations achieved their initial goals of decapitating the governing regimes in those countries, neither mission has met the overall goal of creating security and stability—at least not yet, more than a decade after they began.

New Beginnings

The first post–Cold War era was marked by President George H. W. Bush's address before a joint session of Congress on September 11, 1990. In it, he outlined his vision of a "new world order," arguing that the end of the Cold War and the imminent launching of a multilateral military operation to liberate Kuwait from Iraqi forces offered the nations of the world "a rare opportunity to move toward a historic period of cooperation." Events over the next several years seemed to validate his prediction: The ensuing Gulf War offered a model for multilateral military interventions; the Madrid Peace conference raised the tantalizing hope that a general peace settlement for the Middle East might be in reach; and a "third wave" of democratization spread throughout Eastern Europe, Latin America, East Asia, and parts of Africa. Over the same period of time, the Soviet Union collapsed, while the EU was born, and the WTO came into existence.

Moreover, the dire predictions of some realists that, with the demise of the USSR, new rivals would emerge to challenge the United States proved to be unfounded. Many theorists predicted the rise of a US-Japanese rivalry, given assessments that Japan's economy was about to surpass that of the United States. For many reasons, not least of which included a mutual defense treaty, the threat posed to Japan from neighbors such as China, North Korea, or even Russia (which is why Japan accepted the stationing of US military forces in Japan), shared democratic values, and an important trade relationship, security relations actually improved, and the US-Japanese alliance became closer rather than fraying.

The optimism of the early 1990s was based on the assumption that globalization would knit the nations of the world into a global community espousing common values and shared interests, backed up by a rising tide of prosperity that would "lift the boats" of all nations and eliminate the need for zero-sum perspectives in world affairs. Some thinkers, as well as American leaders, also expected this process to be accompanied by an alignment of other nations with US values and interests, with tacit support for Washington's continued leadership of the community of nations. Writing in *Foreign Affairs* in 1997, Josef Joffe declared, "There is a much bigger payoff in getting others to want what you want, and that has to do with the attraction of one's ideas, with agenda-setting, with ideology and institutions, and with holding out big prizes for cooperation, such as the vastness and sophistication of one's market."[48]

The 2000s were a wake-up call to the optimists. Terrorist attacks exposed homeland security vulnerabilities, the US invasion of Iraq caused global opinion of the United States to plummet, and the 2008 financial crisis challenged American-style capital markets. Diplomatically, the UN Security Council vacillated among those espousing humanitarian interventions versus those committed to defending state sovereignty. International conferences meant to further liberalize trade among the nations or find a common approach to dealing with climate change foundered on the shoals of new divisions between rising powers such as China and status quo powers such as the United States. The 1990s wave of liberal democracy crested, with neopopulist and neoauthoritarian governments gaining ground and demonstrating greater willingness to defy Washington and its prescriptions.

Fifteen years into the era defined by counterterrorism, a new gap has opened up between the confident expectations of the 1990s and the realities of the 2010s. As the United States moves out of the counterterrorism era, there is an opportunity to avoid the pitfalls of threat-centric grand strategies. But not all lessons should be forgotten. Thomas Nichols recognizes there is a positive role for the United States to play that is inspired by the Cold War but applied to counterterrorism: "Acknowledging the power of ideas and retaining a conviction in the possibility of victory should nonetheless be central in conducting" future conflicts.[49]

Because of the realist predisposition to see countries as rivals, China is often identified as the most likely candidate to emerge as the next peer competitor to replace the vanished Soviet Union. Some even argue that the United States and China are already at war, albeit in cyberspace, the currency markets, and influence in developing countries.

Without a doubt, China is a large country with a growing economy and developing military that is deploying naval and ground forces outside of Asia. With contrasting political systems and regular disagreements at the UN over how the global order ought to be structured, there is tension between the two countries. Further, China has territorial disputes with several treaty allies of the United States that could trigger conflict, given US commitments to defend the territorial integrity of its partners. Some see it as inevitable that the United States and China will clash. If so, then the most prudent strategy would be to contain China before it becomes too powerful.

To be sure, China's rise is a significant phenomenon, yet its authoritarian future and a clash with the United States are not preordained. Unlike the Soviet Union, which was under economic sanction by the United States, China and the United States are important trading partners. Unlike the Soviet Union, which actively promoted insurgency and authoritarianism, China has a strict policy of noninterference that does not create challengers to the current international order. And unlike the Soviet Union, which traded with a small group of countries within its sphere of influence, China is a global trading country and member of the WTO. In the words of noted China scholar David Schambaugh, "China is a global actor but without (yet) being a true global power."[50] It is not positioning itself to take on the mantle of the Soviet Union. Some argue, therefore, that China's rise can be accommodated within the parameters of the US-defined international order, with China becoming, in former World Bank president Bob Zoellick's phrase, a "responsible stakeholder" in the system. And the rising powers have no reason to destroy the international system that has facilitated their own ascension.

Thus global anarchy is unlikely, given the vested interests of the major powers in preserving some of the advances made by globalization, which continue to contribute to their prosperity and position. It is very true that the emerging powers of the Global South and East are resistant to the idea of a single rulebook for the world's nations, which drove proposals for the creation of the WTO and the renovation of the UN system, and particularly if the rules of the global order are drawn up largely in Washington. However, no other power or group of powers is positioned to produce an alternative global system that can provide many of the same benefits. Thus the impetus to challenge the US-led order will recede with emphasis instead placed on gaining more influence within it. As this occurs, the new world order will end up looking a lot like the old one where the United States incidentally leads.

Given this reality, the United States can indeed afford to retrench and become more selective in where and when it chooses to engage in the rest of the world. Fear of global collapse is unfounded, and a change in the maximalist deployment of US power will not invite a collapse of an international order favorable to US interests. With domestic politics restraining an activist agenda, we saw the country avoid war with Syria in 2013.

There are, of course, different ways in which this broad strategic outline might be implemented in practice. Focusing on the Asia-Pacific region (and achieving a workable détente with China), while expecting Europe to take full responsibility for its own security and for extending a zone of security and prosperity across the Mediterranean, and forging a closer partnership for Brazil for stabilizing the Americas might be one way. A US concentration on the Western Hemisphere while playing more of an offshore balancing role in Europe might be another. In whatever form it takes, however, the sustainable grand strategy for the United States going forward is greater selectivity on America's part, combined with truly national interests, to avoid the self-fulfilling prophecy of a future China threat.

Notes

1. Quoted in "San Francisco Conference: History of the United Nations," UN website, www.un.org/en/aboutun/history/sanfrancisco_conference.shtml.

2. Winston Churchill, "The Sinews of Peace," in *Winston S. Churchill: His Complete Speeches 1897–1963; Volume VII, 1943–1949*, ed. Robert Rhodes James (New York: Chelsea House, 1974) 7285–93.

3. J. F. Dulles, "Policy for Security and Peace," *Foreign Affairs*, April 1954.

4. Michael Roskin, "From Pearl Harbor to Vietnam: Shifting Generational Paradigms and Foreign Policy," *Political Science Quarterly* 89, no. 3 (Fall 1974): 563.

5. Michael J. Carden, "National Debt Poses Security Threat, Mullen Says," American Forces Press Service, August 27, 2010.

6. Undersecretary of Defense (Comptroller), DOD Budget Request, www .comptroller.defense.gov/budgetmaterials.aspx.

7. Thirty-two percent of the total 2014 requested base budget, or just over $170 billion, will go to pay and benefits. See Karen Parrish, "Hagel Presents Defense Budget Request to Congress," American Forces Press Service, April 11, 2013. In 2012, China spent $166 billion, Germany spent $45.8 billion, and India spent $46.1 billion on defense. Defense budgets are available at SIPRI, www.sipri.org/research/armaments/milex/recent-trends.

8. Andrew Kohut, "American International Engagement on the Rocks," Pew Research on Global Attitudes Project, July 11, 2013, www.pewglobal .org/2013/07/11/american-international-engagement-on-the-rocks/.

9. Josef Joffe, "How America Does It," *Foreign Affairs* 76, no. 5 (September/October 1997): 27.

10. Walter Russell Mead, *Power, Terror, Peace, and War: America's Grand Strategy in a World at Risk* (New York: Knopf, 2004).

11. Sun Guoxiang "A New Era in China-U.S. Relations: Our Leaders Have Learned That It Is Better to Be Partners than Rivals," *Wall Street Journal*, January 16, 2014.

12. Robert M. Gates, *Duty: Memoirs of a Secretary at War* (New York: Knopf, 2014), 582.

13. For detailed analysis of nation-building efforts, see James Dobbins, *America's Role in Nation-Building: From Germany to Iraq* (Washington, DC: RAND Corp., 2003).

14. See, for instance, Naazneen Barma, Ely Ratner, and Steven Weber, "A World without the West," *National Interest* 90 (July/August 2007).

15. "Joint Statement of the Fifth BRICS Summit in Durban," March 2013, available at Council on Foreign Relations, www.cfr.org/emerging-markets/joint-statement-fifth-brics-summit-durban-march-2013/p30341.

16. International Energy Agency, *World Energy Outlook 2012* (Paris: International Energy Agency, 2011).

17. Eugene Gholz, Daryl G. Press, and Harvey M. Sapolsky, "Come Home, America," *International Security* 21, no. 4 (1997): 5.

18. Derek S. Reveron and Nikolas K. Gvosdev, "Rediscovering the National Interest," *Orbis* 58, no. 3 (Fall 2014).

19. Hans J. Morgenthau, *The Impasse of American Foreign Policy* (Chicago: University of Chicago Press, 1962), 191.

20. The White House, "Remarks by the President in Address to the Nation on Libya," www.whitehouse.gov/the-press-office/2011/03/28/remarks-president-address-nation-libya, accessed on October 24, 2012.

21. Ibid.

22. Derek S. Reveron and James L. Cook, "From National to Theater: Developing Strategy," *Joint Force Quarterly*, no. 70 (3rd Quarter 2013).

23. P. H. Liotta, "To Die For: National Interests and the Nature of Strategy," in *Strategy and Force Planning*, 4th ed., ed. Security, Strategy, and Forces Faculty (Newport, RI: Naval War College Press, 2004), 114.

24. Derek S. Reveron, *Exporting Security: Engagement, Security Cooperation, and the Changing Face of the U.S. Military* (Washington, DC: Georgetown University Press, 2010).

25. Charles Hooper, "Going Farther by Going Together: Building Partner Capacity in Africa," *Joint Force Quarterly*, October 2012, 8.

26. Richard M. Nixon, "First Annual Report to the Congress on United States Foreign Policy for the 1970's," February 18, 1970, Presidency Project, www.presidency.ucsb.edu/ws/?pid=2835.

27. For the critical contemporary works on grand strategy, see Peter Feaver, "Debating American Grand Strategy after Major War," *Orbis* 53, no. 4 (Fall 2009): 547–52; John Lewis Gaddis, *Surprise, Security, and the American Experience* (Cambridge, MA, and London: Harvard University Press, 2005); Charles Hill, *Grand Strategies: Literature, Statecraft, and World Order* (New Haven, CT: Yale University Press, 2010); William C. Martel, "American Grand Strategy after November 2012," *Society* 49, no. 5 (2012): 433–38; William C. Martel, "Why America Needs a Grand Strategy," *Diplomat*, June 18, 2012; Walter Russell Mead, *Special Providence: American Foreign Policy and How It Changed the World*, 1st ed. (Routledge, 2002); Williamson Murray, ed., *The Shaping of Grand Strategy: Policy, Diplomacy, and War* (New York: Cambridge University Press, 2011); Barry R. Posen, "The Case for Restraint," *American Interest* 3, no. 1 (November/December 2007): 7–17; Eugene Gholz and Daryl G. Press, "The Effects of Wars on Neutral Countries: Why It Doesn't Pay to Preserve the Peace," *Security Studies* 10, no. 4 (Summer 2001): 1–57; Christopher A. Preble, *Power Problem: How American Military Dominance Makes Us Less Safe, Less Prosperous, and Less Free* (Ithaca, NY: Cornell University Press, 2009); Christopher Layne, *The Peace of Illusions: American Grand Strategy from 1940 to the Present* (Ithaca, NY: Cornell University Press, 2006).

28. Gholz, Press, and Sapolsky, "Come Home, America," 48.

29. These include Posen, "Case for Restraint," 7–17; Gholz and Press, "Effects of Wars," 1–57; Preble, *Power Problem*; Layne, *Peace of Illusions*.

30. Christopher Layne, "From Preponderance to Offshore Balancing: America's Future Grand Strategy," *International Security* 22, no. 1 (Summer 1997): 114.

31. Stephen M. Walt, "Offshore Balancing: An Idea Whose Time Has Come," *Foreign Policy Online*, November 2, 2011, http://walt.foreignpolicy .com/posts/2011/11/02/offshore_balancing_an_idea_whose_time_has_come.

32. Kohut, "American International Engagement."

33. Robert Art, "Selective Engagement in the Era of Austerity," in *America's Path: Grand Strategy for the Next Administration*, ed. Richard Fontaine and Kristin M. Lord (Washington, DC: Center for New American Security, 2012), 17, www.cnas.org/files/documents/publications/CNAS_AmericasPath_Fontaine Lord_0.pdf

34. Daniel Deudney and G. John Ikenberry, "Democractic Internationalism: An American Grand Strategy for a Post-Exceptionalist Era," Council on Foreign Relations working paper, November 2012, 8.

35. Mackubin T. Owens, "A Balanced Force Structure to Achieve a Liberal World Order," *Orbis* 50, no. 2 Spring 2006, 312.

36. Stephen Brooks, John Ikenberry, and Robert Wohlforth, "Don't Come Home, America: The Case against Retrenchment," *International Security* 37, no. 3 (Winter 2012–13): 7–51.

37. Quoted in Melvyn P. Leffler, *A Preponderance of Power: National Security, the Truman Administration, and the Cold War* (Stanford, CA: Stanford University Press, 1992), 18–19.

38. Stephen M. Walt, "American Primacy: Its Prospects and Pitfalls," *Naval War College Review* 15, no. 2 (Spring 2002): 9–28.

39. For instance, the belief that the spread of democracy makes the United States more secure found expression in President George W. Bush's calls for America "to build and preserve a community of free and independent nations, with governments that answer to their citizens, and reflect their own cultures. And because democracies respect their own people and their neighbors, the advance of freedom will lead to peace." George W. Bush, *State of the Union Address*, February 3, 2005, www.cnn.com/2005/ALLPOLITICS/02/02/sotu .transcript.5/. The primacist mindset—that the United States can only be safe if it has no near-peer rivals—was expressed in President Barack Obama's 2010 strategy, which affirmed, "We maintain superior capabilities to deter and defeat adaptive enemies and to ensure the credibility of security partnerships that are fundamental to regional and global security." Barack Obama, *National Security Strategy of the United States* (Washington, DC: White House, 2010), 17–18, www.whitehouse.gov/sites/default/files/rss_viewer/national_security_strategy .pdf.

40. Public Law 99-433, Section 104, "Goldwater-Nichols Department of Defense Reorganization Act of 1986," 99th Cong., October 1, 1986.

41. Reveron, *Exporting Security*.

42. Colin Dueck, "Hegemony on the Cheap," *World Policy Journal* 20, no. 4 (Winter 2003–4).

43. Jeffery H. Michaels, "Dysfunctional Doctrines? Eisenhower, Carter, and U.S. Military Intervention in the Middle East," *Political Science Quarterly* 126, no. 3 (2011): 491.

44. Quoted in "1898: The Birth of a Superpower," Office of the Historian, Department of State, http://history.state.gov/departmenthistory/short-history/superpower.

45. James Monroe, "Seventh Annual Message to Congress," December 2, 1823, Library of Congress, http://memory.loc.gov/cgi-bin/ampage?collId=ll ac&fileName=041/llac041.db&recNum=4.

46. "New Policies for Latin America, Asia," Office of the Historian, Department of State, http://history.state.gov/departmenthistory/short-history/newpolicies.

47. Jimmy Carter, "State of the Union Address," January 23, 1980, Jimmy Carter Library and Museum, www.jimmycarterlibrary.org/documents/speeches/su80jec.phtml.

48. Joffe, "How America Does It."

49. Thomas M. Nichols, *Winning the World: Lessons for America's Future from the Cold War* (Westport, CT: Praeger, 2002), 236.

50. David Schambaugh, *China Goes Global: The Partial Power* (New York: Oxford University Press, 2013), 8.

The Authors

Derek S. Reveron is professor of national security affairs and the EMC Informationist Chair at the US Naval War College in Newport, Rhode Island. He is also a faculty affiliate at the Belfer Center for Science and International Affairs at Harvard University where he coteaches a course on contemporary national security challenges. He specializes in strategy development, nonstate security challenges, intelligence, and US defense policy. He has authored or edited eight books, including *Cyberspace and National Security* and *Exporting Security: International Engagement, Security Cooperation, and the Changing Face of the U.S. Military*. During graduate school, he formulated, implemented, and evaluated democracy promotion programs for the nongovernmental organization Heartland International. He received a diploma from the Naval War College and an MA in political science and a PhD in public policy analysis from the University of Illinois at Chicago. He is a veteran of Afghanistan.

Nikolas K. Gvosdev is a professor of national security affairs at the US Naval War College and currently serves as the director of the Policy Analysis subcourse in the National Security Affairs Department. He was the editor of *The National Interest* magazine and a senior fellow of strategic studies at the Nixon Center in Washington, DC. He is currently a senior editor at *The National Interest* and is a weekly columnist for *World Politics Review*. He is a participant in the Dartmouth Conference Task Force on US-Russian relations. Dr. Gvosdev is the author or editor of a number of books and monographs, including *Russian Foreign Policy: Interests, Vectors and Sectors* (with Christopher Marsh); *Parting with Illusions: Developing a Realistic Approach to Relations with Russia*; *Imperial Perspectives and Policies towards Georgia, 1763–1819*; and *The Receding Shadow of the Prophet: The Rise and Fall of Political Islam* (with Ray Takeyh). He also coedited the twelfth edition of the Naval War College's *Case Studies in Policy Making* and authored several of the cases in it.

Mackubin Thomas Owens is the editor of *Orbis*, the quarterly journal of the Foreign Policy Research Institute, and former professor of national security affairs at the US Naval War College. He has written widely on national security affairs, focusing primarily on the development of US strategy, force planning, and US civil-military relations, including *US Civil-Military Relations after 9/11: Renegotiating the Civil-Military* and a 2009 monograph on Abraham Lincoln as war president. He is a Marine Corps infantry veteran of Vietnam and retired from the Marine Corps Reserve as a colonel in 1994. He served as a national security adviser to Sen. Bob Kasten and directed legislative affairs for the Nuclear Weapons Program of the Department of Energy during the Reagan administration. He also served as a long-range strategist for the Plans Division of Headquarters Marine Corps and on the J-5 (Strategic Plans and Policy) staff of the Joint Chiefs of Staff. Dr. Owens earned his PhD from the University of Dallas, his MA in economics from Oklahoma University, and his BA from the University of California, Santa Barbara.

Index

Figures, notes, and tables are indicated by f, n, and t following the page number.